MASTERS OF SOCIOLOGICAL THOUGHT

Dr. S.S. Ralhan
Dr. S.R. Lambat

Commonwealth

Masters of Sociological Thought

Edition : **2023**

ISBN 81-311-0043-X

Published by :

COMMONWEALTH PUBLISHERS
4831/24, Prahlad Street,
Ansari Road, Darya Ganj,
New Delhi - 110002
Ph. : 23275511, 23257835
Fax : 91- 011- 23257835
e-mail : commonwealthbooks@gmail.com

Typesetting by :

Rishu Computers
Delhi

Printed at :
Roshan Offset Printers
Delhi

Preface

In this volume, only four major sociologists of the west have been included. They are : (a) Auguste Comte; (b) John Stuart Mill (c) Herbert Spencer (d) Karl Marx.

Of all of these, the major world wide influence on social systems has been of *Karl Marx*. What this amounts to is that in his science of society, Marx quite distinctly maintained that societies could, like other phenomena, be classified into types, each having its own laws of relationships between its parts and that these typical characteristics could be classified by considering in detail the most normal case.

It is regretted that more important masters like Max Weber and Praeto could not be included in this volume, but efforts have been made to include names in historical perspectives.

Dr. S.S. Ralhan
Dr. S.R. Lambat

Contents

1

Introduction

The period in which sociology emerged teemed with writers of distinction. The 'Physiocrats', rooted in Montesquieu, made contributions of brilliance in many directions. Turgot, Quesnay, Mirabeau: all deserve mention. The 'Scottish School'—including writers such as Lord Kames, with his remarkable *Sketches of World History,* Adam Ferguson, Dugald Stewart, Adam Smith, Hutcheson, and many more—did much to further the making of a science of society. Our treatment of the directions and developments of social thought has therefore been highly selective—with the single aim in mind of achieving clarity in seeing the major elements and tendencies which constituted the 'beginnings' of sociology.

It must be the same, now, in moving on to make clear the '*foundations*' of the subject.

Other writers than the ones I have selected contributed much that was indispensable. They were important participants in the ongoing argument. Saint-Simon, for example, formed a necessary part of the development of Comte's ideas—even negatively, in his clashes with him, besides contributing much in his own right. De Tocqueville might be said by some to have contributed more, in his substantive study of American society, than did John Stuart Mill whose work he greatly admired and with whom he corresponded. T.H.Huxley and many other fiery Victorians made contributions in discussing the application of the idea of 'evolution' to the study of society and morality and the new assessment of 'Man's place in Nature' as well as Herbert Spencer. Feuerbach, the French Socialists, and many others, as well as Hegel whom we have already mentioned, made contributions which were important in themselves as well as being at the roots of the ideas of Marx and Engels. And many others in philosophy and literature, in politics and economics, in anthropology and history, took part in the surge forward during the nineteenth century of the new exploration of thought and knowledge which was transforming man's picture of his own nature and the nature of the world.

Even so, I believe that it is by a careful selection of certain authors that the nature and elements of sociology which were founded during the nineteenth century can best be laid bare. The ideas of Comte, Mill, Spencer and Marx together with their influences upon certain American writers will tell us all that we need to know for a full and clear comprehension of the system of sociology which was then established; of the basic elements of the new science of society which, by the end of the century, had been successfully founded.

It would be possible to divide these ideas and contributions in various ways. For example, Comte and Mill had much more to say about definitions, concepts, methods—about logic and methodology generally—than did Spencer and Marx; and the latter thinkers might be said to have offered more substantive and detailed theories of the nature of society and social change than did the two former. But any such division, though perhaps expedient for certain purposes, would not be strictly true. Comte, for example, in addition to his methodological discussions, undertook very substantial historical studies. Only Mill, among them all, confined himself specifically to a *logical critique* of sociology; and he did this only in the service of accuracy and, as he himself put it, with a knowledge of his own limitations, and of the limited state of advancement of certain components of the subject (e.g., psychology) at the time. The characteristic which all these men shared, however, and which underlay their concern for accuracy of method in founding a science of society, was their concern about, and involvement in, the social and political dilemmas which men were facing, and their passionate and powerful persuasions about certain theories which, they thought, would help men to understand their situation and so help them towards effective political judgment and action.

In short, they were concerned to understand and explain the facts of human nature, society, history, and social change, in order to judge and to act wisely in relation to them; and their efforts to create a scientific way of 'studying' these facts was part and parcel of this committed quest. They were not men who wanted to be 'social scientists' as such. They were not 'professional' scholars. They were not men to sit in universities fabricating vast skeins of concepts. They wanted a true understanding of the facts of man and society because they *needed* it; and they needed it because they felt themselves responsible, among other men, in grappling with the issues and struggles of human destiny in their own time.

I have therefore thought it the best thing of all to deal with each man's work in its own right, and each in turn. They will be seen to be all connected. And our account will not be a chronological story only. As we proceed, the interconnections, the related developments of conceptions and methods will become clear, and, at the end, we shall be able to see very clearly the firm foundations of the new science of sociology which had been accomplished by the end of the nineteenth century.

2

Auguste Comte: Positive Science and Sociology : A First Synthesis

Comte was born in 1798 during the ferment of the French Revolution, that vast complex of events which heralded the birth of the modern world. He died just over a hundred years ago, in 1857. He was one of the greatest thinkers during this period notable for its great contributions to human thought, and he grappled with the human situation of his day with a power of mind and a dedication which was unsurpassed. His was a great attempt to analyse the nature of, and the reasons for, the decline and disruption of Christendom; to consider the ways in which human society should be reconstituted and revitalized; and to provide that system of knowledge and moral guidance which would make this possible.

To understand Comte's ideas fully, one has to understand clearly those problems which confronted and preoccupied him; about which he was passionately concerned.

Comte lived in the aftermath of the French Revolution. He was continually disturbed and distressed by the disorder of his time, and by the material and cultural poverty of the people. His fundamental and lifelong preoccupation was how to replace disorder by order; how to accomplish the total reconstruction of society. He saw the French Revolution as a crucial turning-point in the history of human affairs. The *ancien regime* was gone, fallen to pieces, shown to be totally inadequate for the new trends and conditions of scientific knowledge and industrialization. There was no adequate order of institutions for the new changes in society. The social action of men was ungoverned and ill-directed. The thought of men was disorientated. There were great cleavages between belief and knowledge. And the feelings of men lacked coherence, confidence, and worthwhile objectives. In the spheres of social loyalty, traditional allegiance, moral purpose, men were adrift.

A new polity—a new order of feeling, thought, and action—was necessary for the new complex, industrial society. But this social reconstruction needed a reliable basis of knowledge. And—and this was the crucial point for Comte—it rested upon man's assumption of his own responsibility. It was no longer possible to fall back upon Gods, metaphysical forces and destinies, traditional modes of belief and feeling. Man was now responsible for his own destiny. Man must make his own society. Man must consciously and responsibly make himself.

On what basis of knowledge and action could this be done? Religion, too, had been disrupted. What values and beliefs could now provide an adeuqate bond of co-operative citizenship in the new society?

Comte was convinced of a number of things:

(1) that this juncture of human affairs was by no means a momentary and temporary crisis, nor was it of significance only in France, but that
(2) it was the unavoidable culmination of the long process of change and development in the history of mankind which had now arrived at a qualitively new level of human thought, experience, and social organization.
(3) It was unlikely, therefore, that the problems raised would be easily solved by political thought and policies previously tried.
(4) New kinds of social action were not likely to be effective unless they rested upon a new and more reliable knowledge of human nature and human society, and
(5) the desired changes in human institutions would not come about of themselves. They would not be achieved unless there was a positive moral desire, commitment, and effort on the part of the people. Social recons-

> truction would only be possible, Comte thought, if supported by the moral convictions, even the religious feeling of the people. This could only be achieved, given the decline of traditional religion, by the clarification and acceptance of a new 'religion of humanity'—in which the improvement of human conditions, the qualities of culture and the qualities of individual character should be the goals of man's endeavours and aspirations.

Comte's work, in its entirety, dealt with these preoccupations. It was a thoroughly worked out answer to the question: how are we to deal with this qualitatively new situation that faces mankind? The relevance of his work to our own time the relevance of sociology to ourselves, is—at once—perfectly clear. For those are the problems which still confront us. They are not, by any means, over yet. We have still not solved them.

It was in the work of Comte more than in that of any other single writer, that all the many earlier lines of thought which we have considered were brought together into a unified, systematic statement. In doing this, Comte achieved a synthesis which was, and is, without any question, of great and permanent value.

In his statement of the nature of 'positive science' he drew upon the epistemological ideas of Hume and Kant, and, indeed, upon the substantive knowledge of all the individual sciences. His range of knowledge in phiosophy and in all fields of science was extraordinarily wide. In creating Sociology, and providing a new basis for social and political thought and practice which has, even yet, not been fully worked out, he brought together the work of Aristotle (who, as we have seen, had attempted an empirical comparative study of political constitutions), Montesquieu (who had done the same, and had also explored and developed the notion of 'laws' of society and social development), and Condorcet (who had written his history of the progress of the human mind in the context of stages of institutional development). But he was also thoroughly acquainted with the contributions to the philosophy of history of Vico, Kant, Hegel and Turgot. He knew the many-sided contibutions to social science and social philosophy of the Scottish School. He was familiar not only with the work of

Hume, but also with that of Adam Smith (he valued highly Adam Smith's treatment of the division of labour; indeed, Smith was the only economist with whom he had much patience) and that of Adam Ferguson—whom he commended for some of his accounts of the historical changes of social institutions. In working out the ritualistic aspects of his new religion, Comte also made much use of De Maistre, especially his 'Du Pape'; not—one might think—the happiest of influences, but, nonetheless, indicative of Comte's wide scholarship.

The work of Comte was thus a great synthesis in the history of human thought. Bringing together important contributions in Moral and Political Philosophy, the Philosophy of History, Epistemology and the history and methods of the particular sciences—he worked these into a new systematic statement which was, at once.

(*a*) a unified system of knowledge, inclusive of the methods required for its attainment, maintenance and expansion.

(*b*) a systematic basis for social analysis and social action, and

(*c*) a systematic basis for religious feeling and moral effort.

Furthermore, there was no finality about Comte's statement—a fault in many other large 'systems' of thought. It was a system that carried within itself the necessity of continual testing, the prospect of continual expansion, and the prospect of a continuing increase in man's control over his material and social environment, which itself entailed, Comte argued, the increasing possibility of moral progress: the extension of distinctively human qualities (reason, knowledge, social co-operation, and altruistic feeling) over man's animal qualities (limited, self-centred impulse).

This 'synthesizing' nature of Comte's work should not blind us to his originality. Originality is rarely pure innovation. As human thought develops, there are many and continuous changes of degree, but—on occasion—various existing contributions are brought together to produce changes so considerable as to constitute a difference in *kind.* Comte's contribution was of this order. Before his work, as we have seen, many areas of human inquiry were still open to unchecked speculation and religious dogma; and none more so than the realm of human nature and human society. After his time—these areas were, and are, open to such unchecked dogma and speculation no longer. Theology still fusses, but is all the time trying to clothe itself in scientific dress so that it can walk respectably through the streets of the twentieth century. Everyone now has to come to terms with the kinds of methods which Comte laid down. His work, as he himself would rightly appraise it, is representative of a crucial point of historical development in human thought, feeling, activity, and social organization.

It is impossible to do justice to Comte's many-sided contributions in summary fashion, but I shall outline as clearly as possible the chief ideas in his system, then touch upon and emphasize certain important aspects of his work which, I believe, are nowadays scarcely known, and rarely, if ever, attributed to him, but which I believe to have been of essential importance in the making of the subject.

The Three Stages of mental and social development:

the co-ordination of feeling, thought and action in individuals and society

There are three important aspects of our nature, Comte said, which, in our individual lives, must be brought into some sort of satisfactory working relation with each other:

1. *Our feelings*—the impulses and emotions which prompt us to, and are attendant on, activity.
2. *Our thought*—which is undertaken in the service of our feelings, but helps also to govern them, and
3. *Our actions*—which are undertaken in the service of our feelings and in the light of our thought.

Also, as it is with our individual—so it is with our social life and behaviour. For the existence and continuity of *society* (a system of shared and regualted behaviour amongst individuals) there must be some order of institutions, knowledge, values, and beliefs which successfully relate the *feelings, thought,* and *activity* of its members.

In the history of mankind—during which the social order bringing these elements into relation with each other has been worked out—three 'types' of solution, three 'stages' of development, can be distinguished. The first is what Comte called the *Theological Stage.* It is characterized by the fact that feeling and imagination dominate in man's search for the nature, causes, and ends of things. Explanations take the form of myths concerning spirits and supernatural beings. Comte discussed three levels of mental development within this stage.

1. Fetishism—when everything in nature is thought to be imbued with life analogous to our own,
2. Polytheism—in which unrestrained imagination peoples the world with innumerable gods and spirits, and
3. Monotheism—in which a simplification of many gods into one god takes place, largely in the service of awakening reason, which qualifies and exercies constraint upon the imagination.

In this stage of thought (the theological), social organization is predominantly of a military nature. It is military power which provides the basis of social stability, and conquest which enlarges the bounds of social life. It is important to realize that Comte did not, in relegating this stage to the past, deny its value. He believed that feeling and imagination were (and are) the chief elements of experience moving men to inquiry; it was they that pressed for understanding and explanation in the condition of human experience before any accumulation of systematic knowledge could have taken place. Once the philosophical (reflective) tendencies leading to monotheism have taken place, however, they cannot be held in check. They lead to a second stage of critical thought, which is transitional.

This is the *Metaphysical Stage,* and it is characterized by the dominance of 'ratiocination'. Indeed, ratiocination plays a much more unbridled role here than in the later stage of science proper. Just as in the theological stage, feeling and imagination are unrestrained and undisciplined, so in the metaphysical stage, speculative thought is unchecked by any other principle. Men now pursue meaning and the explanation of the world in terms of 'essences', 'ideals', 'forms'; in short, in conceptions of some 'ultimate reality. The institutional changes correlated with this stage of thought are, chiefly, the development of defensive militarism and the extension of established law which lays down a more secure basis for co-operative civil life.

Neither of these two ways of relating feeling, thought and action in society, however, is stable or adequate; they are found to be wanting as society changes. Intellectually, they show themselves inadequate in that, over many centuries, they move no nearer to conclusiveness; they never resolve problems. Their problems, in fact, turn out to be incapable of solution. But they also fail when brought to the test of practical experience. As human society becomes in all respects more complicated (particulary because of industrialization) theological and metaphysical systems of thought become increasingly inadequate. They cannot provide the basis of reliable knowledge which—for their manifold purposes: technical, economic, political etc.—men need. Men therefore abandon them, and they are superseded by the third 'stage' of thought and social development: the *Positive stage.*

At this stage of thought, men reject as useless all supposed 'explanations' in terms either of gods or essences. They cease to seek 'original causes' or 'final ends' because (*a*) it becomes clear that these are *not* explanations at all (Comte mentioned as an example of such pseudo-explanation Moliere's satire that opium causes sleep because of its 'dormitive virtue' or its 'soporfic essence'), and (*b*) they can neither be checked against facts nor utilized to serve our needs. Men cease looking for 'causes' of any kind, and seek merely *'laws'.* And it is very important to see that, by 'laws' Comte merely meant statements about the ways in which, in our experience, we find facts to be connected with each other; *that is all.* The crucial factor distinguishing the propositions which go to make up 'positive knowledge' is that in addtion to possessing logical validity, they sould all be submitted to the test of careful observation, and, where possible, to exact experiment.

For Comte, all knowledge is inescapably *human* knowledge; a systematic ordering of propositions concerning our human experience of the world. The *only* knowledg we can have, as distinct from unsupported conjecture, is knowledge of observed facts. Our practice in both individual and social life, if it is to be effective and reliable, must rest upon theories about the interconnections of facts. To go beyond this is pointless. Questions raised about the nature of the world beyond our experience of it cannot possibly be answered.

Positive Science and Positive Philosophy

Comte has been much criticized for his dogmatism, his assertiveness, his sweeping claims on behalf of positive science and his equally sweeping rejection of theology and metaphysics, but a careful examination of his work shows that he was not only right, but also that his claims on behalf of positive science were, in fact, modest rather than overweening. His claim concerning the nature of positive science was only a common-sense admission of human limitations and a philosophical clarification of them; and then, on this basis, a claim that this—after all—is all that we require for our effective action and fulfilment in the world.

Theological and metaphysical questions, said Comte, are set aside simply because they cannot be answered; that is all. Positive Science confines itself to seeking the 'laws' of *phenomena:* statements of the ways in which facts are linked.

These are (1) *laws of co-existence*—statements about the universally found interdependence of elements which distinctively comprise the phenomena being studied (e.g. planetary systems, biological species, human societies, etc.) and (2) *laws of succession*—statements about concrete historical changes, or about facts as they are connected in temporal sequence. Every subject thus has its 'statical' and 'dynamical' aspects, both of which are necessary and both of which are closely dependent upon each other.

In stating these 'laws', however, Positive Science is very careful never to claim completeness, comprehensiveness, or certainty. Comte, indeed, went to great lengths to demonstrate the *limitations* of the claims of science.

All human knowledge, he insisted, *must* be considered limited for two simple reasons:

(1) because of our 'organization' and 'situation' as a species. Our knowledge cna only deal with the world as we experience it through the media of our own human senses, and from our own position in the natural world and in society. If we had *different* natural endowments (for example, if we did not possess the sense of sight) the world would appear differently to us, and consequently our knowledge would different. And:

(2) because social change and the cumulative nature of human knowledge make final certainty extremely unlikely, if not impossible. At the same time, since it permits of continuous growth and systematization, and is continually subjected to the checks of observation and experiment, positive science provides us with the most reliable basis we can obtain for 'prevision' or 'prediction'. Though limited, therefore, it nonetheless provides (and this—without question) the only reliable basis for effective *action* in the world and in society, in the pursuit of all our ends.

Before moving on from this simple outline of Comte's description of positive science. I want to pick out and emphasize several aspects of his treatment. He is often misrepresented as having proposed a simple-minded method of 'induction' in scientific method. He is often thought to be guilty of 'historicism': his conception of 'laws' concerning social facts being said to be grandiose predictions of 'inevitable trends of history'. He is often thought to be guilty of some peculiar kind of finality. And, because of his egotism, and his assertive style, he is often thought to be dogmatic in all his intellectual work. Comte could be defended against all these and many other criticisms. Here I shall stress what I think are some of the more important points for our own purposes—namely, to see what dimensions he clarifies in his conception of science in general, and of the new science of society.

(a) Feeling and imagination in science

Though Comte said that feeling and imagination become 'necessarily subordinate to observation' in positive science, it is certainly not true that his account of 'positivism' discounted the role of imagination in science and came to think of science only as a simple, colourless collection of facts. Comte said quite definitely:

'Nevertheless, there is always plenty of important work for imagination to do in positive speculation; for it has to form and improve the hypotheses, definitive or provisional, by which phenomena are to be connected.'

Furthermore, he attacked the 'erroneous interpretation' of the subordination of imagination to reason as having:

'... been most improperly used to degrade real science into a sort of barren accumulation of unrelated facts, with no merit except that of accuracy. It is therefore important to understand that the true positive spirit is at bottom quite as far removed from empiricism (*i.e.* mere fact-collection) as from mysticism... Science really consists in the laws of phenomena. Facts themselves, however exact and numerous they may be, can only furnish the indispensable *materials* of sicence.' '...true science, far from consisting of bare observations, always tends to dispense as much as possible with direct exploration, and to substitute for it that rational prevision which is, in all respects, the principal characteristic of the positive spirit...'

Clearly, Comte thought of science as a questing, imaginative, hypothetical study exactly as modern philosophers of science do.

(b) The role of Hypothesis in Science

Comte was perfectly clear, also, about the part played by hypothesis in science. In *no* sense did he hold a naive notion of 'induction' or 'empiricism'. At the very beginning of his 'Course of Positive Philosophy', he said:

'If it is true that every theory must be based upon observed facts, it is equally true that facts cannot be observed without the guidance of some theory. Without such guidance, our facts would be desultory and fruitless; we could not retain them; for the most part we could not even perceive them.'

But consider the following, bearing in mind the modern exposition of scientific method. Discussing the nature of hypothesis, Comte said that neither inductive nor deductive procedures would help us:

'... even in regard to the simplest phenomena, if we did not begin by anticipating the results, by making a provisional supposition, altogether conjectural in the first instance, with regard to some of the very notions which are the object of the inquiry. Hence the necessary introduction of hypotheses into natural philosophy...without it all discovery of natural laws would be impossible in cases of any degree of complexity; and in all, very slow. But the employment of this instrument must always be subjected to one condition, the neglect of which would impede the development of real knowledge. This condition is to imagine such hypotheses only as admit, by their nature, of a positive and inevitable verification at some future time—the precision of this verification being proportioned to what we can learn of the corresponding phenomena. In other words, philosophical hypotheses must always have the character of simple anticipations of what we might know at once, by experiment and reasoning, if the circumstances of the problem had been more favourable than they are. Provided this rule be scrupulously observed, hypotheses may evidently be employed without danger, as often as they are needed, or rationally desired...if we try to reach by hypothesis what is inaccessible to observation and reasoning, the fundamental condition is violated, and hypothesis, wandering out of the field of science, merely leads us astray.

Again, when discussing methods appropriate to Biology, Comte wrote:

'It is permissible to form the most plausible hypothesis as to the unknown functions of a given organ, or the concealed organ of a manifest function. If the supposition be in harmony with existing knowledge, if it be held provisionally, and if it be capable of a positive verification, it may contribute to the process of discovery, and is simply a use of a right of the human mind...'

And, having upheld the worth of the hypothetical method in a particular piece of work by Broussais, he went on:

'Whether he was mistaken or not, is not the question. His hypothesis being open to unquestionable confirmation or subversion, it gave a great impulse to the study of pathology in a positive manner...'*

All that Professor Karl Popper is now saying about 'conjectures and refutations' and the 'hypothetico-deductive method'; all that Talcott Parsons is now saying (in Sociology) about 'theory before empirical investigation'; was stated with perect clarity by Comte.

(c) The Nature and Importance of Prediction

It is often thought too, or appears to be thought by some sociologists and philosophers, that Comte thought of 'prediction' purely in a historical fashion—as a matter of 'predicting the future', and especially in sociology, of predicting 'future states of society'; as though he wished sociology to possess a kind of historical 'clairvoyance'. But his notion of 'prevision' or 'prediction' was in every way the same as that of contemporary science.

'Prevision', he says, 'is a necessary consequence of the discovery of constant relations between phenomena, and it is the unfailing test which distinguishes real science from that empty erudition which mechanically accumulates facts without aspiring to deduce them from one another... Thus the true positive spirit consists above all in seeing for the sake of foreseeing; in studying what *is*, in order to infer what *will be,* in accordance with the general dogma that natural laws are invariable.'

But such prevision is not confined in any simple-minded sense to the foretelling of future events, natural or social.

'The truth is', wrote Comte, 'that whether the aim is to explain or to foresee, in either case it is the establishment of a connection. Every real connection, whether statical or dynamical, discovered between any two phenomena enables us both to explain them and to foresee them, each by the means of the other. For prevision, in the scientific sense of the word, is not confined to the future; it may evidently be used also of the present and even of the past. It consists in the knowledge of a fact indirectly, by virtue of its relations with other facts already known, without needing to explore it directly.'

This, surely, is perfectly clear. And Comte maintained, of course, and rightly, that this scientific 'prevision' is the firmest basis for our actions and policies in dealing with either the material world or the institutions of society.

'From science comes prevision: from prevision comes action.'

But we must now consider Comte's conception of the *content* of Positive Science and Positive Philosophy.

The Hierarchy of Sciences

Comte maintained that an examination of the growth of the several established sciences showed not only that human thought in general had passed through the three stages we have mentioned, but also that each particular subject had developed in the same way. This appeared, therefore, to be a necessary order of the unfolding of human inquiry; three stages in the development of the human mind in seeking knowledge of the world and of itself. Now that science (i.e., in his time) had been successfully applied to the study of organic life (biology), and now that the extension of science to the study of man and society was seen to be necessary, it was possible to arrange the sciences systematically in a way which coincided with:

(*a*) the order of their historical emergence and development,

(*b*) the order of their dependence upon each other ('each rests upon the one that precedes it, and prepares the way for the one that follows it'),

(*c*) their decreasing degree of generality and the increasing degree of complexity of their subject-matter, and

(*d*) the increasing degree of modifiability of the facts which they study.

His final arrangement of the sciences on this basis (elaborated in the 'Positive Polity') was: Mathematics, Astronomy, Chemistry, Physics, Biology, Sociology, and, finally, Morals—by which Comte really meant a study of Man the Individual (a study which followed upon sociology and was a mixture of psychology and ethics).

Certain points in Comte's discussion of this 'hierarchy' are worthy of note.

(*a*) Comte thought that each science came into being not arbitrarily, but in order to seek the'laws' of a particular kind, or level, of facts which man had encountered in his experience of the world; which could not be adequately analysed or explained in terms of the 'laws' of the other already existing sciences; and which were seen to require particular methods for their study.

(*b*) This meant that Comte—though he passionately sought a systematic arrangement of the sciences which would give a reliable picture of man's total situation—was also led to guard jealously the independent sphere of each science, and to oppose rigorously the naivety of what we now call 'reductionism'.

(c) It led him also to insist upon the freedom of each science to consider and develop methods appropriate to its own subject-matter. Consequently, he had no naive notion of *one* 'scientific method' which was the same in all sciences, neither did he naively equate in with the methods employed in *one* particular (dthe most exact) science.

Finally,

(*d*) since he has been criticized for the inadequacy of his 'hierarchy', on the grounds that other border-line sciences have emerged since his time, it might be noted that Comte was extremely modest and tentative about the proposed 'hierarchical scheme' and did not suggest any finality in this respect. Since 'Man's very feeble intellect has to be applied to a very complex universe', and since it seems likely that the phenomena of the several sciences will never be brought under one universal 'law', and 'hierarchy' which he proposed had, he said, the merit at least of utility and convenience. It did at least serve to bring scientific knowledge together in a systematic whole, and to give rise to speculative inductions and deductions between the sciences.

(*e*) A fifth point of both interest and importance is that Comte considered the study of 'Man—the Individual' the most complex study of all (more complex than the psychological attributes that are *common* to all men, and more complex, even, than the study of 'social structures'), and thought that it waited upon the achievement of adequate sciences of Psychology and Sociology, but required elements of Philosophy too. This, in my opinion, is a more satisfactory point of view than that held by many psychologists and sociologists now.

Sociology

It is now necessary to see in what ways Comte conceived of the new Science of Society (Sociology—he chose to call it), and in what ways it was important to him.

First, it is clear in terms of objective fact that the other sciences, even including biology, do not, and cannot possibly explore at their own level, the 'laws' (i.e., interconnections of social facts) of human society. The subject-matter of all these other sciences are certainly involved in, and certainly affect, the nature of man and society, but their 'laws' cannot give an adequate account of this new complex level of societal facts in human experience. Biology, said Comte, studies 'man—the animal', but does not take into account the complex cumulative institutions and traditions of his social life. The chief thing distinguishing man from other animals (besides greater intelligence and adaptability) is the growth and development of a historical tradition. Human society is a cumulative process of institutions, knowledge, skills, traditions, values, beliefs, and neither biology nor any other natural science can study these. Neither can the changing nature of these social phenomena be simply deduced from the nature of man as a biological individual. Sociology is necessary, therefore, as a new science, because man has become aware of a new level of phenomena which cannot be adequately studied by existing sciences. It emerges because man recognizes a new level of objective facts which he cannot explain, but which he needs to explain in order to deal effectively with them.

Comte was quite clear then that the distinctive subject-matter of sociology was the 'social system', and the varieties of social systems in the world. A society was a system of interconnected parts. This system was something more than, something other than, the individuals within it, and therefore it required special study. Indeed, individuals could be understood only within the context of the societies of which they were members. Comte was very definite about this. 'Sociology', he wrote, 'consists in the investigation of the action and reaction of the different parts of the social system... This view condemns the practice of contemplating social elements separately as if they had an independent existence; and it leads us to regard them as in mutual relation, and forming a whole which compels us to treat them in combination.' Sociology was, then, the scientific study of the nature and the different forms of societies; of social systems.

And Sociology, in addition to the methods appropriate to the other sciences—observation and experiment—must also, because of the peculiar nature of social facts, use both the *comparative* and the *historical* methods.

When discussing the comparative method, Comte quite distinctly meant:

'The comparison of the different co-existing states of human society on the various parts of the world's surface—those states being completely independent of each other. From the wretched inhabitants of Tierra del Fuego to the most advanced nations of western Europe, there is no social grade which is not extant in some point of the globe, and usually in localities which are clearly apart.'

This knowledge might suggest some ideas concerning social change and evolution, said Comte, but then, the careful use of the historical method could supplement these ideas and check them. And by the historical method, Comte was far from meaning simple chronological narrative. He spoke, for example, of 'the rational use of social series'. And again, drawing upon Condorcet, he said that—for clearness—we may suppose a single nation to which we may refer all the consecutive social modifications actually witnessed among different peoples. This, he said, is a 'rational fiction', but, 'as a scientific artifice merely', he would 'employ this hypothesis, and on the grounds of its manifest utility'. In short—Comte both used and advocated the construction of models, of ideal types, for the exploration of hypotheses.

These methods are appropriate for the statement of sociological 'laws' (i.e. connections between social facts).* If, further, these 'laws' pertaining to social aspects of human nature could also be supported by deductions from the 'laws' pertaining to the biological facts of human nature, they could then be regarded as being as certain and reliable as we could manage to attain—though, let it be remembered, they would never be held to be final, but still open continuously, to test.

Like other sciences, sociology should be divided into 'statics' and 'dynamics'. It must be remembered here that Comte thought that the 'consensus' or the 'nature of the interdependence' of the phenomena being studied should be borne in mind in deciding upon the most appropriate methods of study to be employed.

In organic studies, it might be possible to study 'parts' or 'bits' of material data, and then move towards knowledge of the whole in an 'additive' way. In Biology, however,—in studying the living organism; or in sociology—in studying systems of social institutions; the 'consensus' of facts immediately required that 'the whole' should be the focal concept (the governing orientation) of study, since the parts could only be properly investigated and understood in terms of their interdependence in the whole system. It was of very *nature* of the 'parts' that they co-existed in certain ways in the 'whole'. 'Statics' in sociology thus consisted of clarifying the interconnections between those social facts which appear to be universally necessary for the existence of a society of any kind: the nature of , and connections between, the family, the division of labour, property, govern-ment, religion, morality, and so on. 'Dynamics' then consisted of studying and tracing the interconnections between these many aspects of society as they actually existed and changed in the many types of society in the cumulative processes of history. It was a study, that is, of the actual varieties of societies existing in the world. 'Statics' is therefore chiefly 'analytical,' 'Dynamics' is chiefly 'empirical'. 'Dynamics' applies the analysis of 'Statics' to the study of actual societies.

Sociology was necessary, firstly, then, because of the existence of a distinctive level of objective facts which required study.

Secondly, however, sociology was also a matter of objective necessity for Comte as a body of testable knowledge on which reliable policies for social reconstrcution could be formulated.

But there is a third interesting aspect of the place of Sociology in Comte's system which brings to a head much that had been said earlier—especially by Hume, and, in Comte's own time, by John Stuart Mill—and this is the role it plays in the 'subjective' orientation of all the sciences. We know, said Comte, that the hierarchy of sciences reflects the nature of the 'objective' world only in the most sketchy and tentative way. But there is another way of conceiving and arranging the sciences which provides a certain and unassailable unity of order. This is what Comte called the 'subjective' way of regarding them. *All* knowledge, in *all* the sciences, is *human* knowledge. All the sciences have had a complex historical development within the growth of human society. Consequently, it is clear that all the other sciences fall into place in this one unifying science. Just as all the data of the several sciences are involved in the phenomena of man and society, and all the sciences are necessary for a full understanding of the situation of man, so all these sciences have developed within human society and are themselves part of the full scope of the science of man.

'It is quite otherwise', said Comte, having discussed difficulties of the 'objective' ordering of the sciences, 'when we consider scientific knowledge from the subjective point of view, that is to say when we look at human theories as having their origins in ourselves, and regard them as naturally resulting from the mental evolution, both in individuals and society, and as having for their aim the normal satisfaction of our cravings of every kind. When thus regarded in relation not to the universe but to man, or rather to Humanity, the diverse branches of real knowledge have on the contrary an evident and natural tendency towards a complete systemization not only logical but scientific.

It is easy to see, therefore, why Comte maintained that this full system of positive science and philosophy provides the intellectual basis for the unity, order and progress of the life of man in the modern world. His system brought into a unified whole all the many directions of human science and thought which had hitherto developed in what one might call an 'inarticulated' way. On the basis of this system alone, Comte claimed, could man understand his place both in the natural world and in historical scoiety, and proceed, consciously and effectively, to reconstruct his social and individual life.

It is worthwhile to note here, too, that when Comte spoke of Sociology as the 'crowning edifice' of the hierarchy of sciences, he had this general unifying and orientating nature of the science in mind. He did not mean that it is in any sense 'superior' to any other science; but only that it serves to bring all other sciences into relationship with each other, in the overall intellectual history of man. With Psychology and Sociology, man finally comes to establish positive knowledge not only about the world about which he thinks, but also about his own mind which is doing the thinking. The framwork of knowledge is thus rounded out and complete.

It was Comte's further contention that this growing system of knowledge and attendant institutions which can give each individual the opportunity for his greatest fulfilment, is clearly a cumulative product of many generations throughout history and of all contemporaneous human groups and nations. It is a co-operative product of mankind at large—what he liked to call 'Humanity'—a collective reality which is greater than individuals themselves. And this led him to other considerations.

For Comte, this achievements of a system of positive science including the science of man in society, was only the solution to *one* aspect of the problem of man in the modern world—that aspect relating to thought and knowledge. But, in itself, it is not enough for the reconstruction of a social order whose old foundations have gone. In order that it should be effectively employed in active reconstruction, it has to be coupled, he said '...with two other fundamental conditions—a *sufficient conformity of feeling,* and *some convergence of interests.'*

Social Interests

Comte saw the required convergence of interests in the growth and spread of industrialization. In particular, he placed much hope in the working class—the proletaries. Industrialization forces men to accept the viewpoint; of positivism and inclines them to reject theological and metaphysical explanations of nature. The day-to-day activities of life in industrial society, he said, are directed to the practical improvement of man's condtiions; and this industrial life, devoted to mundane interests, 'is at bottom in direct contradiction with all providential optimism, since it necessarily assumes that the order of nature is so imperfect as to require incessant amendment by man..' Also, in all industrial operations, 'we must needs regard the external world not as directed by arbitrary wills of any kind, but as subject to laws enabling us to exercise a sufficient foresight, without which we should have no rational warrant for exerting oursleves at all.'

Comte thought that manual workers were more likely to be won over to positivism than 'managers', because they were working directly upon material nature, whereas 'managers' or 'capitalists' were much more engaged in taking decisions with regard to people. Comte thought also that working men, though having little leisure, had, nonetheless, minds which were free from the preoccupations which burdened a busy bourgeoisie, so that they could come with fresh minds to positivistic ideas. Also—a very important point for Comte—their minds had not been spoiled by the stupidities, of formal education: bedevilled by classical inanities, squeezed small and petty by the narrow absurdities of specialization, or, above all, unfitted for life and thought by the academies.

Much of this, of course, smacks of Karl Marx. Marx did, in fact, read Comte's work. How much he was influenced by Comte it is difficult to say. What is certain, however, is that Marx's emphasis upon the importance of the role of the proletariat in the shaping of the modern industrial world is far from being as original as is commonly supposed.

Comte had also much of value to say about education—to be based upon systematic instruction in the hierarchy of sciences—but it is impossible to discuss this element of his thought satisfactorily here.

Religion and Morality

The aspect of *feeling* which would inspire and sustain co-operative activity and citizenship in the reconstituted industrial society, could be provided, Comte thought, by the 'Religion of Humanity'. It is on this score that Comte has been most attacked, even by many who are prepared to accept the rest of his system. One cannot help but feel, however, that, in rejecting his ideas about positive religion so completely, they have not taken sufficient care to distinguish between two aspects of Comte's thought.

On the one hand, there are Comte's views concerning the worthwhile objectives of human effort and aspiration—indeed, human devotion. On the other, there are the over-elaborate ritualistic prescriptions connected with all this in the 'Positive Polity'—which was clearly saturated with his obsessive devotion to Madame de Vaux. One can, it seems to me, readily accept the one without the other.

To put the matter as briefly as possible (and, it must be confessed, by so doing to eliminate many of his extravagances), Comte believed that—now that the inadequate foundations of the existing religion had been exposed and displaced—the true core of religious feeling and duty remained. Indeed, it was now freed from its supposed dependence upon dubious doctrines, and made much more clear. And this was no more and no less than a compassionate concern for mankind; an aspiration towards the achievement of the highest human ideals; and a direction of one's efforts to the improvement of both the conditions of man and his nature. 'Love is the principle', reads Comte's slogan, 'Order is the basis, Progress is the end.' It is the moral commitment, in feeling, thought, and activity, to the service of mankind, which is the true core of religion.

'It is', says Comte, 'the only religion which is real and complete; destined therefore to replace all imperfect and provisional systems resting on the primitive basis of theology.' It is '...the substitution of Love of Humanity for Love of God... To love humanity may be truly said to constitute the whole duty of man.'

It is true that this essential core of his teaching is obscured by the detailed prescriptions in the 'Polity'. Indeed, it is perfectly clear that in this last exercise of zeal, Comte—always extreme; unstable in mind and temperament—was carried away by the power of his feelings, his love, for Clotilde de Vaux. George Henry Lewes, for example, wrote.

'It was in the early days of this attachment (i.e. to Madame de Vaux) that I first saw him, and in the course of our very first interview he spoke of her with an expansiveness which greatly interested me. When I next saw him he was as expansive in his grief at her irreparable loss; and the tears rolled down his cheeks as he detailed her many perfections. His happiness had lasted but one year. Her death made no change in his devotion. During life she had been a benign influence irradiating his nature, for the first time giving satisfaction to the immense tenderness which slumbered there... Her death rather intensified than altered this influence... The remainder of his life was a perpetual hymn to her memory. Every week he visited her tomb, every day he prayed to her and invoked her continual assistance. His published invocations and eulogies may call forth mockeries...'*

Well, the mockeries have come. It is this, chiefly, that has given rise to distaste amongst all serious critics. For the same obsessive reason, Comte was led to write in far too fulsome a way about the whole matter, parading his private love in the public enunciations of his system.

Nonetheless, the core of what he had to say is true enough, and I am convinced that it is the ground of morality of the majority of people in the mid-twentieth century. Comte's major error, perhaps, lay in thinking that since this concern for human welfare and human values was, at heart, a religious feeling, its dissemination depended upon ritualistic trappings akin to those of the old religions whereas, in fact, with the temper of positive science and appropriate education, perhaps anything redolent of the old religious trappings strikes false, is such as to engender distaste rather than make an appeal, and the required elements of humane feeling can better be inculcated with less pomp and more quietness. Still, the last word has not been said on this matter.

Comte said much about the nature of the positive priesthood, and about the special role of women, which now seems to verge on the absurd, and, indeed, to contain some elements of reaction—as with regard to the status of women in society. Still, if one has patience, even in the most extreme ideas there is always sufficient in what he said to make a critical reconsideration worthwhile. Besides, Comte had an unhappy knack of writing about these elements of sublime feeling with such direct naivety and exaggeration as almost to *force* a sense of distaste upon the reader. He tried to unburden his intense poetic feeling in severe, exacting, meticulously argued prose, and the result is frequently embarrassing. The truth which lies at the heart of what he had to say about religion was obscured, spoiled, and even made unpalatable by the melodramatic way in which it was stated. It was a great pity.

These, then, were the essential ideas which Comte elaborated and wove together in his system of knowledge (including the science of sociology), and though we have dealt with each as briefly and clearly as possible, I hope that their interrelatedness, as parts of a *system* of ideas, has been made quite evident. Comte was, in fact, one of the most systematic of thinkers. From his diagnosis of the problems of his time, throughout the critical construction of his whole scheme of knowledge, throughout the creation of his science of sociology, right up to the devising of an actual polity and the making of proposals for an extensive international programme of political action, all Comte's ideas were devetailed into each other with a fantastic degree of rational inter-connectedness and articulation. And, as we have seen, this included not only a system of his own devising—in the sense of something which was concocted purely from his own ideas, but a systematic bringing together of all the many contributions to scientific and social thought whose significant relationships with each other he had clearly seen.

Indeed, his pride, towards the end of his life, lay in the fact that he did indeed accomplish the gigantic task of intellectual synthesis which he set himself ealry in his youth. His Course of Positive Philosophy outlined the systematic way of achieving the knowledge on the basis of which social reconstruction could take place. His System of Positive Polity extended this, elaborated the nature of sociology in particular, and set out the outlines of a new polity which, established first among the nations of the West, could ultimately be extended to embrace all the nations of the world—bringing material security, peace, justice, and the conditions for continual improvement—and so achieve the unity of mankind.

It was, in fact, a great achievement.

These essential ideas aside, however, Comte has many other far from incidental merits and contributions which deserve critical reappraisal. These we cannot fully explore because they are not central to our purpose, but a few of them should at least be indicated because they have some relevance to the ideas and purposes which were taken up by subsequent sociologists, and to which we shall refer later.

First of all, it is worthwhile to note that Comte adopted a very definite position with regard to the relations between psychology and sociology, and that this position had certain distinct merits, and posed important problems, even if it was not altogether free from ambiguity. Comte's views lie decidedly on the side of those whose dictum is: 'All psychology is *social* psychology'—at least as far as man is concerned. Biology (and psychology related to this) can provide us with a basic knowledge of the elements of experience and behaviour attendant upon the facts of anatomy, physiology, and the like, which comprise the inherited endowment of human nature. These alone, however, cannot possibly explain the many differing qualities of experience and behaviour which are brought into being *in* individual lives by virtue of their membership of a social and cultural tradition. They do not explain the detailed differences of religious experience, political experience, language, aesthetic experience, among individuals from society to society. For the explanation of *these* elements of perception, feeling, motivation, thought, action, an analysis of *society* is necessary. However, two other points must be made perfectly clear.

Though emphasizing the *social* context of human experience and behaviour, Comte by no means wished to exclude or to deny the importance of, the fundamental bio-psychological elements of human nature. On the contrary, he wished to establish the 'fundamental laws of life and mind' at this level so that they could be related—deductively and hypothetically—with 'laws' at the *societal* level. It is worth remarking very clearly that Comte insisted upon the close relationship between the two levels in order to achieve as complete as possible an explanation and understanding of man in society.

The other very important point is that Comte insisted upon the necessity of a close relationship between not only psychology and sociology, but also between these two and moral philosophy, in any satisfactory study of 'Man the Individual'. He was surely right in maintaining that the *social* framework of reference is necessary for the psychological study of the individual, and that sociology and psychology should work in the closet combination: but this additional point, that neither sociology nor psychology can properly understand the actuality of human nature in isolation from the study of moral and social philosophy, is one which—though unfashionable—is well worth consideration. Here, we can only note that Comte stated and developed this persuation very fully.

It is also important to note that, in his analysis of the chief components of 'social systems', Comte emphasized especially the central significance of the 'Division of Labour' in society. Indeed, his entire analysis of the nature of society: its 'units', its elements of 'strucutre', its 'apparatus', and their inter-relationships within the 'system' of society as a whole; and his entire analysis of the changes and developments of societies; rested upon the central fact of the 'division of functions' and the 'combination of efforts' which came into being as a community came to terms with its environment. Comte's acount was a completely clear 'structural-functional' analysis of the nature of social order and social change in relation to environmental circumstances.

Comte claimed that Aristotle was the first to lay down this basis for the analysis of society.

'Aristotle,' he wrote, 'laid down the true principle of every collective organism, when he described it as the distribution of functions, and the combination of labour. Strangely enogh, our modern economists claim the discovery of this luminous conception, whilst narrowing it, with metaphysical empiricism, to a mere law of industry. The first of philosophers repudiated this particular application of the theory. In its original form, he gave it the wide extension required for its systematic use...

...when society is organized in active co-operation, and this is the characteristic of civil society, this itself becomes a constant source of differences, mental and moral. And these would ever tend to destroy the association altogether, were it not preserved by some appaaratus adequate to maintain the organization. Accordingly, the ground plan of Social Statics as a whole ultimately rests on the principle of the distribution of functions... Thus sociology is finally furnished with an invaluable centre for its Statical work, and its Dyanamical will be in reality nothing but the development of this central principle to its necessary conclusions. In fact, the principle of distribution of functions usually employed to explain the earliest rise of civil society, has now been shown to be the ground on which we may ultimately construct our entire theory...'

This particular emphasis in Comte's scheme of sociological analysis is worth noting, not only because it demonstrates with the utmost clarity the oudinig and adoption of a 'structural-functional' analysis of social systems at the very foundation of the subject, but also because it will serve later to demonstrate the clear continuity in the development of the subjet. We shall see that Emile Durkheim made his own contributions to the making of sociology by taking up certain of these fundamental points of emphasis stated by Comte, and developing them further. This is true both of Comte's emphasis upon 'social psychology' and his emphasis upon the 'division of functions' and the 'division of labour' in society.

Indeed with this prospective reference to Durkheim in mind there is one other special aspect of Comte's 'structural-functional' analysis of social systems which is worth mention: that is his suggestion that (as in biology, so in sociology) the 'normal' functions of the parts of a society might well be clarified by a study of their 'pathology'. As we can become more clearly aware of the function which a part of the body is normally performing within the organism as a whole, when it breaks down, or ceases to function, or comes to be diseased in its functioning, so we may be able more clearly to know the function which a social institution normally performs in the social system as a whole by studying the consequences of its breakdown, or its degrees of 'mal-functioning', brought about by various causes.

The study of the 'pathological' as well as the 'normal' was therefore given a special place in sociological method by Comte, and this too was seized upon by Durkheim and developed in his own rules of sociological method. The *raison d'etre* for this method—namely, the progressive clarification of the functions of the units, or parts, of the social system—has not commonly been fully appreciated.

Comte was also extremely jealous of the central persuasion of sociology, that all the institutions of society had to be seen in their interrelatedness, in their 'consensus', if any one of them, or all of them, or any changes in them, were satisfactorily to be understood. He was was strongly opposed to any facile development of supposed 'specialisms' in sociology. He wrote as follows:

'There can be no scientific study of society, either in its conditions or its movements, if it is separated into portions, and its divisions are studied apart. The methodical division of studies which takes place in the simple inorganic sciences is thoroughly irrational in the recent and complex science of soceity...It is no easy matter to study social phenomena in the only right way—viewing each element in the light of the whole system. It is no easy matter to exercise such vigilance as that no one of the number of contemporary aspects shall be lost sight of. But it is the right and the only way...'and '...by any other method of proceeding, we shall only find ourselves encumbered with special discussions, badly instituted, worse pursued' and 'accomplishing no other purpose that that of impeding the formation of real science.'

With this, as with every point one makes about Comte, his relevance for the problems of sociology in our own time becomes patently clear.

It is the same with his strictures on an ill-considered 'empiricism'. Though the collection of information is obviously important, Comte opposed altogether the idea that an 'empirical' sociology was a kind of 'social arithmetic'; that it consisted of collecting and counting *facts* in contemporary society; that it was empirical because you actually went out, with notebook and pencil in hand, and looked through your eyeballs at what was *there now;* that it was *scientific* in that it was accurate.

Comte would have made two points: first, as we have seen, that this conception of empiricism is a misconception of science as such, and second, again, that social facts are eseentially historical, and that the idea that you can observe and understand contemporary social facts independent of historical perspective is an illusion. No history, says Comte, no sociology, and it is perfectly clear what he meant.

Even in his concern for morality and political action, which, as we have seen, was so extravagantly overlaid and overdressed by his proposals for the ritual ordering of his new religion, Comte made points of considerable importance, and took the trouble to apply himself to the working out of a definite programme of political reform which foreshadowed much of what is only now coming into being.

Comte argued that in the past social sympathy had been too much restricted to the idea of the Nation, and that it would become the duty of the nations of Western Europe in particular to move beyond their nationalities to form a European Union as a preliminary step in seeking the union of humanity as a whole.

'Wise and generous intervention of the West on behalf of our sister nations who are less advanced, will form a noble field for Social Art, when based on sound scientific principles. Relative without being arbitrary, zealous and yet always temperate; such should be the spirit of this intervention; and thus conducted, it will form a system of moral and politcal action far nobler than the proselytism of theology or the extension of military empire. The time will come when it will engross the whole attention of the Positive Council...'

It is this, of course, which is now coming increasingly to engross the attention of our councils, in Europe and in the United Nations.

The work of Comte, then, quite apart from providing the first systematic statement of the foundation of sociology as a science, positively bristles with ideas which are both relevant to, and correctives of, many conceptions and practices of our time.

It is perfectly true that Comte was unbalanced as a person in many respects, that he was precocious, egotistical in the extreme, and possessed of an almost boundless megalomania. It is true that his personal qualities and personal affairs led him to quite outrageous extravagances in his elaboration of some of his ideas. Yet, if we have the patience and fair-mindedness to set these elements aside, there is a core of very considerable importance in his work. Edward Beesly, one of Comte's translators, wrote:

'I am not sure that the intelligent reader has always the patience to consider whether he has really grasped Comte's full meaning. Never was there a writer whose every word requires to be so carefully weighed.'

And Gilbert Murray, a man of the soundest judgment, was of the same opinion.

'Whatever the failures imperfections of his actual statement,' he wrote, 'I cannot but feel, first, that his system forms a wonderful achievement of sincere and constructive thinking and, secondly, that the thing he is trying to say, if only he could succeed in saying it, is not only sublime, but true.'

These judgments, I believe, are wholly sound.

It is only fair, too, to say that Comte encountered personal difficulties, and possessed personal qualities, which were such as to do much to offset the less fortunate aspects of his nature which are commonly emphasized by critics who wish to derogate his ideas by pointing a finger of scorn at him.

Comte was, of course, mentally ill, and extremely so, during some periods of his life, and experienced family and other circumstances that explain much.

He was the son of Royalist and Roman Catholic parents. Grappling, with desperate honesty, with the radical changes of thought in the revolutionary situation, he had continually to resist parental wishes and criticisms as boy, youth, and man. His mother, in particular, must have exerted powerful emotional pressure upon him, hoping to see him remain within the religion of his birth. The extent of the parental pressures he encountered may be conjectured from an incident relating to his marriage.

Comte, because of his beliefs, had resisted his parents' wish to solemnize his marriage by a religious ceremony. During a period in which he was suffering severe mental illness, whilst he was still violently unbalanced, his mother, with the aid of a zealous Abbe and the Archbishop of Paris, contrived to have her son and his wife undergo the ceremony of marriage—conducted by a priest—before leaving the asylum. It is a shocking, harrowing story; an almost unbelievable instance of how far maternal love (if that is the right word) and clerical malpractice (if that is a sufficient word) can go.

And on his side in the matter of personal qualities two things might be remembered. First, he was not a man only to talk. He did not only advocate, for example, the free scientific education of working men. From 1830 to 1848, on Sunday afternoons and without fees, he delivered annually a course of lectures to them. Second, his compassion for the unfortunate among mankind was deeply and genuinely felt. As a young man of eighteen and nineteen, wandering about the streets of Paris during the time of carnival, his wonder and comment was—how it was possible that people could so forget that thirty thousand human beings around them had barely a morsel to eat. Similarly, at the very end of his life, living very frugally, and, again, with an almost absurd asceticism, 'at the close of dinner he daily substituted for dessert a piece of dry bread, which he ate slowly, meditating on the numerous poor who were unable to procure even that means of nourishment in return for their work'.

'The world, ' said John Morley, 'has strong self-protecting qualities. It will take what is available in Comte, while forgetting that in his work which is as irrational in one way as Hegel is in another.' This is true. But the world might, at the same time, be gracious in its understanding of the probable causes of such irrationality, and exercise some magnaimity in considering the work of a man who dedicated himself to the service of mankind more than most. Despite its great extravagances, Comte's contribution is one of considerable and enduring worth. The foundation of the new science of sociology—seen to be so necessary, by so many, for so long—was clearly and firmly accomplished at his hands. This was a great achievement.

Summary

With the aim of complete clarity in mind, let us summarize the chief elements of the first systematic statement of Sociology by Comte in order to see the ways in which it constituted an advance upon the early social theories and common sense in which it was rooted. If we follow this practice in relation to each contributor, we should finally achieve a clear picture of the nature, scope, and main elements of the subject as it had been created by the end of the nineteenth century.

(a) Scientific knowledge: a clear delimitation

(I) THE LIMITATION OF SCIENTIFIC KNOWLEDGE

Following the ideas of Hume and Kant, Comte achieved a very clear statement of what science could achieve, and should attempt. The scope of scientific knowledge was precisely delimited. Scientific knowledge consisted of such propositions about the regularities of connection between phenomea as could be subjected to test. Anything going beyond this, even the idea of 'causes' as being something lying 'behind' phenomena, forcing them to be what they were, was abondoned. Knowledge consisted of statements of regularities found in the world of our experience.

(II) SCIENTIFIC 'LAWS'

These propositions were of two kinds: *(a)* 'uniformities of co-existence' (about the interdependence of parts in the phenomena one was studying), and (*b*) 'uniformities of succession' (about the actual changing varities of such phenomena in the world, which we sought to explain).

(III) STATICS AND DYNAMICS

Statics was that part of a science devoted to the careful analysis of its subject-matter, the analysis of the 'consensus' of parts in the whole, (i.e. in the 'organism' in Biology, or the 'social system' in Sociology), thus producing 'uniformities of co-existence'.

Dynamics, applying this analysis, was the study of the actual changing forms of the subject-matter existing in the world, thus producing 'uniformities of succession'.

(IV) A CLASSIFICATION OF THE SCIENCES

All sciences were of this nature, and could be classified in accordance with the order of their emergence and development, the order of their dependence upon each other, the degree of complexity of their subject-matter and the degree of exactitude possible, and the degree of modifiability of the facts which they studied. There was no *one* kind of scientific method and technique. Each science uncovered 'laws' appropriate to its subject-matter; at its own 'level' of facts. The propositions of no science could be 'reduced' to another, through deductions from knowledge in one could furnish hypotheses for another; and the levels could therefore be connected.

(V) A BASIS FOR PREDICTION AND ACTION

Such knowledge, though circumscribed and limited, was bounded by clear criteria. It was, therefore, just because of its prescribed limitations, the most exact and reliable basis for (*a*) *prediction* and (*b*) the *guidance of action.*

(VI) SCIENTIFIC KNOWLEDGE NEVER FINAL

Such knowledge was not final, but 'relative' to human nature and its circumstances. Though 'relative', however, it was not *arbitrary.* It rested on the most carefully considered criteria of which man was capable at any particular time.

(b) Scientific knowledge of society: Sociology

(I) SOCIOLOGY: A SCIENCE

Sociology was one science among others, so defined. It had become necessary because a specific 'level' of facts had become recognized in human experience which existing sciences could not sufficiently explore or explain.

(II) THE EXISTENCE OF 'SOCIAL SYSTEMS'

It had become recognized that groups and institutions existed in some relationship of interdependence in societies as wholes, and that they could only be properly understood within this perspective. Sociology was necessary, therefore, as the scientific study of 'social systems'.

(III) THE NECESSITY OF THE METHODS OF SCIENCE

Testable knowledge (as distinct from opinion or speculative conjecture) about 'social systems', as about any other facts in our experience, could only be achieved by using the methods of science.

(IV) THE ABANDONMENT OF METAPHYSICAL' EXPLANATION

Sociology therefore abandoned explanations of social systems in terms of 'final ends' or 'ultimate purposes', or even 'causes' which 'lay behind' social phenomena.

(V) THE DELIMITATION OF SOCIOLOGY

Sociology deliberately confined itself to discovering and stating regularities about the nature of social systems; the interconnections between their parts in whole societies; and the relations between such societies themselves. 'Whole societies' were related to each other to some extent and in certain ways within 'human society' as a whole throughout the world, and had come to be what they were within the cumulative processes of history. Sociology was concerned to establish knowledge about this entire fabric of social interdependency.

(VI) SOCIOLOGICAL 'LAWS'

The propositions of sociology would state regularities of at least two kinds: (*a*) 'uniformities of co-existence' (about the nature of the 'social system' as a subject-matter, and the relations between the parts of society and the whole; about the kind of 'consensus' of facts a 'social system' was) and (*b*) 'uniformities of succession' (about the changing nature of actual societies in history).

(VII) SOCIAL STATICS AND SOCIAL DYNAMICS

Sociology was (like all sciences) divided into Social Statics: devoting itself to the conceptual analysis of the nature of social systems; their parts, their functions, their interrelations; and Social Dynamics: devoting itself to the application of this analysis to achieve an understanding and exaplanation of the varieties of societies in the world. Statics and Dynamics were *not* distinguished as having separate subject-matters, they were only two different aspects of method and theory.

(VIII) SOCIAL STATICS (1) : STRUCTURAL-FUNCTIONAL ANALYSIS

The complex nature of a society could be analysed in terms of 'structures' and their 'functions'. Its 'units' (groups and institutions) and their 'apparatus' could be described and analysed and their functions clarified. The normal functions of units might be illuminated by studying 'pathological' conditions of social systems, when institutions had, by the aggravation and intensification of certain normal processes, broken down; or for some reason had been brought into disorder and disorganization.

(IX) SOCIAL STATICS (2): SOCIAL INSTITUTIONS AN ORDERING OF FEELING, THOUGHT, AND ACTION

These elements of 'structure' and 'function' could be understood by focusing upon the central fact that they brought the *feeling, thought,* and *action* of men into satisfactory relationship with each other whilst, as members of the community, they were dealing with the material and organizational problems related to their environmental situation.

(X) SOCIAL STATICS AND SOCIAL DYNAMICS LINKED: THE CONSTRUCTION OF MODELS

This kind of analysis could provide the framwork for a detailed study of the varieties of societies and the processes of historical change, by facilitating the construction of clear 'models' or 'types' of social system. The 'theological', the 'metaphysical', the 'positive' stages of social organization were three such 'types' of social order (three kinds of institutionally patterned organi-zation of feeling, thought, and action) in terms of which the actual changes of society in history could be illuminated and understood.

(XI) SOCIAL DYNAMICS : A TYPE OF HISTORICAL SEQUENCE

These 'types' did not exist as pure, actual societies. Every society, at different periods, could be understood as a blend of them. Also, societies in history were interconnected in wide cultural movements and epochs in which changes from a predominance of one 'type' to the predominance of another, took place. It was possible, therefore, against conceptually, to employ the 'scientific artifice' of conceiving of human history as a 'rational series', or a 'rational fiction', drawing upon the many actual societies and their modifications which we can observe, and by this means understanding the sequence of social change through the three types. The 'models' of social order also implied a 'model' of social change—and was of the nature, therefore, of a hypothesis.

(XII) TYPES OF SOCIAL ORDER AND SOCIAL CHANGE FOCUSED UPON MIND AND KNOWLEDGE IN SOCIETY

The construction of these types of social order and social change was focused upon the development of thought and feeling, of mind and knowledge, in society, because these could be seen to be crucial for the orientation of the institutional activities of men; and therefore all social institutions could be expected to be correlated with them.

(XIII) DEDUCTIONS AND HYPOTHESES, SUPPORTING EMPIRICAL GENERALIZATIONS, YIELDED EXPLANATIONS

Also. these 'types' of social order and social change rested *both* upon deduction from what was known about the biological and psychological aspects of human nature, *and* upon empirical generalizations about the actual interdependence of social institutions found in history. Deduction and hypotheses therefore supported empirical generalizations to provide 'explanations'.

(XIV) METHODS OF SOCIOLOGY

The methods of sociology, in this entire task, included those of the other sciences: observation, description, classification, comparison; experimentation in so far as it was possible; and, in addition, and uniquely, the historical method. The historical method was necessary because human societies were different from other 'facts' in nature in being historical, cumulative, cultural sequences of feeling, thought and action. The classificatory and comparative method and the historical method thus supported each other.

(XV) THE KNOWLEDGE OF SOCIOLOGY NEVER FINAL KNOWLEDGE

The knowledge established by Sociology would not, and could never claim to be, 'final' or 'absolute'. It would always be 'relative' to the nature of man and his circumstances. At the same time it would not be 'arbitrary', but based always upon the clearest criteria of testable truth which men could achieve in their time. As in all positive sciences, it would be continuously open to objective test. It would be capable of continuous extension in range, and improvement in accuracy. And only if this was so could the degree of men's responsible and effective control over their environment and social organization be capable of improvement.

(XVI) A BASIS FOR PREDICTION AND SOCIAL PRACTICE

The knowledge of sociology would, therefore, though deliberately limited by its own criteria, be the most exact and reliable basis we could achieve for *prediction,* and for the making of *practical policies* in society.

The nature and scope of sociology was now outlined with meticulous clarity. The nature of its subject-matter, and the nature of its methods were laid out in a completely systematic fashion. A mode of analysing social order and, thereafter, of investigating and explaining social change was clearly outlined. And social theory was linked with the practical tasks of politics with which men were confronted. Properly pursued, sociology promised a basis of the most reliable knowledge possible on which practical judgment and decision could rest.

Sociology, then, even in this—its firts statement—could clearly be seen to go beyond the assumptions and dilemmas of common sense, and beyond the earlier theories of man and society. It provided not only a new perspective on the nature and development of society, but also a framework for the testing of its own pronouncements; a basis for the continuous growth of its knowledge.

Out of the many roots which had preceded it, the science of society was, at last, *made:* clear and complete as a system of analysis. All the main components for a satisfactory knowledge of society—the study of government, of religion, of education, of property, of social classes and their conflicts, of all those institutions which were the sources of men's troubles—now found their place within this new perspective: *the only perspective within which they could be understood.* From this point on, the sociological perspective was *the only satisfactory perspective.* Those who rejected it, had to provide one more reliable. So far, in the century that has followed, they have raised only a great cloud of dusty argument which still drifts across our vision, but an alternative and more reliable perspective has not yet been produced.

Meanwhile, the foundation so successfully laid by Comte has been built upon and enriched in many ways.

3

John Stuart Mill : A logical Critique of Sociology

John Stuart Mill, one of the greatest and most humane thinkers of the nineteenth century, indeed of any century, is very well known for his contributions to ethics, political philosophy, economics and logic, to mention but a few of the subjects to which he devoted himself. Curiously, however, his contribution to the making of sociology is little known and has been considerably under-estimated. Unlike Comte, Mill did not even attempt a substantive theory of man in society. He was conscious of the fact that the human sciences were too little advanced, in his own time, for any complete statement. Instead, he undertook a logical clarification of the methods most properly to be employed in these sciences, and the kinds of generalization and the degree of exactitude which it was reasonable to expect them to attain.

In a correspondence with de Tocqueville, for example, Mill refused his invitation to construct the science of society whose methods he had (so de Tocqueville thought) so clearly proposed, because, he said, it was so difficult and so little advanced. And in the sixth book of his own *System of Logic* he said that he was quite well aware of how little could be done towards the substantive creation of this science in what was, as he put it, a *mere* treatise on logic. However, he thought that something could be done to suggest the outlines of such a science; to make clear the kinds of methods that were most appropriate to it and the kinds of methods that ought from the outset, to be rejected.

Mill approached the study of the social sciences from at least three points of view.

Firstly, like Comte, he was persuaded that the problems peculiar to human society since the French Revolution—the disruption of the old social order, the new problems created by complex industrial development, the problem of replacing the established traditional authority of both religion and Government by some more rationally based morality, and the like—could only be dealt with effectively on the basis of a new body of *knowledge* about man and society, and this could only be achieved by the use of scientific method. In the preface of his book on logic, Mill said that the last section of his work was: 'an attempt to contribute towards the solution of a question which the decay of old opinions and the agitation that disturbs European society to its inmost depths, render as important in the present day to the practical interest of human life as it must at all times be to the completeness of our speculative knowledge—whether moral and social phenomena are really exceptions to the general certainty and uniformity of the course of nature, and how far the methods by which so many of the laws of the physical world have been numbered among truths irrevocably acquired and universally assented to, can be made instrumental to the formation of a similar body of received doctrine in moral and political science.'

Mill's primary object then, in considering the establishment of a science of man and society, was that of being in a position to deal adequately with the problems confronting mankind in the modern world. His concern, like that of Comte, and most previous philosophers, was ethical and practical, as well as being speculative in a purely intellectual sense.

Secondly, however, Mill was also much aware of and much in sympathy with the desire of Hume to see a science of man formulated, and at the end of his book on logic, having considered the application of scientific method to the study of man, he commented in the following way.

'Notwithstanding', he said, 'the extreme generality of the principles of method which I have laid down, I have indulged the hope that to some of those on whom the task will devolve of bringing those most important of all sciences into a more satisfactory state, these observations may be useful. Should this hope be realized, what is probably destined to be the great intellectual achievement of the next two or three generations of European thinkers will have been, in some degree, forwarded.'

Thirdly, Mill was amongst the first thinkers in Britain, or in any other country for that matter, to be thoroughly acquainted with the work of Comte, and to concern himself with a critical assessment of his ideas, and the furthering of his proposals for a science of sociology. In this sense, Mill was responsible for giving the work of Comte wide publicity in Britain and, indeed, he was one of a number of Englishmen who actually helped to maintain Comte financially during a particular, important and problematical period of his life.

Much emphasis, however, must be placed not only upon Mill's methodology of social science as such, but also on his study of logic proper.

Mill was concerned with a very specific problem here. The natural sciences had developed over the previous two centuries, and had without any question, demonstrated their worth in producing testable and reliable knowledge about all aspects of the nature of the physical world. Curiously, however, the kind of *logic* which men still considered as being productive of truth, the only kinds of *inference* which they still considered to constitute a pattern of clear thinking, was the syllogistic logic which had been little changed since the time of Aristotle. There was an odd gap between the procedures of inference which men actually used in science, and the philosophical account of such logic as could be employed. Mill was therefore very much concerned to clarify the new procedures of inference used in the natural sciences. He wanted to discover, and to state as clearly as possible, the ways in which men actually produced testable knowledge of the world of their experience.

His main emphasis in his whole study of logic was that the earlier conviction that knolwedge of the world could be produced from completely *a priori* assumptions and propositions, was false, and that—no matter how conjectural some generalizations or hypotheses might appear—*all* of them, without any question, were derived from human *experience*. They were, that is to say, *inductive,* rather than *a priori* and *deductive,* in origin. This is not to say, by any means, that Mill thought deduction played no part in science and its procedures of inference. On the contrary, he thought it was extremely important. His chief point was only that the propositions and generalizations which men established about the nature of the world—whether produced by clear and systematic methods, by the deliberate assembling of as many facts of a particular kind as possible, or whether purely by a rough-and-ready analysis of our common sense experience—were all *drawn from experience.* As we shall see later, however, this does not mean that Mill, as many critics have said, was guilty, in any sense, of a naive notion of induction or of 'inductive logic'.

In addition to insisting upon this experiential basis of all human knowledge; the foundation in empirical experience of all worthwhile procedures of inference; Mill then went on to undertake a detailed examination of all those procedures of experimentation or comparison, all those procedures of inference, of handling data in order to produce conditions of test, of judging evidence, whereby scientists actually attained their results. Having clarified these procedures as they had, in fact, been developed, and as they were, in fact, used in the natural sciences, Mill then, in the final book of the *Logic,* applied them to the study of man and society, in order to see whether and how far, they could be fruitfully employed in this kind of study. Mill's concern in the *Logic* then, though having a very important bearing upon the development of sociology, a 'general science of man in society', was much wider than this. His book on logic can be said to be among the most important contirbutions in this field since the time of Aristotle.

For *our* purposes, however, it is Book VI of the *Logic* which is of the greatest importance, and it will be most rewarding, for understanding the development of sociology, to analyse Mill's main proposals and arguments in this book.

The state of 'knowledge' concerning man and society

Mill began by claiming how backward, when compared with the degree of exactitude established in the natural sciences, was man's knowledge about his own nature and the nature of his own society. Having shown how successful the various sciences which establish 'laws' about the natural world had become, Mill claimed that the laws of mind and, to an even greater degree, those of society, were so far from having attained an even approximate degree of certainty in their formulation, and an even partial degree of recognition among scholars, that it was still an open controversy whether they were capable of becoming subjects of science at all in the strict sense of the term. And, he claimed, those who were agreed on this point disagreed on almost every other!

'If a more general agreement is ever to exist among thinkers,' he wrote, 'if what has been pronounced the proper study of mankind is not destined to remain the only subject which philosophy cannot succeed in rescuing from empiricism, the same process through which the laws of many simpler phenomena have by general acknolwedgement been placed beyond dispute must be consciously and deliberately applied to those more difficult enquiries.'

Man's knowledge concerning his own nature and his own society was still very much, even in the mid-nineteenth century, in the realm of *opinion* rather than that of testable knowledge, and the only way in which this situation could be improved was that the methods of science should at least be applied as far as this proved possible.

The only thing it is salutary to notice, before leaving this, is that Mill's words are almost as applicable to our own time as to the time in which he was writing. The situation is not too different some hundred and twenty-five years afterwards. This alone should cause us to stop and take very seriously the question Mill was raising.

A first objection : the freedom of will

Before trying to clarify the methods most appropriate to the study of man and society. Mill first dealt with what he thought was a genuine obstacle to many people; a problem which, for many, seemed altogether to preclude the possibility of a scientific study of man. And it is worthwhile to look at his discussion of this problem very closely, since it is a source of disquiet to many people still. It is the old question of the freedom of the will.

If, as many people believed, Mill said, human individuals possessed free will; if they could exercise deliberate choice; how was it possible to establish generalized knowledge about them which would allow *predictions* to be made? How could a *scientific* knowledge of men and societies be possible? If people could exercise choice, no matter how carefully we made predictions about them, they would always be able to act differently if they so wished, and thus confound our predictions. Furthermore, if a man possessed free will and could exercise choice, how was it possible to claim that his nature was causally determined; was the outcome of *causes?*

Mill treated this question in what seems to me an admirable and well-nigh conclusive way.

He began by arguing that it was an error to discuss the question of free will in too abstract a way. No one believes, for example, that a human being 'possesses' a 'will' in the same sense that he possesses a brain or heart or lungs or any other part of his body. When we use the word 'will', we are speaking not of some part of man, but of his capacity for exercising choice; the ability to exercise conscious deliberation, and, subsequently, to control his conduct. Similarly, when we want to maintain that human beings possess *'free'* will we never think that, in their exercise of choice, they are *completely* free; free without any reference to limitations. The idea of freedom, indeed, can never really be held as a complete abstraction. It is always a question of being free *to do* something, or being free *from* something; and it is always *to some extent.*

To put the matter briefly, Mill maintained that the best way of considering this question was to reduce it to more modest and sensible terms. Instead of asking: do men possess free will? it is better to ask: can men exercise choice? And, if so, does this prevent us from claiming that human nature and conduct are the outcome of causes about which we can establish scientific knowledge?

His first point was then the straightforward one that there is no inconsistency whatever in maintaining *both* that man's character is the outcome of causes *and* that he is capable of exercising choice, for the simple reason that, in human experience and behaviour, the choices that men make are themselves among the causes of their subsequent character and behaviour.

It is true that a man is born into a particular social environment; a complex set of circumstances. He is brought up within a family and is educated in a certain school. He grows up surrounded by the beliefs, values, ideals, institutions of society. His nature is therefore, quite obviously, to a very large extent shaped by these influences. But, throughout his experince of these influences, as he is growing to maturity and afterwards, he reflects upon them to some extent, changes his ideas about them to some extent, and chooses ways of behaving which, upon reflection, he has to some extent worked out for himself. Without at all pressing the matter so far so to argue that the individual can achieve *entire* self-determination, it is quite clear that the choices he makes have a determining influence upon the ways in which he behaves and the kind of character he becomes afterwards. For example, if a boy, on leaving school, chooses to follow one career rather than another, this will have an enormous determining influence upon the circumstances which will exert subsequent influences upon him for many years to come; and this will therefore have a determining influence upon aspects of his behaviour and character. If he chooses to become a soldier, a civil servant, a university student, each of these choices will have a very different effect upon his behaviour, his habits, his mode of life, and his character in future.

It seems clear then, Mill argued, that the choices a person makes are among the causes of his behaviour, and, therefore, that if we could know *all* the antecedents of a man's present character, it would be possible to give a causal account of his whole development; since his deliberations and his choices were themselves causes (among other kinds of causes) of the ongoing changes in his nature. It turns out, then, that there is no inconsistency whatever in saying that, to some extent, a man can shape his own character, but, also, that his character is the outcome of causes.

Mill claimed that the discussion of the 'free will versus determinism' issue in the past had been bedevilled by an unwarranted element of 'necessitarianism' in the idea of 'causal determination'. It had come to be thought that to say that a causal account could be given of a man's character and behaviour, was to say that the causes, including his choices, of a man's life and conduct were, in some sense, *inevitable*. The choices were only apparent choices, because, in fact, they could not possibly have been any different.

Mill completely rejected this 'necessitarian' idea as an undemonstrable and unnecessary metaphysical assertion, and claimed that a man could reflect and choose in his life, but, nonetheless, that these reflections and choices were among the causal influences shaping his subsequent nature, and that if we knew all about them we could give a full causal account of his development. The reason why we are always unable to give such a complete causal account of any individual is simply that we do not, and cannot, know all the factors and events which were antecedent to his present nature. We shall return to this point later.

Having clarified this, however, Mill went on to make his second important point. This that—although a man may exercise choice, and although we need not deny some degree of freedom of the will—his choices are nonetheless, in fact, very considerably circumscribed by at least two factors. A man's choices are never completely free; they are always exercised within constraints which can be specified and known.

First of all, from the beginning of his life, an individual gradually develops a *settled character*. His inclinations, his dispositions, his attitudes, his habits, are never completely arbitrary. They come to have a certain stable and settled form, a certain pattern, in his character. This character will be partly the outcome of his responses to all that he imbibes from his social environment; but it will also be the outcome of his own efforts to achieve the kind of character which other people desire of him, or that he himself, in the context of other people's judgments, desires. We do find, in fact, that when we know a man's character sufficiently well, we can predict with a large measure of accuracy how he will exercise his choice, and how he will conduct his deliberation upon various matters. We can predict how he will choose. And this is not because he is not free to choose. It is simply that, knowing him well enough, we know *how* he will exercise his freedom. Taking Mill's earlier point into account, it is important to see that the man we know will, in fact, be judging freely, in accordance with his own convictions, his own principles. He *could* choose to do something else if he wished to do so; he could deliberately flout our predictions if he wished; but he will not, in fact, do anything else because of the particular nature of his character.

We do not, therefore, need to regard a man as a machine, as an automation, before we can predict about him. Of course, a man may do something totally unexpected; incalulable; but, in our experience, this is so exceptional as usually to astonish us. And, if it happens, we conclude that, after all, we did not know this person's character as well as we had thought. We frequently say of a person who has done something unexpected: 'I never knew that he had it in him'. But in the normal, usual, sequences of a man's life we can, in fact, predict a good deal about him. We all know that when we know a person intimately, it is possible to predict in this manner and, furthermore, all our expectations in social intercourse are based upon such predictions.

Also, without being at all cynical, it is surely true that none of us are rational and reflective to the point of totally disentangling ourselves from our earlier experience. Our qualities of character have been very considerably engendered by the influences and pressures of our early environment. Even the most reasonable and reflective of us are aware of deep-rooted dispositions which more or less have their own way with us; which almost insist upon themselves in our behaviour, and determine our reactions, even when we think we think we have achieved rational control over them. Indeed, it is possible to be perfectly conscious that we possess some disposition in our nature and still be unable ourselves to govern it. Again, it is the case that the exercise of choice is a matter of degree, and thus this degree is within the context of settled dispositions of character.

Mill's second circumscribing factor is the immediate set of circumstances in which a person is placed. We are never able to exercise choice among an *infinity* of alternatives. We can exercise choice only among those limited alternatives which actually confront us in a given situation; and it is perfectly obvious that all social situations carry constraints which limit the things we would like to do. To give a simple example : if a man is employed in a factory which recognizes the practice of the 'closed shop', he can exercise choice only in a very limited number of ways. He can either leave the factory, or join the trade union, or work at the factory, not join the trade union, and put up with the misery and discomfort of being any, 'cont to Coventry'. He is not free to do *anything* that he likes. The range of his choices is *finite.* His choices are always limited in accordance with the immediate circumstances.

Mill claimed firstly, then, that though a man can choose, this does not preclude a causal account of his nature, since the choices are themselves causes; and, secondly, that a knolwedge of a person's character and of those social and physical circumstances in which he is placed, enables us to predict to a specifiable degree about the way in which, in fact, he will exercise his choices.

Many other things, of course, could be said about this issue between free will and determinism, but it seems to me that Mill treated it with an adequacy completely sufficient for his purpose, and for ours, which is that of showing that the fact that man can choose does not stand in the way of establishing testable scientific knowledge about him. It will be noted that—so far—this argument has been entirely concerned with individuals, though the specific study of social circumstances has entered. However, social facts, elements of social organization themselves, such as the legal system, the governmental system, the religious system of a community, can obviously be observed and described even more easily than individuals, and therefore, on the face of it, there seems to be no obstacle whatever in applying science either to the study of men as individuals or to the study of the institutions of their social life. Freedom of the will does not stand in the way of a science of man and society.

Before leaving this point, it is important to notice that Oxford historians, theologians, and others, who maintain that freedom of the will *does* stand in the way of science of society are obliged to come to terms with Mill's argument and to say, clearly, on what grounds they do not accept it.

The natural sciences and the human sciences

Having shown that a scientific study of man was, in principle, possible, Mill's next argument was to show that the human sciences (and their problems) were not so diferent from the physical sciences as was commonly supposed. To do this, he compared them briefly with three physical sciences—

meteorology (the science of the weather), tidology (the science of the tides) and astronomy.

In meteorology and tidology he showed that even though the underlying laws which govern the weather and the tides are known with considerable exactitude (the relationships, for example, between pressure and temperature: the influence exerted by the moon on the seas, etc.), it is still, nonetheless, beyond the power of the meteorologist and the tidologist to predict with precision what the weather or the level of tides will be at any particular spot and at any particular time. This is because they do not know, in sufficient exact detail, all the antecedents of the particular instances about which they are making predictions. We may know exactly the 'laws' of temperature and pressure which produce particular kinds of weather, but we cannot predict with exactitude what the weather will be like in East Anglia next August 3rd at 4.0 in the afternoon, simply because we cannot possibly know all the antecedents before that occasion. Similarly, though we may know exactly the extent of the attraction of the moon upon the sea and the way in which this produces the tides, we find it extremely difficult to predict what the level of the tide will be at Clacton on the second Thursday in May a year hence because we do not know all the other detailed circumstances that may be involved: the force of the wind at that time, or the local irregularities of the ocean bed (which may have changed before that time). What this amounts to, then, is that even in some physical sciences, though the underlying laws which govern the behaviour of the facts which they study are exactly known, and can be exactly demonstrated in laboratory conditions, it is still impossible to predict certain specific events of nature because, in any such particular situation, all the relevant antecedent facts cannot possibly be known.

Astronomy, on the other hand, is a precise science because *both* the general laws of the movements of the planets *and* the specific antecedents which cause the local perturbations in the orbits of particular planets are known. In this case, there has been sufficient time, and the phenomena are sufficiently simple, to allow knowledge of all the particular antecedents to particular planetary movements to be known as well as the general laws which govern the large-scale movements of the planets.

Logically, therefore, said Mill, there is no reason at all why the human sciences should be considered fundamentally different from these natural sciences. There may well be universal characteristics about human nature and human society. There may be similarities in all human societies, in certain institutions—let us say in the family, or religion. There may be universal laws of character development in human nature. But none of these would, in themselves, enable us to predict precisely about any particular person at any time, or about a specific change in any particular society. For precision, for exactitude, here, we would need as detailed a knowledge as we could get of all the peculiar local circumstances of the individual, or of the social order we were concerned to study, and this we can never hope to achieve completely. Mill maintained then, that the human sciences are in the condition of meteorology and tidology—where general laws may be ascertained but where precise exactitude in particular predictions seems likely to remain impossible.

However, the *degree* of exactitude of our particular predictions will become greater as our knowledge of the antecedents of these events increases. We can, that is to say, move the human sciences ever more closely to the kind of exactitude that astronomy has achieved, though without ever hoping to achieve the same degree of precision. This *imprecision* of our knowledge of human nature, however, is *not* because the thinking, feeling, acting of individuals are not consequent upon causes. It is only because we cannot possibly foresee all the particular *circumstances* in which individuals or societies will be placed, and because we cannot know with complete detail all the dimensions of the *characters* of the individuals and groups involved. These aspects of individuals and social behaviour are never altogether alike in different cases. Hence, a science of man and society can only, at the best, consist of empirical generalizations ('general laws') and statements of tendencies. Even so, our knowledge of these tendencies will, and can, be more or less exact, depending upon the methods of study we use. Furthermore, some aspects of human nature may be common to all of us even though other aspects may differ considerably.

'Inasmuch,'said Mill, 'however, as many of these effects which it is of most importance to render amenable to human foresight and control are determined (like the tides) in an incomparably greater degree by general causes than by all partial causes taken together, depending in the main on those circumstances and qualities which are common to all mankind, or at least to large bodies of them, and only in a small degree on particular or peculiar idiosyncrasies, it is evidently possible with regard to all such effects to make predictions which will almost always be verified, and general propositions which are almost always true.

'And whenever it is sufficient to know how the great majority of the human race or of some nation or class of persons will think, feel and act, these propositions are equivalent to universial ones.'

It would not be enough, however, simply to state these generalizations concerning the common aspects of human nature and human behaviour. They would, in addition, have to be explained.

Psychology: the essential basis of a science of man

Having thus shown that a scientific study of man and society was, in principle, possible, and was not, in principle, different from some natural sciences, Mill then proceeded to examine the possible nautre of a science of man, and undertook an exacting discussion of the methods most appropriate to it.

The starting-point of his views, and one which was very distinctive and on which he insisted, was the fundamental persusation that all *social* phenomena are rooted in the nature of human *individuals;* that all phenomena of *society* are, when properly considered, phenomena of human psychology.

'All phenomena of society', he says, 'are phenomena of human nature generated by the action of outward circumstances upon masses of human beings...The laws of the phenomena of society are, and can be, nothing but the laws or the actions and passions of human beings united together in the social state. Men in a state of society are still men. Their actions and passions are obedient to the laws of individual human nature. Men are not, when brought together, converted into another kind of substance with different properties as hydrogen and oxygen are different from water.'

Mill's first point, then, was that psychology was of the most fundamental importance for any kind of social explanation. He said relatively little about the actual nature of psychology, knowing very well that the subject was very much in its infancy, and being too sensible to attempt the establishment of knowledge when no knowledge really existed. However, he had some very interesting points to make about a science of psychology.

His first point of importance was that the science of psychology must be a science of observation and experiment. We could not, he claimed, know anything with any degree of certainly about human nature, human experience, and human behaviour, unless we followed the methods of observation and experiment. For too long, suppositions about human psychology had rested upon unsubstantiated opinion. Rigorous observation and rigorous experiment were therefore necessary.

Secondly, Mill had interesting points to make about the relationship between physiology and psychology. Clearly, he said, our psychological experiences—our emotions, motives, thoughts, purposes, sensations and the like—depend upon and rest upon certain bodily states. A knowledge of such bodily states is therefore necessary. However, he claimed, no amount of knowledge of the physical basis of psychological experiences can ever make an investigation of these experiences themselves unecessary. Physiological knowledge is knowledge additional to that of psychology; it is necessary and useful knowledge; but it is an error to think that it can altogether replace it. To put this another way, Mill argued firmly that psychological knowledge can never be *reduced* to 'explanations' in terms of physiological processes, and this, I think, is a point which deserves much emphasis at the present day in view of some developments of so-called 'Physiological psychology' which, strictly speaking, are nothing more than physiology proper.

A third point which Mill made clearly, was that environmental influences play a very great part in shaping or engendering qualities of human experience. He was strongly persuaded that, among human beings, differences in family circumstances, education, in all outward social situations, were capable of affording an adequate explanation of a considerable portion of personality and character formation, but he thought that if we knew more about inherited differences, about differences in the acuteness of the senses and perception, about differences in the inherited instincts and emotions, among individuals, that these might well yield a greater explanation of some differences of qualities of personality than we now think. For example, he thought that a great acuteness of the senses (a quick and subtle susceptibility to sense impressions) may lead to such qualities in personality and character as a love of the beautiful and moral enthusiasm, whereas a mediocre sensibility may be connected with a love of scienctific or abstract truth; and a person with such a limited sensibility might be deficient to some extent in artistic feeling and taste, and in moral fervour. It is important to say, however, that Mill did not *assert* these matters—he simply suggested them as possible examples of his view that if we knew more about these fundamental aspects of human sensation, impulse, emotion, they might be able to add a good deal to our explanations of human nature in addition to our knowledge of those environmental circumstances which play upon it.

The chief point of importance here, however, is simply that Mill was quite frimly convinced that psychology is an essential basis for the construction of a science of human society, and this was a very definite and basic component in his outline of such a science.

The scientific study of society

In addition to the study of individuals, Mill then said, it is obviously also necessary in any adequate science of human nature to study the facts of *social life:* 'the actions of collective masses of mankind, and the various phenomena which constitute society'.

In addition to our knowledge of individual feeling, thinking and acting, we need also, by observation and experiment, in so far as this proves possible, to establish a knowledge of the social institutions, the forms of social organization, within which men find themselves. Later, as we shall see, Mill described what he considered to be the main elements of social structure in any society when he spoke of the basic conditions for the existence of a society. For the moment, however, we can simply note that he believed a knowledge of social structure, of the institutional organization of society, to be a necessary component in a science of man, in addition to a knowledge of the nature of the individuals who live within it. However, it is very important to note here that Mill still maintained his strong belief that institutions do not exist, and cannot be said to exist in any sense, independently of individuals.

'All phenomena of society', he wrote, 'are phenomena of human nature generated by the action of outward circumstances upon masses of human beings: and if, therefore, the phenomena of human thought, feeling and action are subject to fixed laws, the phenomena of society cannot but conform to fixed laws, the consequence of the preceding. There is no hope that these laws, though our knowledge of them were as certain and complete as it is in astronomy, would enable us to predict the history of society like that of the celestial appearances for thousands of years to come. But the difference of certainty is not in the laws themselves, it is in the data to which these laws are to be applied.'

It is quite clear, then, that Mill required in his science of man *both* a knowledge of the structure of social institutions within which men carry on their social life and activities, *and* a knowledge of the psychological characteristics of individual human nature. Having insisted on this, he then went on to argue, however, that some *other* component is necessary in any science of human nature to investigate and explain the interaction between these two.

Ethology: the science of personality and character formation and of 'collective' psychological facts

This third component Mill called Ethology, and, as he described it, it is what modern psychologists would think of as a compound of personality psychology and social psychology. It is the scientific study of the way in which (given a basic knowledge of perception, motivation, emotion and other basic endowments of human nature) character and personality is developed by the influence of the groups and institutions within which individuals are born and brought up to maturity, and within which they continue to pursue their associational activities as adults. Mill believed that ethology was predominantly, indeed wholly, a deductive science.

On the one hand, observation and experiment can give us a basic knowledge of the psychological endowment of individuals. On the other, observation can give us a clear knowledge of the structure of groups and institutions within which individuals are born and grow to maturity. Ethology studies the way in which character formation takes place through the action of the institutional setting upon the basic psychological endowment. Mill believed, therefore, that ethology should follow deductive procedures in the sense that it should be possible to deduce, from a knowledge of psychology, what kind of character development would be likely to take place if certain specified conditions of social life were given. The validity and truth of this deduction could then be tested against our observations as to whether, in these specific social circumstances, this kind of character was, in fact, brought into being.

The science of ethology provides, therefore, what Mill called the 'middle principles', the '*axiomata media*', linking the observational sciences at either extreme.

An adequate science of human nature must therefore include these three necessary components: (1) a basic psychology, (2) a descriptive and analytical knowledge of social structure, and (3) a hypothetical study of social psychology and personality and character development, linking the other two.

To put this in a slightly different way, in order to point to other important dimensions, ethology would be necessary in order to show how the individuals within a community came to possess certain settled dispositions of character and personality; settled ideals, beliefs, attitudes, social purposes; and this knowledge would be necessary in order, further, to explain how changes in *some* institutions reacted upon people's dispositions in such a way as to bring about changes in others. This is an extremely important point to which we shall come back later.

In all this, it is most important to bear in mind that Mill certainly did not expect ever to be able to achieve the degree of exactitude in the human sciences that was possible in the natural sciences. He was only concerned to say that we should try to achieve the greates degree of exactitude that lay within our power. And he was continually reiterating that an amount of knowledge quite insufficient for prediction may be most valuable for guidance. The science of character—Ethology—may not permit of absolute precision. Nonetheless, it is the science on which the most important art of education rests, and Mill was always pointing out that, in spite of inexactitude, people in society *do* have very definite opinions as to what kind of family upbringing, what kind of school experience, what kind of instruction and training is most likely to bring about certain ends and qualities of character. Now these suppositions must rest upon implicit 'theories' about character development, and the only thing that we can possibly do to make our suppositions as reliable as we can, is to make these 'theories' as explicit and exact as possible, and to test them. Only on our most reliable *knowledge* of the facts of character-development can our arts of family unbringing and education be reliably based and effective. Only if they rest upon reliable knowledge are the methods we use in upbringing and education likely to bring about the ends that we desire. More broadly speaking, this same knowledge is necessary for the wise exercise of the art of government.

Having briefly outlined this three-fold nature of a general science of man and society, Mill then turned to the question as to what its methods should most properly be: which methods were obviously inappropriate, and which methods, on the other hand, would have to be followed if knowledge was to be established.

Methods appropriate to a study of man and society:

(1) Methods rejected

In one of the most important sections of his work, Mill then critically considered the extent to which the various methods of inductive study which he had earlier elaborated in his *Logic*, could be effectively applied to the study of man. Some of these methods he rejected outright, others he qualified, arriving finally at a conception of method in sociology which was closely in agreement with the one already elaborated by Comte. First of all let us look at the methods he rejected.

(a) The Chemical (Compound) Experimental Method

The first method which Mill completely, emphatically and, indeed, hotly rejected was what he called the 'chemical' or 'compound' method in social science, including the various 'experiental' methods attendant upon it.

Now this precise heading of Mill's chapter—which appears to equate the 'chemical' and the 'experimental' in speaking of this particular method—has, I believe, given rise to a considerable degree of misunderstanding of Mill's position. Furthermore, I believe that the point Mill was at pains to make in this section is of the very greatest importance, and I therefore think it is necessary to make it luminously clear. Later, we shall see that Durkheim, in criticizing Mill, actually falls into the error which Mill here warns against, and gives rise to much ambiguity as a result. The understanding of this matter here will be a valuable basis for understanding much that comes later.

Firstly, let us consider this term—the 'chemical' method; which seems rather curious in our modern ears. It seems odd to use the word 'chemical' to refer to a particular scientific method. What Mill essentially meant by this term was this.

There are some social scientists, indeed people in all walks of life, economists, politicians, clergymen and the like, he maintained, who speak as though they believe that social institutions or any other actualities of political and economic affairs (such as, for example, a tariff barrier or the bank rate) have an actual existence, as entities, over and above the heads of individuals, and are actually involved in a network of cause-and-effect relationships between each other without involving men and women as individuals—as, as it were mediators of social experience and action—at all. Mill was concerned to attack this idea root and branch! He thought it was a completely false way of conceiving the nature of society, and that it gave rise to a completely false method of exploring human interactions in the context of social structure and social change.

Let me try to make this absolutely clear.

Mill was *not* saying that elements of social structure such as a form of government, a form of industrial organization, an administrative structure of the Health Service, a form of the family and marriage, a system of education, and so on, which have characteristics other than those of individual psychology, do not exist. This he was perfectly ready to admit, and indeed, as we have already seen, he believed that empirical generalizations could be made about social organization, at this level of 'social' facts. What he was particularly concerned to make clear and emphasize beyond doubt, however, is that these elements of social organization cannot, by any stretch of imagination or any stretch of scientific methodology, be conceived as having cause-and-effect relationships between each other as self-existent entities. If a change in one of these institutions is followed by changes in other institutions, it is not that *it* has caused *them,* though we may sometimes speak in a convenient, shorthand way, as if this were the case. It can only be because the first change has been mediated through the experience and action of *people* in such a way as to bring about the subsequent changes. The first change has an impact, an influence, upon the settled dispositions, ideas, qualities of character of the individuals living in that society. It is then through their responses to this influence in relation to other aspects of their lives, that changes in other kinds of social institutions have occurred. Again, to be perfectly clear, let us think of an example.

If—a thing common in our experience now—the bank rate is reduced and this is followed by an expansion in productivity in the economy, it is not, Mill would say, that some entity called the 'bank rate' (existing independently of individuals) has *caused* an increase in another entity called the 'level of production in the economy' (also existing independently of individuals), though, in a shorthand way we may conveniently speak like this. What, in fact, has occurred, is that an alteration in the bank rate has influenced the calculations, the expectations, the decisions of the men and women involved in economic activity. The grounds for economic decisions have been changed. It may now be more profitable to borrow cheaper money and to invest capital in productive industry. Manufacturing activities in many directions may be stimulated. And it is because of these reactions of individuals and groups of associated individuals to the change in the Bank Rate that changes in the level of production throughout the economy have subsequently taken place. Mill himself used the example of 'protective tariffs' and whether or not they caused 'prosperity' in society; a question that was much discussed in his time; but any example of this kind makes the point perfectly clear.

What this amounts to, Mill was trying to say, is this.

The kind of view which a chemist might have of the compounds which he is studying—namely that certain molecular *compounds* are qualitatively distinct from the separable components of which they consist, and that they can be studied in terms of causal interconnection at their own level—is quite fundamentally and quite definitely incorrect and false when applied to the phenomena of human society. Though society has a framework of interconnected institutions which have qualities other than those of individual psychology; and though these institutions certainly do have their kinds and degrees of causal influence upon the personality and character formation of individuals; it is still not the case that society is some kind of 'compounding of individuals' into something totally different from and independent of individuals. Individuals, in the context of all the influences which play upon them, remain people—men and women who calculate their modes of life as persons—and any explanation of changing 'institutional regularities' must take this fact into account.

Mill put it like this:

'The laws of the phenomena of society are and can be nothing but the laws of the actions and passions of human beings united together in the social state. Men, however, in a state of society are still men. Their actions and passions are obedient to the laws of individual human nature. Men are not, when brought together, converted into another kind of substance with different properties as hydrogen and oxygen are different from water or as hydrogen, oxygen, carbon and azote are different from nerves, muscles and tendons. Human beings in society have no properties than those which are derived from and may be resolved into the laws of the nature of individual man. *In social phenomena the composition of causes is the universal law.*

'...the method of philosphizing which may be termed chemical, overlooks this fact and proceeds as if the nature of man as an individual were not concerned at all or were concerned in a very inferior degree in the operations of human beings in society.'

It may be specially noted before leaving this point, that it is on these grounds of thinking (i.e. that a consideration of individuals must necessarily be involved in social explanation) that Mill has been charged with what Karl Popper has called 'psychologism'. It is also the case that attempts to elaborate the complex patterns of explanation involved in bringing psychology and sociology properly together, are condemned as 'abstract theory' by those who have not the patience, or qualities of mind, to confront the actual intricacies of human nature and human society. It is interesting to note, therefore, that Mill himself—already, when making this point—ridiculed those who objected to it as 'abstract theory'. The errors of 'abstraction' he claimed, lay rather with those guilty of this unwarranted 'objectification' of institutionalized regularities.

Mill's point about this 'chemical' or 'compounding' conception of society is therefore perfectly clear. Let us turn now to the second term in his title—'The Experimental Method'.

Mill quite definitely rejected the appropriateness of the experimental method in a science of man and society. For this, too, he has been criticized. But again it is of the utmost importance—and this also must be emphasized very greatly—to see that *Mill rejected the experimental method only in relation to this 'chemical', 'compound' conception of the nature of society.*

It is the idea that—given that societies exist as sets of interconnected social institutions, we can then conduct experiments: comparing total societies with each other in order to test the causal efficacy of isolated institutional variables in bringing about certain social effects—that Mill emphatically rejected. This section of his work was extremely complicated, but we must do our best to become quite clear about these experimental methods which he rejected, and about his grounds for rejecting them. This is important not only for its own sake (though, of course, it *is* important simply from the point of view of achieving an accurate understanding of Mill's own ideas) but also because in the subsequent development of sociological theory, some thinkers, without the logical calrity of Mill, nonetheless employed some of the methods he rejected. It is important to understand these methods, and Mill's objections to them, as clearly as possible, so that we can properly assess in the development of the subject many of the contributions (such as those of Emile Durkheim and Max Weber) which followed. This is not, by any means,, to say at this stage, that the contributions of Durkheim and Weber were to any great extent erroneous; only that some of their proposed methods had already been critically assessed by Mill, and had been shown to be questionable. We therefore, need to understand this.

Mill elaborated five experimental methods:

(i) The method of difference.

(ii) The indirect method of difference.

(iii) The method of agreement.

(iv) The method of concomitant variations.

(v) The method of residues.

His objections to all these methods were much the same, but it is important to define each method as clearly as possible.

(I) THE METHOD OF DIFFERENCE

The method of difference, Mill said, is that in which we compare two particular instances which are alike in every respect except the one which is the subject of enquiry. If we could conduct this kind of experiment, we should be able to isolate the effect of this one difference. Applying this to the study of societies, Mill says:

'If two nations can be found which are alike in all natural advantages and disadvantages, whose people resemble each other in every quality, physical and moral, spontaneous and acquired, whose habits, usages of opinions, laws and institutions, are the same in all respects except that one of them has a more protective tariff or in other repects interferes more with the freedom of industry, if one of these nations is found to be rich and the other poor or one richer than the other, this will be a crucial experiment, a real proof by experience which of the two systems is most favourable to national riches.'

Mill then went on to say, however, that though this method might be applicable to the subject-matter of the natural sciences, the supposition that two *nations,* or two total *societies,* possessing such a complete degree of similarity could ever be found, was manifestly absurd. There was, therefore, an undoubted and demonstrable impossibility of obtaining in Sociology the conditions required for the most conclusive form of scientific enquiry. This 'direct' method of studying specific differences and their consequences was out of the question.

Because of this inadequacy, Mill then considered the second possibility, which he called 'the indirect method of difference'.

(II) THE INDIRECT METHOD OF DIFFERENCE

This method is that in which, instead of comparing two *specific instances* which differ in nothing but the presence or absence of one particular circumstance, the investigator compares two *clases* of instances which agree in nothing excepting the presence of the specific circumstances in the one class, and its absence in the other.

For example, we might compare two sets of societies—one which differed in all characteristics excepting that they *possessed* protective tariffs; the second which also differed in all characteristics excepting that they *lacked* protective tariffs. The attempt in comparing these two sets of societies might be to see what effect the presence or absence of protective tariffs had upon the prosperity of these societies.

At first glance, supposing the societies possessing the protective tariff were prosperous and those lacking it were all impoverished, it would seem to be plausible that the tariff barrier had *caused* prosperity. On further thought, however, Mill maintained, it is clear that this result is quite inconclusive, for the simple reason that the prosperity of the one set of countries and the poverty of the other might be due to any one or any group of those other social factors which differed amongst them all. In short, the multiplicity and wide-ranging difference of the factors involved makes any such conclusion, by employing the indirect method of differences, impossible.

Mill then considered a third method: the 'method of agreement'.

(III) THE METHOD OF AGREEMENT

This third method rests upon the canon that:

'If two or more instances of the phenomena under investigation have only one circumstance in common, the circumstance in which alone all the instances agree is the cause of the given phenomena.'

For example, if we found two or more cases, two or more societies which were characterized by prosperity and which possesed tariff protection, but which differed in all other social institutions, then it would be proved—according to this method—that the existence of tariff protection was the *cause* of prosperity.

Mill's objection to this method rested upon the simplicity of its assumptions. There always exists in human societies, he insisted, a *multiplicity* of causes and effects, extremely difficult to disentangle. In the example given, there are are so many and various causes which contribute to, and result in such large social 'effects' as 'prosperity' (for example military security, political freedom, stable government, industrial activity, industrial relations, good education, and so on) that no one of them, even if it is a common feature in the societies being compared, can be claimed to be solely responsible.

'No one cause', Mill wrote, 'suffices of itself to produce any of these phenomena whilst there are countless causes which have some influence over them and may co-operate either in their production or in their prevention. From the mere fact, therefore, of our having been able to eliminate some circumstance, we can by no means infer that this circumstance was not instrumental to the effect in some of the very instances from which we have eliminated it. We can conclude that the effect is sometimes produced without it, but not that, when present, it does not contribute its share.'

What Mill was saying here is that in social matters we always have a plurality of casues, various combinations of which may have a similar result. Now this is a point which merits much argument and criticism, and later we shall see that Durkheim takes Mill to task for it. Let us simply note, however, before leaving it, that Mill is thinking of arguments concerning the causes of large scale social effects such as prosperity, security, poverty, and it is these circumstances of *societies,* as whole *systems of institutions,* which he thinks it impossible to explain in terms of any *single* cause, and especially and single cause in terms of an institutional or aggregate 'entity' without reference to the experience and behaviour of people.

The same kind of objections, Mill thought, had to be raised against the fourth method: the method of 'concomitant variations'.

(IV) THE METHOD OF CONCOMITANT VARIATIONS

This is the method of establishing statistical correlations between aggregates, and it is important in assessing Mill's discussion of this method to notice that he did *not* maintain that correlations between aggregates cannot be achieved, nor did he maintain that these are of *no* value. Indeed, Mill was well aware of the new developments of social statistics and the curious constancies of human behaviour over long periods of time within the same society which they revealed: rates of marriage, murder, suicide, posting letters without stamps, leaving umbrellas in hotel foyers, and so on. Mill was perfectly well aware that, in the aggregate, constancies and correlations of human behaviour could usefully and clearly be established by statistics.

What he was concerned to argue, however, (and I believe that most modern statisticians would uphold him) was that a statistical correlation is always and only a correlation, and a correlation between *aggregates*. It can never claim to be a *causal* statement. Mill emphasized that the aggregates between which statistics establishes its correlations, all consist of individual cases. Since there is such a multiplicity of causes in individual behaviour and social affairs, different causes might be operative in each particular individual case, even though an aggregate correlation bound all these cases together.

To give an illustration: it may be that there is a constancy in the rate of suicide from year to year, and it may be that this constant rate of suicide may be correlated, let us say, with the stability of the economy. That is to say, if there are great instabilities and fluctuations in economic circumstances (whether of sudden prosperity or sudden poverty), the suicide rate may be shown, invariably, to increase. With continued stability, perhaps the suicide rate remains low. But Mill would say that this is only a very general correlation indeed and not, by any means, a sufficient causal statement. For it may be that if we considered Mr. Jones, Mr. Smith, Mr. James and so on, who committed suicide, the actual causes in each case might be very different, and refer to other factors, even though they might be connected with economic circumstances. For example, one man may have committed suicide because he thought he had cancer; another because he had lost his life-savings; another because his wife had left him and taken off his children; another because he was deeply depressed in a new social class with which he was unfamiliar; and so on. Now all these individual causes may be *connected* with, and even attendant upon, the stability or instability of economic circumstances yet the statistical correlation at the aggregate level would not be a detailed uncovering of all the many causes that were involved. For a *full* causal analysis, the factors in each individual case would have to be examined. Mill simply maintained that the multiplicity of causes in human affairs is so great that the method of concomitant variations is limited, though useful, for the exploration of them.

Mill himself wrote:

'Every attribute of the social body is influenced by innumerable causes, and such is the mutual action of the co-existing elements of society that whatever affects any one of the more important of them will by that alone, if it does not affect the others directly, affect them indirectly. The effects therefore, of different agents not being different in quality, while the quality of each is the mixed result of all the agents, the variations of the aggregate cannot bear a uniform proportion to those of any one of its component parts.'

Now it may be that Mill over-emphasized the objections against the method of concomitant variations and underestimated its use in uncovering significant connections in which causal relationships might lie, and we shall return to this method when we consider the work of Durkheim. Let us only note, however, in order to be perfectly clear about this, that Mill was *not* maintaining that empirical generalizations about social aggregates cannot be established by statistical methods. He was only claiming that this is *all* that statistics can do; and that, for a causal explanation of these empirical generalizations, sometimes more, and something more detailed and specific is required. Indeed, empirical generalizations, Mill insisted are not themselves explanations at all. They are simply descriptive statements of general fact which themselves require explanation. Statistical generalizations, such as that the rates of suicide in different societies are related significantly to variations in certain other factors, themselves require explanations of a kind which statistical method itself cannot provide.

A simple example of an empirical generalization in another science would be that in the autumn all leaves, or acorns, or apples, fall to the ground; but this in itself, though a regularity in the behaviour of nature, is not an explanation of anything. It is a generalization which intrigues us and leads us to *look* for an explanation, and this explanation would be found to have many aspects, having something to do, say, with the maturing of fruit, the establishing of a layer of cork between twigs and leaves, the methods of reproduction and dispersal of seeds by trees, the force of gravity, and so on. The same is the case in society. The fact that a rate of suicide is constantly concomitant with certain other elements of social life is not in itself an explanation; it is a generalization which itself requires explantion. Mill was only maintaining this, but we shall look at this point again when we come to consider the ideas of Durkheim.

(V) THE METHOD OF RESIDUES

Mill then considered a final experimental method: the 'Method of Residues'. In this method, he claimed, we examine one instance of a phenomenon only; in sociology—one instance of a human society. We then eliminate all those effects of the causes of which we already possess a clear knowledge. We must then be left with a limited number of effects and causes. And we shall then be able to concentrate on clarifying the relationship between these residual causes and effects, thus being more likely to achieve an elucidation of what is still lacking in our knowledge.

Again, however, Mill maintained that this method was inappropriate for sociology; his reasons being again the wide-ranging multiplicity and the varying combinations of causes in the production of social effects.

This then, though a brief resume, is what Mill had to say about the five kinds of experimental method; and he rejected them all for the study of society, for sociology.

Again, however, it is most important that we should note that he rejected these methods solely with reference to the experimental study of *total societies,* of institutions and *systems* of institutions, which are held to have some kind of cause-and-effect interdependency without reference to individuals. Mill *insisted* upon the experimental method for psychology, and I believe that he would have been prepared to consider the experimental method, though with qualification, if it were conducted at a limited level of individuals, and groups of individuals in specified social situations. It is only this large 'chemical, compound' conception of society which he was attacking here, and it was in relation to this that he thought the experimental method false and useless.

One final point may just be mentioned in this place; again a point to which we shall return. Mill has frequently been criticsed for what has come to be called 'holism'. He has been said to be guilty of considering societies as 'wholes', and believing that societies as wholes have destinies and move in certain directions with historical inevitability—indeed, with an inevitable *progress* in their historical destiny. I hope it is absolutely clear from what has been said, that this criticism of Mill is sheer nonsense. It is totally unfounded. If ever anyone was concerned to maintain the place of the individual, not only in moral philosophy and in political behaviour of a practical kind, but also in the explanation of the most complex social events, it was Mill. No one can possibly have stressed the importance of the place of the individual more than he. This criticism, then, is completely unfounded; and this will be even more clear a little later.

(b) The Geometrical or Abstract (Deductive) Method

The second method of study which Mill completely, and without qualification, rejected, was the 'geometrical' or 'deductive' method. This is much easier to be clear about than the vaious kinds of 'experimental' method, and little time need be spent upon it. By the geometrical method, Mill meant the method of pure deduction: clarifying the conclusions entailed in particular premises, without any resort to empirical testing; the kind of reasoning one gets in a geometrical theorem. It is quite unwarranted, he thought, to offer a whole theory of society which is no more than a set of deductions drawn from some simple premise. Even the premise itself, which may have been drawn from careful personal observation, and may have been established with some care, should never be accepted and adopted without wide and careful checking against the facts of experience. But, and perhaps more important, the corollaries deduced from the premise should never be accepted without emprical checking either.

To give one or two examples: Thomas Hobbes gave an account of the emergence and nature of political sovereignty which was nothing more than a process of logical deduction from what he considered to be the primary motive in human nature—that is, fear, and the suspicion and conflict between human individuals and societies to which it gives rise. Given this fundamental feeling of fear and the 'state of war' which it entails in the absence of social regulation (in the absence of a central political authority) Hobbes then deduced a whole theory as to what the nature of political society should be like. Clearly, this is not, in any sense, a scientific method. Such a process of deduction from some premise (whether a guess, or careful observation, or from whatever source it might have come), would be perfectly all right if it were subsequently submitted to specified conditions of test. But, as we well know, many philosophical theories about the nature of society have lacked this last and crucial element of empirical testing. They have been elaborate systems of pure deduction.

Mill is surely right in casting this method aside, as being not in any sense scientific or reliable. With this method, it is open to anyone to provide any kind of premise and deduce any kind of theory from it. If this is never to be checked against facts, then it is obviously without a vestige of precision. This method, then, can be dispensed with readily.

Methods appropriate to a study of man and society: (2) Methods accepted

Having eliminated what he considered to be unsatisfactory methods, Mill then turned to those which he thought appropriate and correct in the study of man and society. In order to do this as clearly and fully as possible, he began by stating the problems of sociological explanation as he saw them, and in the analysis which follows it will be seen that he was in very close agreement with Comte.

(a) *Two kinds of sociological enquiry*

There are, he said, two fundamental questions which face a science of society.

The first is: 'What are the causes which produce and the phenomena which characterize states of society generally?'

The second is: 'What effect will follow from a given cause, a certain general condition of social circumstances being presupposed?'

That part of sociological analysis dealing with the first of these questions is 'Social Statics'. Social statics is the theoretical understanding of the very nature of society; what its main components are; the needs and functional problems in which they are rooted, in any type of society. It clarifies, as Mill put it, 'the conditions of stability in the social union'. The empirical 'laws' or 'generalizations' appropriate to this branch of sociology will be *'uniformities of co-existence'*. They will be statements about the nature and interconnections of institutions which actually *constitute* a society and make a stable society possible.

That branch of sociological analysis which deals with the second kind of question is 'Social Dynamics'. Social dynamics is the theoretical understanding of the progressively changing nature of the actual historical societies of all kinds which exist in the world; it elucidates the causes of social change. As Mill put it 'The fundamental problem... is to find the laws according to which any state of society produces the state which succeeds it and takes its place. The empirical laws of society produced by social dynamics will be *uniformities of succession'*.

Two points must immediately be made clear:

The first point is that when Mill spoke of 'empirical laws', *(a)* uniformities of co-existence, and *(b)* uniformities of succession, he did not mean that these generalizations were causal laws in the sense of constituting 'explanations'. They were purely descriptive generalizations which themselves required explanation. Moreover, Mill believed that it was a very important aim, or should be an important aim of sociological enquiry, simply to discover and establish such generalizations. And it was for this purpose, for example, that he thought statistical correlations particularly useful and important, and he welcomed statistical methods from this point of view.

'In statistics' he said, 'it is evident that empirical laws may sometimes be traced and that tracing them forms an important part of that system of indirect observation on which we must often rely for the data of science...' And again: 'To collect, therefore, such empirical laws from direct observation is an important part of the process of sociological enquiry.'

As we shall see later, Mill believed that empirical generalizations of this kind were important, both for stimulating the formulation of hypotheses *and* for testing such hypotheses as might be made.

The second point which must be clarified at once, is the way in which Mill used the word 'progress' and 'progressive'. When he was insisting that social phenomena are always in process of change; that societies are essentially characterized by historical change; and when speaking of the task of social dynamics; Mill argued that the processes of history are 'progressive'. But it is most important to note that Mill quite explicitly said that he did *not* mean, by this word, that social change necessarily entailed *moral betterment.* He did think it likely that the developments in history could be shown to entail moral betterment, and that they would be likely to entail moral betterment in future, but he did *not* think that this could be at all *assumed.* This is decidedly *not* what he was meaning when he used the word progressive here.

All he was arguing here was that social change is simply *an ongoing process of difference.* That is to say, the facts in the sequences of historical change are simply *different from what they were before;* and there is no evidence to suggest any cyclical movements in history such as had been claimed by earlier thinkers. Social change, he said, by way of contrasting illustration, is not cyclical, but moves always forward with a kind of *trajectory* movement. Society *changes* and becomes *different.* That is *all.* Social change does not return upon itself.

It is very important to notice this point, because Mill has been charged with the same error as Comte and others in claiming the inevitability of human progress. This charge, as can be seen, is a totally false one. Mill made this claim concerning the nature of historical change purely in order to clarify the nature of the essential historical method that sociology must employ.

Having criticized the cyclical theory of history offered by Vico, Mill wrote:

'The words progress and progressiveness are not here to be understood as synonymous with improvement and tendency to improvement. It is conceivable that the laws of human nature might determine, and even necessitate, a certain series of changes in man and society which might not in every case or which might not, on the whole, be improvements. It is my belief that the general tendency is, and will continue to be, saving occsaional and temporary exceptions, one of improvement, a tendency towards a better and happier state. This, however, is not a question of the method of the social sicence, but a theorem of the science itself. For our purpose, it is sufficient that there is progressive change, both in the character of the human race and in their outward circumstances so far as moulded by themselves, that in each successive age the principal phenomena of society are different from what they were in the age preceding.

'The progressiveness of the human race', Mill says, 'is the foundation on which a method of philosophizing in social science has been of late years erected far superior to either of the two modes which had previously been prevalent, the chemical or experimental and the geometrical modes.'*

Clearly, Mill was referring here to the 'progressive' account of institutional changes offered by Condorcet and borrowed and developed by Comte.

Before clarifying the method which Mill proposed for the study of these questions, let us look firstly at his conception, not only of the nature of social statics, but also of the facts of the social order with which social statics had to concern itself. In the following passages, we shall see that Mill had a very clear conception of the nature of a society, of the major institutions which comprise it, and of their close interconnection. Furthermore, he saw clearly that a functional analysis of the interconnections of these institutions and the ways in which they are rooted in human needs and problems, is necessary. Again, like Comte, he had a completely clear notion of a 'structural-functional' analysis of social systems. The language that he used in these passages as, for example, when speaking of the institutional 'requisites' of a society, are completely modern and thoroughly anticipate such terms as the functional 'pre-requisites' of modern theorists such as Parsons, Merton, and others. Also, in noting Mill's point of view here, let us remember that it is exactly the same kind of conception of the nature of a society, and the social facts of which it consists, as that put forward earlier by Comte, and, as we shall see, that put forward later by Spencer, Marx, Hobhouse, Durkheim, Weber, and others. Indeed, it is the conception put forward by every sociologist of note from the very first foundation of the subject.

Firstly, when introducing the scope of social statics, Mill said that since this analyses what constitutes a 'state of society', it is necessary to fix clearly the ideas attached to the phrase 'a state of society'. He wrote as follows :

'What is called a state of society is the simultaneous state of all the greater social facts or phenomena. Such are the degree of knowledge, and of intellectual and moral culture, existing in the community, and of every class of it; the state of industry, of wealth and its distribution; the habitual occupations of the community; their division into classes, and the relations of those classes to one another; the common beliefs which they entertain on all the subjects most important to mankind, and the degree of assurance with which those beliefs are held; their tastes, and the character and degree of their aesthetic development; their form of government, and the more important of their laws and customs. The conditions of all these things, and of many more which will readily suggest themselves, constitute the state of society or the state of civilization at any given time.

When states of society, and the causes which produce them, are spoken of as a subject of science, it is implied that there exists a natural correlation among these different elements; that not every variety of combination of these general social facts is possible, but only certain combinations; that, in short, there exist Uniformities of Co-existence between the states of the various social phenomena. And such is the truth; as is indeed a necessary consequence of the influence exercised by every one of those phenomena over every other. It is a fact implied in the *consensus* of the various parts of the social body.

States of society are like different constitutions or different ages in the physical frame; they are conditions not of one or a few organs or functions, but of the whole organism. Accordingly, the information which we possess respecting past ages, and respecting the various states of society now existing in different regions of the earth, does, when duly analysed, exhibit uniformities. It is found that when one of the features of society is in a particular state, a state of many other features, more or less precisely determinate, always or usually co-exists with it.'

A second important passage of the same kind begins as follows:

'As already remarked one of the main results of the science of social statics would be to ascertain the requisites of stable political union. There are some circumstances which, being found in all societies without exception, and in the greatest degree where the social union is most complete may be considered (when psychological and ethological laws confirm the indication) as conditions of the existence of the complex phenomenon called a State. For example, no numerous society has ever been held together without laws, or usages equivalent to them; without tribunals, and on organized force of some sort to execute their decisions. There have always been public authorities whom, with more or less strictness, and in cases more or less accurately defined, the rest of the community obeyed, or according to general opinion were bound to obey. By following out this course of inquiry we shall find a number of requisites which have been present in every society that has maintained a collective existence, and on the cessation of which it has either merged in some other society, or recostructed itself on some new basis, in which the conditions were conformed to. Although these results, obtained by comparing different forms and states of society, amount in themselves only to empirical laws, some of them, when once suggested, are found to follow with so much probability from general laws of human nature, that the consilience of the two processes raises the evidence to proof, and the generalizations to the rank of scientific truths.'

It is most important to see, before leaving this initial treatment by Mill of the nature of society, that he regards the generalizations that can be made at the level of functional analysis as being *laws* and *scientific truths* in the fullest sense. They are not only empirical generalizations at the 'societal' level (about the associations, institutions and forms of organization in the social order), but also can be shown to stem from the basic psychological nature of man, the ethological requirements for the growth of human character, and the necessitous social problems which must be confronted and dealt with by all communities. A deductive element of high probability is found to support the empirical generalizations. This we shall come to later when, in speaking of 'functionalism', it will be necessary to criticize those who believe that the premises of functionalism cannot be said to possess any theoretical basis at all.

We must now clarify that method of studying *both* social statics *and* social dynamics which Mill thought most appropriate and correct. Having dispensed with methods he thought false and dangerous, he then outlined the only method which he thought correct and worth pursuing.

(b) The Concrete Deductive Method

Mill declared that the only correct method for a 'general science of society' was what he called the concrete deductive method and this is very close to what is now known, in the philosophy of science, as the 'hypothetico-deductive' method. 'The social science', said Mill, 'is a deductive science, not indeed after the model of geometry but after that of the more complex physical science'. It is most important to emphasize the nature of this hypothetico-deductive method by Mill, since his analysis of inductive *procedures* has been so travestied by critics as being an extremely naive notion of 'inductive logic'.

The concrete deductive method, said Mill, consists of three operations, the first of direct induction, the second of ratiocination, the third of verification. Mill believed that more often than not the first induction, as he called it, stems from some direct observation in our experience, whether an outcome of common experience or of a more meticulous collection of facts undertaken systematically. The essential thing, however, upon which Mill insisted, is that the first step in the concrete deductive method is that we have *some kind of knowledge of facts which we consider significant* from which we then proceed to infer or deduce that, if this is so, then certain other facts should be such and such. This procedure of inference is the second step of ratiocination or deduction. The third step of verification is simply the testing of *both* our initial assumptions *and* our deductions in discovering whether, in fact, our predictions are borne out.

This use of the term 'direct induction' as the first procedure of reliable scientific method ought not to lead us to think that Mill thought of this procedure of induction as merely a collecting of facts without any kind of theoretical presuppositions. The idea that Mill had a naive notion of inductive logic is totally false. When he spoke of 'direct *induction'*, he was simply meaning that our initial premises are always drawn from some kind of *experience* and are not completely *'a priori'* axioms as had been thought to be the case in earlier classical syllogistic thinking. His emphasis really derived from his concern to attack 'a priori' metaphysics as being unproductive of knowledge; and to insist that those axioms or premises which *seemed* of an 'a priori' nature, were, in fact, rooted in our *experience*.

Denying this simple and naive notion of induction as being a collecting of 'facts' without theoretical presuppositions and *condemning* both Bacon's account of it and Kepler's practice of it, Mill claimed that, for him, induction consisted purely in drawing inferences from known facts to those at present unknown. As he put it, induction, 'as distinguished from those mental operations sometimes improperly designed by the name', can be summarily defined as generalization from experience. It consists in inferring from some individual instances in which a phenomenon is seen to occur, that it probably occurs in all instances of that certain class, namely, in *all* those which resemble the instances already observed. When Mill spoke of inductive *procedures* of establishing knowledge, then, he was chiefly concerned to attack the *a priori* syllogistic mode of reasoning of earlier times and to insist that all our knowledge of the world is experiential.

In order to make Mill's conception of the concrete deductive method completely clear, it is necessary to quote what he had to say about the use of hypothesis in science, and, in my opinion, these passages vindicate him completely against the misinterpretations of many of his modern critics.

'An hypothesis', he wrote, 'is any supposition which we make (either without actual evidence, and on evidence avowedly insufficient) in order to endeavour to deduce from its conclusions in accordance with facts which are known to be real; under the idea that if the conclusions to which the hypothesis leads are known truths, the hypothesis itself either must be, or at least is likely to be, true. If the hypthesis relates to the cause or mode of production of a phenomenon, it will serve, if admitted, to explain such facts as are found capable of being deduced from it. And this explanation is the purpose of many, if not most, hypotheses. Since explaining, in the scientific sense, means resolving a uniformity which is not a law of causation into the laws of causation from which it results, or a complex law of causation into simpler and more general ones from which it is capable of being deductively inferred; if there do not exist any known laws which fulfil this requirement, we may feign or imagine some which would fulfil it; and this is making an hypothesis.'

'Any hypothesis being a mere supposition, there are no other limits to hypotheses than those of the human imagination.'

'According to the foregoing remarks, hypotheses are invented to enable the Deductive Method to be earlier applied to phenomena. But in order to discover the cause of any phenomenon by the Deductive Method, the process must consist of three parts—induction, ratiocination, and verification. Induction, (the place of which, however, may be supplied by a prior deduction), to ascertain the laws of the causes; ratiocination, to compute from those laws how the causes will operate in the particular combination known to exist in the case in hand; verification, by comparing this calculated effect with the actual phenomenon. No one of these parts of the process can be dispensed with.'

'Now the Hypothetical Method suppresses the firt of the three steps, the induction to ascertain the law, and contents itself with the other two operations, ratiocination and verification, the law which is reasoned from being assumed instead of proved.'

'This process may evidently be legitimate on one supposition, namely, if the nature of the case be such that the final step, the verification, shall amount to and fulfil the conditions of a new complete induction. We want to be assured that the law we have hypothetically assumed is a true one.' 'It appears, then, to be a condition of the most genuinely scientific hypothesis, that it be not destined always to remain an hypothesis, but be of such a nature as to be either proved or disproved by comparison with observed facts.'

'The hypothesis, by suggesting observations and experiments, puts us on the road to that independent evidence if it be really attainable; and till it be attained, the hypothesis ought only to count for a more or less plausible conjecture.'

'This function of hypotheses is one which must be reckoned absolutely indispensable in science. When Newton said "Hypotheses non fingo", he did not mean that he deprived himself of the facilities of investigation afforded by assuming in the first instance what he hoped ultimately to be able to prove. Without such assumptions, science could never have attained its present state; they are necessary steps in the progress to something more certain; and nearly everything which is now theory was once hypothesis.'

The process of tracing regularity in any complicated, and at first sight confused set of appearances, is necessarily tentative: we begin by making any supposition, even a false one, to see what consequences will follow from it; and by observing how these differ from the real phenomena, we learn what corrections to make in our assumption. The simplest supposition which accords with the more obvious facts is the best to begin with, because its consequences are the most easily traced. This rude hypothesis is then rudely corrected, and the operation repeated; and the comparison of the consequences deducible from the corrected hypothesis with the observed facts suggests still further correction, until the deductive results are at last made to tally with the phenomena.'

'The vortices of Descartes would have been a perfectly legitimate hypothesis, if it had been possible, by any mode of exploration which we could entertain the hope of every possessing, to bring the reality of the vortices, as a fact in nature, conclusively to the test of observation. The vice of the hypothesis was that it could not lead to any course of investigation capable of converting it from an hypothesis into a proved fact.'

'Nevertheless, I do not agree with M.Comte in condemning those who employ themselves in working out into detail the application of these hypotheses to the explanation of ascertained facts, provided they bear in mind that the utmost they can prove is, not that the hypothesis *is,* but that it *may* be true.'

This, then, was the 'concrete deductive method', the most reliable method of science according to Mill, and, in the 'science of society' it would proceed as follows: Possessing (1) knowledge (derived from observation and experiment) of the laws of *psychology,* and (2) empirical generalizations (derived from observation and comparative and historical studies) concerning the *regularities of society* (of associations and institutions and their interconnections in society), the investigator would (3) state a hypothesis in terms of the middle principles of Mill's science of ethology (*personality and social psychology and the exercise of deliberate choices)* as to how certain social circumstances had acted upon the nature of the individuals in society in such ways as to bring about the subsequent event, set of circumstances, or social change, which was being studied, and for which an explanation was being sought. The method is exactly that followed in the other natural sciences, but is applied appropriately with regard to the qualitatively different psychological and social facts which are under investigation, and about which testable knowledge is desired.

In this application to the study of man and society, however, Mill saw that the method encountered two fundamental difficulties, and he examined these carefully.

(c) The multiplicity of causes and effects, and the compounding of laws

As he had argued when rejecting other methods of study, Mill again insisted that the phenomena of man and society are characterterized by their great complexity of causes and effects and by their continuous change. It follows from this that deductive propositions of the kind mentioned are very difficult to frame. To put the matter as simply as possible—in the analysis of any social event, there will always be several, and frequently many, factors to encompass, and we shall have to weigh many causes and effects in arriving at the explanation which seems most satisfactory. An 'explanation' of any social event, or set of social events, in terms of one cause and one effect, as outlined by the relatively simple form of the concrete deductive method, seems completely out of the question. Indeed, when the utmost care has been taken to review all the multiplicity of causes, a realistic appraisal of the difficulties involved leads us to think that our result is likely to be at best, only a *meticulously careful approximation,* a statement of *tendency,* rather than a clearly demonstrable explanatory law. Still, an awareness of those difficulties does not mean that we should abandon the scientific method. We have no alternative but to seek the best degree of exactitude that we can, and if we follow the concrete deductive method as rigorously as possible, bringing all causes and effects together in our investigation, and paying the closet attention both to the correctness of our modes of inference and to the empirical testing of our hypotheses, then we shall attain the best results possible. 'The ground of confidence', Mill wrote, 'in any concrete deductive science, is not the 'a priori' reasoning itself but the accordance between its results and those of observation 'a posteriori'.'

'The effect produced', said Mill, 'in social phenomena by any complex set of circumstances amounts precisely to the sum of the effects of the circumstances taken singly, and the complexity does not arise from the number of the laws themselves, which is not remarkably great, but from the extraordinary number and variety of the data or elements of the agents which, in obedience to that small number of laws, co-operate towards the effect. Sociology infers the law of each effect from the laws of causation on which that effect depends, not, however, from the laws of causation on which that effect depends, not, however, from the law merely of one cause, as in the geometrical method, but by considering all the causes which conjointly influence the effect, and compounding their laws with one another.'

(d) Problems of contemporary and historical study

The second fundamental difficulty in the way of using the concrete deductive method in social science is the extreme difficulty of studying strictly contemporaneous events in society, and many points of the very greatest importance are attendant upon this consideration.

The first point which is very simple but frequently ignored by many sociologists, is that it proves to be almost impossible to observe a strictly contemporaneous event in such a way as to have a full knowledge of all that is involved. People who speak of direct 'observation' of contemporaneous social facts or events are in danger of deceiving themselves. Indeed, social events which are occurring in the *present* are often the most difficult to know. It is only, sometimes, long after the events have taken place, when various documents and other items of evidence have become available, that we can satisfy ourselves that we have, at least, an objective, balanced, and detailed knowledge of them. Curiously, then, the fact seems to be that it is easier, sometimes and in some respects, to observe an event of the past than an event that is occurring in the present. Historians, of course, have long accepted this fact. Furthermore, one's own *personal observation* of a current event must be extremely limited. Only with a later consideration of, and reflection upon, all the factors involved, as can be obtained through scrutiny and interpretation of documents, can one have anything approaching a full coverage of the nature of a social event. What this amounts to then, is that *sociological method* cannot avoid a dimension of *historical method.* The concrete deductive method in sociology must always be concerning itself, in very large part, with events that have already taken place, with data drawn from the past.

This leads to a second important aspect of this question which is, simply, that very frequently, the examples of those social circumstances and problems which most rouble us, which are most important to us, and which we most wish to understand and explain, *have already occurred.* It is during the course of their happening that we have come to realize their urgency, and we are interested in analysing and understanding them in order to be able to deal with them more effectively should they happen to us again. Indeed, we may wish to understand the causes of the events concerned in order to prevent their recurrence. The other examples which we can draw together for comparative study will be, however, chiefly historical examples in other societies which we must cull from the past. Again then, it is clear that sociological analysis must concern itself essentially with a study of historical events, as constituting a very large part of its task, and possibly a larger part of its task than studies strictly of the present moment.

Mill argued, therefore, that it is necessary to qualify the concrete deductive method in its application to the study of man and society in a way which led him to call it the *'inverse'* deductive method.

(e) The Inverse-Deductive Method

Because of this peculiar nature of the data of sociology, that it consists chiefly of past events drawn from various societies, it is usually the case that we have certain empirical generalizations about them before we have made or constructed any hypotheses, and before we have inferred any kind of explanation of them. This means that we have to undertake the concrete deductive method in an inverse manner. Instead of clearly stating our hypotheses, making inferences from them, and then verifying our predictions by submitting them to conditions of test of the nature of an artificial manipulation of facts (as in the laboratory experimentation of the natural sciences), the reverse order has to be followed. We already *have* certain empirical generalizations; and we have to try to produce hypothses and deductions from them which will satisfactorily explain the empirical generalizations about events that have already happened. By using this 'inverse deductive' method alone can we arrive at causal explanations of social processes. Mill further argued that it is only in this way that we can come to have any confidence in our ability to understand and predict events for the future.

The nature of historical events, and the substantial place they must occupy in a science of society, makes necessary, therefore, this inversion in the way in which we conduct the concrete deductive method.

'Instead,' Mill said, 'of deducing our conclusions by reasoning and verifying them by observation, we in some cases begin by obtaining them provisionally from specific experience and afterwards connect them with the principles of human nature by *a priori* reasonings, which reasonings are thus a real verification.'

Mill went on to point out that this was, in fact, the method proposed by Comte, who had regarded it as an inescapable and essential component in the nature of sociological theory.

In order to be as clear as possible, I shall try to summarize Mill's understanding of the nature, and essential parts of a 'science of society' with the aid of a few diagrams.

In the scientific study of society, it is false, he claimed, to think that elements of a social system are entities which have cause and effect relationships with each other without reference to the individuals in society.

We can make empirical generalizations about the way in which elements of social structure are connected with each other in any situation, and the ways in which changes in some follow upon changes in others, as indicated in level (1) SOCIOLOGY, in Diagram (1), but these do not give us a sufficient *causal* explanation. They are purely empirical generalizations at the social level. Similarly, we can establish generalizations about the basic psychological elements of human nature, on the basis of observation and experiment, as indicated in level (2) PSYCHOLOGY. But these two levels are quite distinct and, in this state, unconnected. It is also obviously insufficient to suppose that we can explain the complex changes in social institutions by any simple reference to the psychological qualities of individuals in abstraction from their social experience as in Diagram (1) (ii).

Interrelated changes in the elements of social structure (at level (1)) can only be correctly traced, understood, and explained, by investigating the impact which one change has upon the settled personality and character dispositions of individuals (at level (3) ETHOLOGY) and which therefore gives rise to subsequent changes in other institutions. Diagram (2) is the better indication of the actual kinds of interconnection between institutional changes, individuals as the outcome of their social and collective experiences, and their basic human psychology, than is either version of Diagram (1). To support and explain the empirical generalizations at level (1), we need hypothetical and deductive propositions as to what we would expect the reactions of people to be to specified change in circumstances; and these would be based upon our knowledge of psychology (level (2)), and our derived hypotheses at the level of social psychology (level (3)).

Supposing, for example, a change in economic institutions takes place—say the large-scale development of industrialization, with new forms of property, company organization, factory methods of production, and a complex division of labour; and supposing that this change always seemed to be followed (in all societies which experienced it) by related and distinctive changes in other institutions: in the family, education, political organization, religion, and so on. It would be an *error,* Mill maintained, to say—as indicated in Diagram (1)—that the changed 'Economic Institutions' *caused* changes in the family, education, religion, and government. Statements of institutional interdependence of this sort are only 'empirical generalizations' which *require* explanations. And it would not be sufficient simply to refer blankly to basic 'laws' of individual psychology, as at level (2), as indicated in the second version of Diagram (1).

The only correct procedure of explanation would be by the incorporation of level (3) ETHOLOGY. We should aim at a body of knowledge as to how the institutional patterns of society (level (1)) operate upon the basic elements of human psychology (level (2)) to bring into being the settled dispositions and qualities of personality and character, and their patterns of delibration and choice, in individuals as members of society. With this, we should then explore how the changes in 'Economic Institutions' (Industrialization and its specified characteristics) have an impact upon individuals, and how, mediated in their experience, deliberation, and action, *subsequent* changes in the family, education, government, religion, are brought about. The arrows in Diagram (2) seek to indicate this sequence of explanation.

Mill's essential understanding is that all *these three components are necessary in a satisfactory science of man and society.* There can be no such thing as an 'autonomous' sociology; no such thing as an 'autonomous' psychology. *All* are necessary in this kind of interrelationship for a satisfactory scientific study of all the dimensions of human experience and behaviour in the context of social relationships, which have their own structured interdependencies in the framework of society's organization as a whole. The isolation of any one component is a *wrong* isolation. It is an *error.* And, within this conception, Mill's chief emphasis is that institutions do not exist as entities independent of people and that the changes in one which bring about changes in others are always mediated through the experience, behaviour, deliberation, and action of individuals, and can only be sufficiently explained in these terms.

It may be very strongly noted here, that in Mill's whole system of sociological anaysis, it is the *middle principles,* the hypotheses and deductions in terms of 'ethology' or 'social psychology', which are considered to be of the greatest importance for explanation. *'The laws of collective character',* he wrote, *'are by far the most important class of sociological laws.'* The important hypothetical explanations of social facts are rooted in these middle principles. 'The middle principles,' said Mill, 'the *axiomata media,* of every science, principally constitute its value.' It is these hypotheses which link, in an explanatory way, the empirical generalizations at the level of psychology on the one hand, and the empirical generalizations at the level of social institutions and social regularities on the other. Without them no complete sociological explanation is possible.

Having considered these quite fundamental problems of method, Mill then discussed in more detail the nature of historical facts, the development of societies and social institutions in history, in order to see how far we could have confidence that, apart from other considerations, the subject matter was *manageable* and that we might expect to be able to establish systematic knowledge about it. In all this, he followed very closely the treatment of Comte, and the following points are those which he accepted and emphasized as being important for the making of a science of man and society.

Firstly, Mill accepted Comte's generationalization about the 'three stages' of social development, the three 'types' of social order and he clearly regarded this generalization as being a useful *classification* of 'types of society' for purposes of comparative study.

'Speculation Comte conceives to have, on every subject of human enquiry, three successive stages; in the first of which it tends to explain the phenomena by supernatural agencies, in the second by metaphysical abstractions, and in the third or final state confines itself to ascertaining their laws of succession and similitude. This generalization appears to me to have that high degree of scientific evidence which is derived from the concrrence of the indications of history with the probabilities derived from the constitution of the human mind. Nor could it be easily conceived, from the mere enunciation of such a proposition, what a flood of light it lets in upon the whole course of history, when its consequences are traced, by connecting with each of the three states of human intellect which it distinguishes, and with each successive modification of those three states, the correlative condition of other social phenomena.'

Secondly, Mill accepted that the *consensus* of institutions in human society, and the continuity of this consensus from period to period, or, more specifically, as he put it, from generation to generation, is such as to give us confidence that a systematic and orderly knowledge of institutional development can be achieved.

Thirdly, however, having emphasized the extreme difficulty of seeing some grounds of systematic order in these detailed institutional developments, Mill said that it would be very useful if we could find that there was *some one element* in the complex nature of society which was pre-eminent over all others as the prime agent of social change and social development. Fortunately, he claimed, there was one such factor which we could take as being of central importance; as constituting a central line of development in human society; and about which we could correlate the chnages which had taken place in all other social institutions. This central factor was the growth of human knowledge, the development of the 'speculative faculties of mankind', and this again, of course, was the point made by Comte.

Mill, however, made this point very clearly indeed and with far greater brevity than Comte. He wrote as follows:

'Now, the evidence of history and that of human nature combine, by a striking instance of consilience, to show that there really is one social element which is thus predominant, and almost paramount, among the agents of the social progression. This is the state of the speculative faculties of mankind, including the nature of the beliefs which by any means they have arrived at concerning themselves and the world by which they are surrounded.

'It would be a great error, and one very little likely to be committed, to assert that speculation, intellectual activity, the pursuit of truth, is among the more powerful propensities of human nature, or hold a predominating place in the lives of any, save decidedly exceptional, individuals. But, notwithstanding the relative weakness of this principle among other sociological agents, its influence is the main determining cause of the social progress; all the other dispositions of our nature which contribute to that progress being dependent on it for the means of accomplishing their share of the work. Thus (to take the most obvious case first) the impelling force to most of the improvements effected in the arts of life is the desire of increased material comfort; but as we can only act upon external objects in proportion to our knowledge of them, the state of knowledge at any time is the limit of the industrial improvements possible at that time; and the progress of industry must follow, and depend on, the progress of knowledge. The same thing may be shown to be true, though it is not quite so obvious, of the progress of the fine arts. Further, as the strongest propensities of uncultivated or half-cultivated human nature (being the purely selfish ones, and those of a sympathetic character which partake most of the nature of selfishness) evidently tend in themselves to disunite mankind, not to unite them,—to make them rivals not confederates; social existence is only possible by a disciplining of those more powerful propensities, which consists in subordinating them to a common system of opinions. The degree of this subordination is the measure of the completeness of the social union, and the nature of the common opinions determines its kind. But in order that mankind should conform their actions to any set of opinions, these opinions must exist, must be believed by them. And thus the state of the speculative faculties, the character of the propositions assented to by the intellect, essentially determines the moral and political state of the community, as we have already seen that it determines the physical.

'These conclusions, deduced from the laws of human nature, are in entire accordance with the general facts of history. Every considerable change historically known to us in the condition of any portion of mankind, when not brought about by external force, has been preceded by a change of proportional extent in the state of their knowledge or in their prevalent beliefs. As between any given state of speculation and the correlative state of everything else, it was almost always the former which first showed itself; though the effects, no doubt, reacted potently upon the cause. Every considerable advance in material civilization has been preceded by an advance in knowledge; and when any great social change has come to pass, either in the way of gradual development or of sudden conflict, it has had for its precursor a great change in the opinions and modes of thinking of society. Polytheism, Judaism, Christianity, Protestantism, the critical philosophy of modern Europe, and its positive science—each of these has been a primary agent in making society what it was at each successive period, while society was but secondarily instrumental in making *them,* each of them (as far as causes can be assigned for its existence) being mainly an emanation not from the practical life of the period, but from the previous state of belief and thought. The weakness of the speculative propensity in mankind generally has not, therefore, prevented the progress of speculation from governing that of society at large; it has only, and too often, prevented progress altogether, where the intellectual progression has come to and early stand for want of sufficiently favourable circumstances.

'From this accumulated evidence, we are justified in concluding that the order of human progression in all respects will mainly depend on the order of progression in the intellectual convictions of mankind that is, on the law of the successive transformation of human opinions.'

Fourthly, Mill also accepted Comte's point that human and social facts, as a corollary of their more complicated nature, are not less, but *more,* modifiable than mechanical and chemical facts. Consequently, with our knowledge of sociology, we should have considerable power to alter them. In this, Mill agreed with Comte that the advancement of sociological knowledge should be of use to men in enabling them to formulate effective social policies for the attainment of those kinds of improvements in society that they desired.

Fifthly, Mill also agreed with Comte that history was a cumulative process and that the longer it continued, the more interdependent the various societies of the world would become. Consequently, there would be an increasing similarity in the pattern of institutions throughout the world, and again consequently, the firmer the foundation for sociological generalization would become. He wrote as follows:

'The longer our species lasts and the more civilized it becomes, the more, as Comte remarks, does the influence of past generations over the present, and of mankind *en masse* over every individual in it, predominate over other forces; and though the course of affairs never ceases to be susceptible of alteration both by accidents and by personal qualities, the increasing preponderance of the collective agency of the species over all minor causes is constantly bringing the general evolution of the race into something which deivates less from a certain and preappointed track. Historical science, therefore, is always becoming more possible; not solely because it is better studied, but because, in every generation, it becomes better adapted for study.'

Also:

'... since both the natural varieties of mankind, and the original diversisties of local circumstances are much less considerable than the points of agreement, there will naturally be a certain degree of uniformity in the progressive development of the species and of its works. And this uniformity tends to become greater, not less, as society advances; since the evolution of each people, which is at first determined exclusively by the nature and circumstances of that people, is gradually brought under the influence (which becomes stronger as civilization advances) of the other nations of the earth, and of the circumstances by which they have been influenced. History accordingly does, when judicously examined, afford Empirical Laws of Society. And the problem of general sociology is to ascertain these, and connect them with the laws of human nature, by deductions showing that such were the derivative laws naturally to be expected as the consequences of those ultimate ones.'

By these methods then, Mill maintained that a reliable knowledge of man in society could be established. He realized to the full the great difficulties in the way of achieving precise testable knowledge by the application of scientific method; indeed, he is probably the most painstakingly honest and the most modest theorist in the whole development of sociology; but he pointed out that it is better to pursue that degree of exactitude in knowledge that we find we are capable of, than to leave the study of man and society in the realm of completely unwarranted and unchecked conjecture. And, as we have said before, he continually reiterated: 'An amount of knowledge quite insufficient for prediction may be most valuable for guidance'. If we wish to govern society as wisely and effectively as possible, even though *exact* knowledge is beyond our power to achieve, it is still necessary to secure as reliable a degree of accuracy in knowledge as is humanly possible.

'The aim of practical politics', Mill said, 'is to surround any given society with the greatest possible number of circumstances of which the tendencies are beneficial, and to remove or counteract, as far as practicable, those of which the tendencies are injurious. A knowledge of the tendencies only, though without the power of accurately predicting their conjoint result, gives us, to a considerable extent, this power.'

The making of social policy: science, philosophy and practical experiance

There is one final aspect of Mill's work which deserves attention.

When Comte had outlined his science of society, he proposed that a kind of 'council of social scientists', those who possessed an expertise in the new science, should be the responsible advisers and governors of the modern state, indeed, of the modern world. Mill was much more modest, and much wiser than Comte in this connection. he saw quite clearly that the knowledge of the social sciences cannnot of itself demonstrate *moral* truths. It cannnot determine the ends we *ought* to seek or the moral values in the light of which we *ought* to govern society. It is therefore necessary, said Mill, that the knowledge of the social scientist and the deliberations of the moral philosopher should be considered together and in relation to each other; that *both* should be taken into account. The moral philosopher can do something to clarify the ends and values which ought to guide our legislation; the social scientist brings such knowledge as he can of the means whereby these ends might be successfully achieved, given the present context of social circumstances. But Mill went even further than this, and it is the mention of the 'present social circumstances' which leads us on to this.

Besides the contributions of social scientists and moral philosphers, Mill thought it vitally necessary that those who practise the appropriate arts in society should be consulted too. Those men who are practically engaged in the management of human relationships; in the practice of the several arts—the judge, the doctor, the politican, the artisan; are likely to have qualities of judgment, practical assessments of immediate problems, and spontaneous notions about the means by which they can best be dealt with, which neither the social scientist nor the moral philosopher may possess. If all *three* contributions are carefully considered and taken into account in the making of social policies, then we can at least be as sure as possible that the best approach to the taking of decisions has been made.

In this, as in his purely methodological thought, Mill seems to me to have been admirably qualified, guarded and wise. His contribution to the making of sociology was very great indeed. He publicized, critically assessed, developed, and used, the best of the work of Comte; but his own methodological outline, his own logical critique of what seems unwarranted and what seems possible and worthwhile in sociological theory, remains of the utmost importance, even at the present time. His work certainly constituted a great consolidation and advance in the making of sociology.

Many later sociologists owed much to Mill; many committed the errors against which he had already warned; and many who are thought to have advanced the study of sociology considerably have, in fact, said little, if anything, more than Mill in this preliminary logical outline of the subject. All students of the social sciences would benefit from coming to terms with his work, and considering his various points in meticulous detail. After a profound study of Mill, no-one would be likely to be jejune in his approach to sociological explanation. And even this, if it could be accomplished, would be a great advance.

Summary

Mill's exacting logical critique led him, then, into complete agreement with Comte that a science of man and society was both necessary and possible. Again, in order to achieve a completely clear picture of the development of the subject, let me try to summarize his main conclusions as follows:

(a) *The need for a science of society*

(I) TO ESTABLISH KNOWLEDGE AS DISTINCT FROM OPINION

A science of society was necessary if *knowledge*—as distinct from opinion, or untested conjecture—about it, was to be achieved.

(I) TO PROVIDE A RELIABLE BASIS FOR JUDGMENT AND PRACTICE

A science of society was also necessary in order to achieve the most reliable basis possible for the discussion of political practice; for the weighing, taking, and implementing of important political decisions.

(III) TO CONTRIBUTE TO THE GREATER EFFECTIVENESS OF 'FREE WILL' (OF DELIBERATE CHOICE AND SOCIAL ACTION)

A scientific study of society did *not* deny 'freedom of the will' and did *not* presuppose 'determinism'. A *science* of man and society was logically and actually possible even if men *did* 'possess free will'. Furthermore, if it was successful in establishing 'laws' of human behaviour, or of regularity of institutional connections in society, it did not in any sense strip men of their free will or divest them of a basis for deliberate action. On the contrary, sociology explored the actual dimensions, conditions, and possibilities of the exercise of deliberate judgment and action, and therefore provided a basis of knowledge for their greater effectiveness.

(b) Methods of science appropriate to sociology

(I) METHODS OF SCIENCE CLARIFIED AND ACCEPTED

The careful delimitation of the methods of science—of observing, describing, classifying a specified range of facts; of establishing 'laws' of interconnection among them by means of hypothesis, deduction, and crucial experimental test—were the means of attaining demonstrable knowledge. Such methods alone could produce *knowledge* of society, as well as of nature. And such knowledge alone could form a basis for reliable prediction, and, therefore, for reliable judgment and action.

(II) SOCIAL SCIENCE NOT DIFFERENT FROM NATURAL SCIENCE

A science of man and society was not significantly different from the sciences of nature in encountering difficulties of achieving precise prediction about empirical complexities, even if general 'laws' could be established. Sciences which *had* established general 'laws', could still only achieve precise prediction in so far as they improved to a point of exactitude their methods of attaining information about all the antecedents of the particular events they sought to predict. A science of society was not different from other sciences in any sense of logical principle in this respect; only, perhaps, with regard to the greater complexity of the antecedents with which it had to deal.

(III) AN ERROR TO REGARD 'SOCIAL FACTS' AS 'COMPOUND ENTITIES' INDEPENDENT OF INDIVIDUALS IN THEIR CASUAL CONNECTIONS

Social 'institutions' or 'societies' as wholes, were not to be regarded as definite entities, whose, causal interdependencies could be adequately known and stated independent of individuals with their particular dispositions of personality, character and will. Experimental methods referring to 'social entities' of this kind were to be rejected as being conceptually and methodologically incorrect; as being mistaken with regard to the very nature of social facts, social processes, and their interconnections.

(IV) AN ERROR TO PERSIST IN PAST METHODS OF PURE DEDUCTION

Methods of pure deduction (whether from completely 'a priori' or from experiential premises) which made no use of careful empirical procedures of study, and no reference to conditions of empirical test, were also to be completely rejected, as being totally inappropriate to the pursuit of knolwedge.

(V) METHODS PROPER TO SOCIOLOGY: EMPIRICAL GENERALIZATIONS AND THEIR EXPLANATION

The methods proper to sociology were, as in other sciences, observation, descripton, the establishing of empirical generalizations, and the explanation of these by hypotheses and deductions which were subject to conditions of test. Such generalizations would certainly include statements about 'societies' as wholes, about 'institutions'— the articulation of their parts, and their kinds and degrees of interdependency in both order and change; but they would also include statements about the individuals and groups who pursued sequences of social action and the attainment of certain ends within the context of them.

THE COMPOUNDING OF A MULTIPLICITY OF CAUSES AND EFFECTS

The many causes and the many effects which were simultaneously at work in even the most apparently simple social event, must always mean for for sociology a complex task of compounding them in any full and satisfactory explanation. An 'explanation', in sociology, could never be a *'weighting'* of one institutional *entity* within the context of others. It was always more complicated than that.

THE COMPARATIVE METHOD: THE ALTERNATIVE TO EXPERIMENT

In view of the great and probably insurmountable difficulties of artificial experiment (i.e. of close approximation to laboratory experiment) in the study of society, sociology could do not other than employ, as carefully as possible, the comparative method. This, clearly, also involved the *classification* of societies and social institutions.

THE HISTORICAL METHOD

Since societies, social institutions, and the sequences of action of men in society, were essentially historical phenomena; involving persistence and change in time; the scientific study of society must, *necessarily,* include a historical method. The absence of this would mean an insufficient understanding of the nature of the facts being studied; a falsification and superficial treatment of them; and therefore the great probability of error in the conclusions.

THE INVERSE-DEDUCTIVE METHOD

Because of the nature of society and history, and the limited position of the investigator in the context of his own age and circumstances, the hypothetical-deductive method would have to be of an 'inverse' nature in sociology We were unavoidably in a position of having to seek the most satisfactory hypotheses possible for 'facts' we could already establish, or which were already established, at the level of 'empirical generalizations'. In sociology, therefore, the empirical, comparative, classificatory, historical methods of study were almost bound to be employed in this 'inverse' context. We were almost bound to deduce backwards from empirical generalizations already fairly well established to get at the hypothesis which best explained them. Contemporary comparative studies seemed necessarily to involve the manipulation of historical data.

(c) The nature and components of a science of society

(I) THREE ESSENTIAL ELEMENTS AND LEVELS: THE PSYCHOLOGICAL, SOCIETAL, AND SOCIAL-PSYCHOLOGICAL

A satisfactory science of society must comprise: (*a*) a basic experimental Psychology to establish knowledge of the psychological endowment of human beings, (*b*) a study of social systems; the nature and interconnections of institutions in societies as 'wholes' at the level of societal organization, and (*c*) a 'personality and social psychology' (ethology) to provide middle principles of knowledge concerning the reciprocal influences obtaining between institutions and groups (at the one level) and the psychological endowment of individuals (at the other): manifested in the formation of personalities, the establishment of character dispositions, and the exercise of deliberation and will by individuals in their roles in institutions and as members of groups. Explanations of interconnected changes at the institutional level (i.e., changes in some institutions brought about by changes in others) would then be mediated in terms of the influences of the institutional changes upon the collective dispositions and wills of the individuals involved. Hypotheses and deductions (and any necessary compounding of these to account for complex situations) would be drawn from the levels of psychology and social psychology as well as from the study of institutional interconnections, and *all* these, taken together, could 'explain' the empirical generalizations at the level of institutional regularity and change. The 'middle principles' of social psychology therefore played a central role in Mill's understanding of 'explanation' in sociology.

(II) SOCIAL STATICS AND SOCIAL DYNAMICS

Sociology should, as Comte had suggested, be logically divided into the two parts: Statics and Dynamics; the one providing a detailed analysis of the essential nature of 'society' as the distinctive subject of study; the other consisting (in the light of this analysis) of a detailed empirical study of the concrete varieties of societies in the world and attempts to establish specific theories about them.

(III) STATICS: A STRUCTURAL-FUNCTIONAL ANALYSIS

Social Statics could provide a detailed analysis of social systems (of societies),in terms of those institutional elements which were necessary to satisfy certain functional 'requisites' rooted both in the psychology of human beings and in determinate problems encountered and experienced in communal relationships. The high degree of consonance between these analytical and deductive generalizations and the empirical fact of the universality of these institutions in human societies gave even these the logical status of 'laws' of human nature and human society.

(IV) DYNAMICS: CLASSIFICATION, COMPARISON, AND HISTORICAL STUDIES

Using the guiding framework of analysis provided by 'Statics', the study of the concrete varieties of societies in the world should then be undertaken by the classificatory, comparative, and historical methods already mentioned. Mill agreed that, in this task, the construction of models, and, specifically, Comte's 'three types' of social order and the attendant sequence of social change which they theoretically emphasized, was of great utility. Mill agreed that the 'Law of the Three Stages' as outlined by Comte had much to support it; and he thought that it provided a great unifying thread for comparative and historical studies and was a first great generalization for the understanding of social change.

(V) THE PROGRESSIVENESS OF SOCIAL CHANGE

Mill discarded earlier 'cyclical' (and other philosophical) assumptions underlying the study of social change, and held that sociology could best proceed on the assumption that social change was no more than a certain temporal 'progression': namely that things simply *became different from what they were before*. There were no assumptions here—whether of moral betterment, of cyclical patterns, or of any other expectation—at all. Any such tendencies that might exist would only be *discovered* by empirical study, not introduced by assumption beforehand. This scientific study of the nature of social change would be bound to be more accurate and more reliable than earlier theories.

(VI) KNOWLEDGE IN SOCIETY: A CENTRAL CRITERION

Mill also agreed with Comte that the selection of the development of *knowledge* in society as the central 'yardstick' about which other institutional change could be correlated, was correct and well-justified. He agreed that, of all aspects of society, this, especially, was accessible to clear description. It permitted of analysis in terms of clear criteria: of knowledge as such, and also of the degree of control over the social and natural environment which it provided. Since it was the basis of *all* man's activities, it was also likely to permeate and affect literally *all* the institutions of society.

(VII) SOCIAL KNOWLEDGE, SOCIAL JUDGMENT, SOCIAL PRACTICE

A very clear picture was also provided by Mill of those relations between the social scientist (with his knowledge), the moral and social philosopher (with his clarification of moral principles and moral ends), and the man of practical experience (with his understanding of the immediate actuality and possibility of things) which were necessary if the best deliberations, the best judgments, and the best political decisions and actions on social issues were to be achieved. The knolwedge of sociology was seen therefore not only as something in and for itself, but as a necessary and important contribution within the context of social judgment and utility.

The making of Sociology as proposed and outlined by Comte was therefore defended, validated, and further clarified by this searching logical critique of Mill. Indeed, Mill established the groundwork of the new science much more firmly. He eliminated conclusively that had been thought to be insuperable objections to it—as, for example,the doctrine of 'the freedom of the will'. He showed convincingly that it was in no crucial way different from the natural sciences, or any less valid than they in dealing with its subject-matter. He clarified and exposed certain possibilities of error (such as the attaching of misplaced concreteness to'institutions' or 'socities' as aggregate 'entities' independent of people). And he explored in much more satisfactory detail the several levels of investigation necessarily involved in a science of society: the psychological, the social psychological, and the societal. It is as good a point as any on which to leave our outline of Mill's most excellent and thorough work to note and to emphasize that—for him—*there could be no possible separation of psychology from sociology, or any conflict between them, if they were properly conceived.* Properly understood, a science of man and society *included* psychological, social psychological, and societal studies as *indispensable and co-operating components: no one of which could be sufficient in itself.* This is a point of view which, I shall argue at the the end of our study, is altogether correct, and there is no clearer statement of it in the entire literature than that accomplished by John Stuart Mill. The work of Mill was not only a great contribution to the making of sociology; it is something from which we can still learn much which is of the most fundamental importance in our subject.

Mill, however, and from his own considered choice, confined himself to the study of logical analysis and method. He explicitly withheld himself from any attempt to offer substantive theories of society. He thought that such an attempt would be untimely and impossible, since the state of some of the necessary components (such as psychology) was insufficiently advanced. We turn now to certain nineteenth century thinkers who not only accepted the necessity and importance of a science of society, and who not only attempted to found it, but who also offered substantive theories on the basis of it which were, in their view, vital for the understanding of modern industrial society and the problems which men confronted. These theories were stated within the context of the newly dominant perspective of the nineteenth century—the perspective of 'evolution'. First we shall examine the contribution of Herbert Spencer who, more than any other single figure, was the exponent of 'evolution'. Then we shall examine one very specific theory within this same context—that of Karl Marx.

4

Herbert Spencer: Structure, Function and Social Evolution

A unified scheme of knowledge. Influences of Comte and Mill

Spencer's work was very similar to that of Comte in that he sought to achieve and present a unified scheme of knowledge resting upon a clear philosophical position and embracing *all* the sciences. Spencer was therefore much more than a sociologist. He was a philosopher and a scientist in the widest sense, concerned with as complete an understanding as possible of the nature of things and of the place of man within nature, and he achieved an astonishing body of work.

First Principles clarified the philosophical basis for all the rest of his work, and presented his approach to all the sciences. This outline was then filled out by a *Principles of Biology*, a *Principles of Psychology*, a *Principles of Sociology*, and, subsequently, a *Principle of Ethics*. In addition to these–all of which were very voluminous works–he published a separate book on *The Study of Sociology*, and essays of both a slight and a substantial nature on many themes: moral and political theory, practical social questions such as education and state-education, the changing nature of the political parties, the purpose of art, the origin of music, vaccination, dying, gymnastics, and so on. On every theme, large and small, important and unimportant, Spencer wrote clearly, entertainingly, and always with something stimulating and original to say.

His work could, in one sense, be regarded as a detailed filling-out (in terms of substantive knowledge) of the skeleton 'schema' which Comte had indicated in his 'hierarchy of sciences', were it not for the fact that Spencer himself claimed, and most emphatically, that his work was developed independently of the ideas of Comte, and rested on at least some ideas which were significantly different.

There is little point in arguing whether Spencer did or did not borrow very largely from the work of Comte. Three things, however, may he said.

Firstly, it is clearly quite wrong to think of Spencer as being simply a *successor* to Comte, or a *successor* to the logical critique of Mill. Spencer was, in fact, an early contemporary of both Comte and Mill. His own work was developed at much the same time though, of course, he outlived both of them and continued his writing on sociology and on political questions a good deal longer than they did.

Secondly, there is no doubt whatever that Spencer did know of the work of Comte; knew also of the critical assessment of his work in Mill's book on *Logic;* and utilized the ideas of both men extensively. That this is so may be clearly seen in the actual phrasing of many of his ideas. A good example of this can be taken from his essay on education. In his extremely interesting discussion of the inadequacies of the study of history in his time, Spencer argued that a *sociological* study of history was the only kind of history worth while.

'The thing it really concerns us to know', he wrote, 'is the natural history of society. We want all facts which help us to understand how a nation has grown and organized itself.'

Amongst these social facts, said Spencer, would be the government–its structure, principles, methods, and not only central but also local government; the ecclesiastical organisation in society; superstitions and myths; the system of social classes–including the titles, salutations, and forms of address that accompany it; leisure activities; the nature of the family, the regulation of the sexes; the relations between parents and children; the economic system–including the division of labour, guilds, associations between employers and employees, the means of producing and distributing commodities; the means of communication in society; the nature of art, literature and the mode of daily life of the people; and also, finally, the system of morals in society. Having briefly indicated the kinds of facts that would go into a natural history of society, he then continued:

'These facts, given with as much brevity as consists with clearness and accuracy, should be so grouped and arranged that they may be comprehended in their *ensemble,* and contemplated as mutually-dependent parts of one great whole. The aim should be so to present them that men may readily trace the *consensus* subsisting among them; with the view of learning what social phenomena co-exist with what others. And then the corresponding delineations of succeeding ages should be so managed as to show how each belief, institution, custom, and arrangement was modified; and how the *consensus* of preceding structures and functions was developed into the *consensus* of succeeding ones. Such alone is the kind of information respecting past times, which can be of service to the citizen for the regulation of his conduct. The only history that is of practical value, is what may be called Descriptive Sociology.

'And the highest office which the historian can discharge, is that of so narrating the lives of nations, as to furnish materials for a Comparative Sociology; and for the subsequent determination of the ultimate laws to which social phenomena conform.

'But now mark, that even supposing an adequate stock of this truly valuable historical knowledge has been acquired, it is of comparatively little use without the key. And the key is to be found only in Science. In the absence of the generalizations of biology and psychology, rational interpretation of social phenomena is impossible. Only in proportion as men draw certain rude, empirical inferences respecting human nature, are they enabled to understand even the simplest facts of social life; as, for instance, the relation between supply and demand. And if the most elementary truths of sociology cannot be reached until some knowledge is obtained of how men generally think, feel and act under any given circumstances, then it is manifest that there can be nothing like a wide comprehension of sociology, unless through a competent acquaintance with man in all his faculties, bodily and mental. Consider the matter in the abstract, and this conclusion is self-evident. Thus: Society is made up of individuals; all that is done in society done by the combined actions of individuals; and therefore, in individual actions only can be found the solutions of special phenomena. But the actions of individuals depend on the laws of their natures; and their actions cannot be understood until these laws are understood. These laws, however, when reduced to their simplest expressions prove to be corollaries from the laws of body and mind in general. Hence it follows, that biology and psychology are indispensable as interpreters of sociology. Or, to state the conclusions still more simply: all social phenomena are phenomena of life--are the most complex manifestations of life--must conform to the laws of life--and can be understood only when the laws of life are understood.'

There is absolutely no doubt of the fact that these paragraphs were written with the ideas of Comte and with Mill's *system of Logic in* mind. The insistence upon a recognition of the interdependence of social facts in societies as 'wholes'; the tracing of the kind of 'consensus' that exists among them; the clear acceptance of a 'social statics' and 'social dynamics' and of the methods of classification and comparison; the desire to support empirical generalizations about *social* facts by deductions based upon biology and psychology; are all clearly rooted in these two writers. The phraseology, let alone the ideas, are almost exactly the same. We can be quite clear in our minds then that Spencer did, in fact, consider critically the ideas of Comte and the ideas of Mill, and that, to some extent, his own work was additional to them and a development of them. Indeed, in addition to such textual knowledge of Spencer's indebtedness to Comte and Mill, we know that he was a friend of people like George Henry Lewes and George Eliot, also of T. H. Huxley, some of whom were among the first people in Britain, together with Mill, to appreciate the work of Comte and to do everything in their power both to publish and to publicize it, though not, of course, uncritically.

The third point, however, is that no matter how extensive Spencer's indebtedness to Comte, Mill, and others might have been, there is no doubt whatever that, from the beginning of his thought, he had been moving towards a similar conception of a science of society, and, furthermore, that he had a power of mind, a power of sustaining long, serious, painstaking study in the development of his system, which was itself a source of great originality and independence. In this sense, his work is not derivative by shows an originality, a thoroughness, a clarity, and a tenacity of mind which are altogether to be admired.

As with so many of the thinkers we have already considered, Spencer has been much caricatured. His point of view, or indeed his many points of view, have been much over-simplified, and then criticized adversely on this false basis. A full understanding of Spencer's treatment is such as to enhance one's admiration of the detailed way in which he worked out his systematic comprehension of things.

Furthermore, Spencer's initial statement of the foundation of philosophy, the distinction between religion and philosophy, and, within this context, the place and the nature of science, was profound, clear, and in some ways preferable to that of Comte. It was perhaps less dogmatic than the position of Comte, though I would not want it to be thought that I was making this a major distinction.

Comte, of course, denied the fruitfulness of metaphysical and theological speculation once positive science had come to be established, even thought he readily acknowledged their utility in science, in the sense that the exercise of imagination and speculation within them might furnish important insights, and hypotheses. Spencer agreed that positive science was the only method whereby testable knowledge could be achieved, but, nonetheless, he maintained that men would continue to ponder, and quite understandably, about the more fundamental questions concerning the nature of the universe and man which scientific knowledge could not possible solve. He did not maintain that we could establish *knowledge* about these questions, but, simply, that we could not stop thinking about them, and that *something* of the nature of metaphysical speculation, *something* of the nature of religion, would always continue to exist in human thought and feeling.

A little later we shall see what he had to say about the development of ecclesiastical institutions, the place of religion in society, and the state of agnosticism to which he thought religious development in a scientific age must lead. This, I believe, is one of the clearest statements of the present culmination of the religious quest that has been given. Apart from being true, it is very apposite to the problems which we face now, in our own time.

Spencer, then, was a great original thinker of the nineteenth century–one of the great Victorians–and there is no doubt whatever of the importance of his contribution to the making of sociology: both as a system of analysis in its own right, which can still hold its own against any other system within sociology, and as a system of concepts and ideas which had a tremendous influence on subsequent thought.

The position which Spencer held with regard to what constitutes *'knowledge,'* and the kinds of methods by which we can arrive at it, was in complete agreement with that of Comte and Mill, and with the earlier notions of Hume and Kant, though he worked it out and expressed it rather differently.

Everything in our experience, he thought–the regularity and order of everything in nature, the necessitous relationships and the orderly processes of the world–led us to be persuaded that there did, in fact, exist some *actuality,* some fundamental *reality,* in which everything was rooted, out of which all things proceeded, or *of* which all things were changing forms and manifestations, which possessed dimensions and qualities going beyond our own perceptions of it. We could not bring ourselves to believe that our own *experience* of the world really exhausted or fathomed all aspects of the actual nature of the world. Furthermore, all the ways in which we spoke of our 'knowledge' were such as to confirm this persuasion. When we recognized that our experiences or propositions were 'partial' or 'relative,' our language implied that there was some 'whole' or 'entirety' of which we could see only a 'part', or some 'absolute' reality of which we could have only a 'relative' view. It was at least plausible, then, that there was some inscrutable reality the full nature of which transcended our own partial experience.

However, the simple truth was that we could find no way whatever of stating propositions about this reality excepting in terms of *how it appeared to us:* as a world of objects, people, relationships conveyed by our senses and systematically connected by our reasoning. We could do no more, then, than admit that there was a realm of the 'Unknowable', but then confine our attention to the 'Knowable'.

We could make accurate statements about all the aspects of the world as we experienced them, and we could arrange these statements to form a coherent, systematic and testable body of knowledge. Commonsense began with a disconnected set of statements. The various sciences went beyond these in a reflective and more accurate way, but each science was still a 'partial' segment of knowledge. Philosophy brought all the sciences into relation with each other and provided a 'unified' scheme of knowledge embracing all the dimensions of our experience.

'Knowledge of the lowest kind', wrote Spencer, 'is *un-unifed* knowledge; Science is *partially-unified* knowledge; Philosophy is *completely-unified knowledge.*'

Spencer's aim, therefore, was to produce a new unification of all knowledge which the new developments of science had made possible, and this included a scientific knowledge of man in society. He claimed that, following the emergence of the methods of science, man could only provide himself with a true and satisfactory perspective of his place in the wider nature of things; a true picture of his place and destiny in the world; if he undertook and achieved a 'Synthetic Philosophy' of this kind,

The central enthusiasm at the heart of Spencer's effort towards this system of knowledge, however, the central significance of the 'system' which he offered, was that he believed he had discovered a conception which did, in fact, pervade the whole of nature and unify the whole of knowledge. His 'unifying' or 'synthetic' philosophy was by no means simply a 'collection' of the knowledge of all the special sciences. It was an illumination of the actual unity, connectedness, and coherence of all knowledge by the use of a conception which pointed to, and then analytically explored, the central process which lay at the very heart of, and characterized all the actualities and transformations of nature, human nature, and human society. This was the concept of 'Evolution'.

The Concept of Evolution

Spencer's entire schema of knowledge rested upon this persuasion that 'evolution' was the key concept for the understanding of the world as a whole and of man's place within it, and it is therefore absolutely essential to achieve a full understanding of what he meant by it. Spencer's system of 'explanation' in all sciences, including sociology, simply *cannot* be understood without a primary understanding of his concept of evolution–because his principles and grounds of explanation are rooted in, and derived from it.

It is because of this wide employment of the concept of evolution that Spencer's work has been subjected to much criticism that is quite fundamentally erroneous. A chief criticism, entirely trivial, is that Spencer falsely extrapolated from the biological theory of evolution for the purpose of sociological explanation. That is, it is commonly thought that Spencer *derived* his theory of social evolution from the *biological* theory of evolution, and that this was therefore a false application of the concept of evolution in sociological explanation. This criticism is totally unfounded; it is a complete misunderstanding of Spencer; and, because of it, is necessary to make completely clear what the fundamental basis of Spencer's evolutionary conception actually was.

We must bear in mind Spencer's basic persuasion that the *origins* and the *'ultimate'* nature of the reality which forms the basis of all our experience are inscrutable and remain in the realm of the unknowable. Science can do no more than deal with a careful analysis and exploration of our actual experience of nature without ever being able to plumb the fundamental depths of how that nature came to originate in the first place or what its ultimate purposes, if any, might be. For Spencer, then, scientific knowledge consisted simply of careful, systematic, testable propositions about all aspects of the world of our experience.

When we consider all the varieties of objects in nature of which we do have perceptual experience–planetary systems, oceans and mountain-ranges, storms and earthquakes, trees and grasses, fishes, reptiles, birds and men, and the civilizations of men in history–we realise, as a fact of the most fundamental nature, that all these phenomena are *forms* and *transformations* of the same basic material substance. Nature consists of a vast variety of continuing forms into which its basic substance and energy is compounded. Furthermore, all these forms–differently according to their nature–are sequences and processes of creation, growth, development, death and dissolution in time.

The forms of the world emerge out of the basic substance of existence, have their pattern of growth and change, and are then dissolved into their original basic elements. The very nature of the variety of things in the world is an appropriate pattern of transformation of the basic substance of which the world consists.

In some sense, then, an explanation of all aspects of the world as we experience it must consist in an understanding of what these processes of transformation are: what are the components, sequences, and grounds of their occurrence; how, and according to what principles, do they occur? A knowledge of the world will be a systematic and testable body of propositions about these several *patterns of transformation:* which *are* the world, as we experience it.

In all this, Spencer had two fundamental ideas. Firstly, that since all forms of nature were transformations of material substance, the pattern of them must be evident in the processes of material substance, and evidenced, then, in the basic postulates of physics. Secondly, though the world manifested many *forms* of transformation, *the basic process of transformation itself* was common to them all, and was the central characteristic of the entire nature of things. Whitehead's later dictum that 'reality' is 'process' and that 'existence' consists of the actualization of 'forms' of process, is right at the heart of Spencer's thinking–as, indeed, it has been a central philosophical persuasion from Plato, to Bergson, and Whitehead himself.

The basic process of transformation, at the heart of the nature of all things, Spencer called 'Evolution', and the clarification of it, and what was involved in it (and in a satisfactory explanation of it), could only, he maintained, be gained by examining the basic formulations of physics.

It can be seen already, and at once, how totally absurd is the notion that Spencer simply borrowed the idea of biological evolution for use in sociology. His position was rooted in a far more fundamental philosophical persuasion than that.

It would be too detailed a task to go into all the ramifications of Spencer's explanation of the laws of physics, but a simple statement of the propositions he accepted and used, is this:

(1) There is a persistence of force in the world; a persistence of some sustaining energy in which all phenomena are rooted, upon which all phenomena, rest, but which itself

lies beyond our knowledge. This is a major, irreducible fact which we cannot explain, but which we are obliged simply to accept.

(2) The basic elements of matter and energy in the world are neither created, nor destroyed, but 'conserved'. There is a basic 'indestructibility' of the elements of matter.

(3) There is a perpetual continuity of motion in the world. All things continue in motion.

(4) There is a persistence of certain relations among forces in the world.

The force, the elements of matter, the continual motion in the world is not a chaos. There exists a uniformity or regularity of relationships among *defined phenomena* in the world.

These are ordered, recurring manifestations of events in the natural world, and the forces, elements of matter, and relations of motion existing among them have a definite regularity.

The world is an *order* of elements.

(5) Changing manifestations of these regular forms and processes of nature take place as a transformation and equivalence of forces.

The force, the elements of matter, the motion, are never lost or dissipated entirely in a process of change, but are merely transformed into the manifestation of some other event or some other form of existence.

(6) The directions of change and movement among the phenomena of the world; the direction of motion of the elements of phenomena; are a resultant of the fact that all forces and elements move along the line of least resistance, or greatest attraction.

(7) All phenomena in nature have their own particular rate and rhythm of movement; of duration and development.

Each has its appropriate pattern of transformation; this is attendant upon the nature of the organisation of its force, elements of matter, and pattern of motion.

Phenomena are manifestations of certain rhythms of motion.

These basic propositions are stated very simply here, bare of detail, but it will be clearly seen that they entail a pattern of explanation. The defined phenomena of the world rest upon certain dispositions of force, elements of matter, and patterns of motion, and all exist in a condition of interdependence. A certain 'equilibrium' of forces and elements obtains within and among them. The explanation of *each phenomenon*–a planetary system, a tree, a species of animal, a civilization–will consist of an analysis and clarification of that disposition of forces and elements which constitutes its 'order' and sustains its equilibrium. This order, of course, will itself be a 'moving equilibrium' since all phenomena are in a continuous condition of interdependence in motion. The explanation of *changes* in and among phenomena will consist of an analysis and clarification of the factors which have brought about a disruption or alteration of the normally persisting disposition of forces and elements, and a tracing of the new *re-ordering* of forces and elements which takes place as a new disposition of them, in a new condition of equilibrium, is arrived at.

Whatever phenomena we are analysing, then–physical, chemical, biological, psychological, social–this yields a very clear system of description, analysis, and explanation. But Spencer went considerably beyond this.

First of all, he derived from these basic propositions his 'law' of evolution. When we examine the nature of both order and change in any kind of phenomena in the world, we find, he insisted, that the pattern of transformation is the same, and could be formulated like this.

'Evolution is an integration of matter and concomitant dissipation of motion, during' which the matter passes from relatively indefinite, incoherent homogeneity to a relatively definite coherent heterogeneity and during which the retained motion undergoes a parallel transformation.

According to Spencer, all the phenomena of nature–the stars and planetary systems, the earth and all terrestrial phenomena, biological organisms and the development of species, and all the changing psychological and sociological processes of human experience and behaviour–followed this definite pattern of change. All processes of change are similar, in that they emerge our of the physical stuff of the world, have their own patterns of transformation and change, and, according to these patterns, in due course decline and dissolve. In this, they move from a condition of simplicity to a condition of organized complexity; from a condition of indefiniteness to a condition of definiteness; from a condition in which their parts are relatively undifferentiated to a condition of increasing specialization, in which their parts are characterized by a complex differentiation of structure and function; from an unstable condition consisting of a large multiplicity of very similar units, relatively incoherent and disconnected in their behaviour, to a stable condition consisting of relatively fewer phenomena now so intricately organized and articulated that their behaviour is regular, coherent and predictable.

All phenomena in nature are what they are in the context of reciprocally interacting environmental conditions. They change within such a context of forces, and appropriately. In this process of accommodation, all phenomena, without exception, grow and change from relatively simple units and processes which are very similar to each other and relatively incoherent in their connections and relations with each other, to more complicated forms which, though developing internal differentiations of structure and function, also manifest a greater degree of articulation in the organisation of their parts, and of regularity of behaviour–both among their internal parts, and, externally, in relation to the elements and conditions of their environments.

This was how Spencer conceived and described his 'law' of evolution , and it can be seen that it is perfectly clear; providing a universally applicable *system* of analysis and knowledge, linking all the phenomena in the world our experience and the orientations of all the sciences in exploring them. There is no doubt or ambiguity whatever, then, in what Spencer meant by 'unified scheme of knowledge' or a 'synthetic philosophy' which the sciences and critical philosophy could now provide.

Following this initial statement, this outline of his framework, Spencer then proceeded to apply it in his investigation of all fields of knowledge, actually trying to achieve the scheme of knowledge which he had proposed. Naturally, he failed. One lifetime is not enough for such a project, and Spencer's accomplished work was chiefly within the range of the biological and human sciences–psychology and sociology–which were more at the centre of his concerns. The fact that Spencer could not exhaustively *complete* his scheme is not, however, any criticism of the nature and validity of the scheme itself. As with Comte's proposals for a system of positive knowledge, so with Spencer's scheme, it is arguable that it is, indeed, this kind of systematization of knowledge alone which can provide man, today, with a meaningful picture of his place within the scheme of things and with a reliable basis for responsible action in changing the nature of the world and of society, If such a scheme is beyond the capacity of one man to complete in all its detail–which it most certainly is–it is not beyond the capacity of many co-operative scholars; and perhaps it is still something at which we should aim in an effort to prevent the fragmentation and disorientation of specialist knowledge as our society becomes ever more complicated.

With regard to this question of the *validity* of Spencer's scheme, one or two other preliminary points must be made before leaving this brief outline of his concept of 'evolution'.

First of all, it will be seen how supremely important it is *not* to make the error of thinking that Spencer simply extended any particular theory of biological evolution to other fields of study in which it was not applicable. And it is worth noting that Spencer's outline of the centrality of 'evolution' in the nature of things was stated *before* Darwin's *Origin of Species* was published. It is also worth noting that though Spencer *did* conceive of any phenomenon as being continuously in a condition of having to accommodate itself to its environment, and sometimes spoke of the 'struggle for existence,' he was *not* committed to the strictly Darwinian account of biological evolution in terms of genetic transmission and 'natural selection', and the application of this account in fields going beyond biology. On the contrary, Spencer's conception was *broader* than that of Darwin, and provided for the exploration of the patterns of transformation *appropriate* to all kinds of phenomena–plants, planets, people, societies–as they accommodate themselves to their environmental contexts.

And this leads to a vital point: that, even if Spencer's particular description of 'evolution is found to be insufficient or inaccurate in this or that detail, it is still the case that his unified scheme of analysis for relating the sciences, and the knowledge they provide, holds good. Phenomena of all kinds *are* forms of material substance, persisting as certain concatenations and dispositions of elements.

They *do* exist in a 'moving equilibrium' of inter-dependence with their environments. They *do* have appropriate sequences of transformation of their elements in their pattern of emergence, growth, development, and dissolution. The changes that beset them, or occur to or among them, *are* related to changes in environmental conditions and *do* consist of a re-ordering of their elements into a qualitatively changed form.

It is important to see, then, that the scheme of analysis which Spencer provided still offers a luminously clear programme for the pursuit and unification of knowledge, even if his own particular notion of 'evolution' fails before certain criticisms. Having said that, however, it is doubtful–once Spencer's notion of 'evolution' is freed and disentangled from that of Darwin–whether it does fail to withstand criticism, and I will come back to this later.

One other very important point, however, remains to be made.

It might be said, by way of criticism of Spencer, that–even if 'evolution' as he described it is central to the processes of nature–it is still the case that his 'law' of evolution is *not* an *explanation* of anything at all. It is, in fact, simply a *descriptive* statement, an *empirical generalization* only, which itself requires explanation.

Now in so far as we have described it already, this criticism would appear to have weight, even though, as we have seen, Spencer's conception did imply quite a clear system of analysis and explanation. In fact, however, Spencer went far beyond the descriptive account we have given (what he called the 'inductive' grounds for his statement), to consider principles of deductive explanation which make this criticism quite beside the point. Here, we need only note these grounds of explanation, but–when we come to consider Spencer's account of the nature of society and social evolution–we will return to them to give this criticism and the rebuttal of it, full weight.

It is enough now simply to note that, having described this centrality of 'evolution' in nature, Spencer did in fact search for grounds of explanation rooted in the fundamental proposals he had outlined. Given the persistence of force, the indestructibility of the basic elements of material substance, the continuity of motion, and the like: *why* were the changes of phenomena from the homogeneous to the heterogeneous? from the relatively incoherent to the relatively coherent? from the simple to the complex? from the undifferentiated to the differentiation of specialized structure and functions. The following are the more important factors which he emphasized.

Explanations of Evolution

(a) The instability of the homogeneous

The condition of homogeneity, Spencer argued, is, in fact, a condition of unstable equilibrium.

When an aggregate of many similar units exists, and extends its number over a larger area, two factors making for changes and differentiations among them are present. Firstly, they cannot maintain their arrangements unaltered: they have to change their relations to one another. Secondly, the several parts of the aggregate are exposed to different forces, different conditions (whether of kind, or quantity, or intensity) and are therefore differently modified.

'The homogeneous', said Spencer, 'must lapse into the non-homogenous...' and he gave illustrations drawn from all phenomena. For the moment, let us note briefly what he said about the differentiation of species in biology.

'We have abundant materials for the induction that each species will not remain uniform–is ever becoming to some extent multiform; and there is ground for the deduction that this lapse from homogeneity to heterogeneity is caused by the subjection of its members to unlike circumstances. Tending ever to spread from its original habitat into adjacent habitats, each species must have its peripheral parts subject to sets of forces unlike those to which its central parts are subject, and so must tend to have its peripheral members made different from its central members.'

Spencer gave excellent examples of the same principle at work in human societies, too, but we can come to these later. It is enough for now to see that the movement from initial homogeneity to relative heterogeneity is not only described but *explained*.

(b) The multiplication of effects

Secondly, Spencer argued, once differentiation and diversity begins; once it emerges; a cumulative rapidity of increasing diversity and differentiation is set in motion. Diversity feeds upon itself, so to speak, and makes for increasing complexity. A brief quotation makes Spencer's conception completely clear:

'Each differentiated division of the aggregate becomes a centre from which a differentiated division of the original force is again diffused. And since unlike forces must produce unlike results, each of these differentiated forces must produce, throughout the aggregate, a further series of differentiations.

'This secondary cause of the change of homogeneity to heterogeneity obviously becomes more potent in proportion as the heterogeneity increases. When the parts into which any evolving whole has segregated itself, have diverged widely in nature, they will necessarily react very diversely on any incident force–they will divide an incident force into so many strongly contrasted groups of forces. And each of them becoming the centre of a quite distinct set of influences, must add to the number of distinct secondary changes wrought throughout the aggregate.

'Yet another corollary must be added. The *number* of unlike parts of which an aggregate consists, is an important factor in the process. Every additional specialized division is an additional centre of specialized forces, and must be a further source of complication among the forces at work throughout the mass–a further source of heterogeneity. The multiplication of effects must proceed in geometrical progression.'

Again, Spencer gave illustrations from all fields of knowledge, and later we will look at those he selected to illustrate social processes in particular.

(c) Segregation

This is not easy to clarify briefly, but it is enough for our immediate purposes to say that, once differentiation occurs within the units of an aggregate, a tendency towards the 'specialization' of parts will develop. To any particular influence, units which are alike will respond in a similar fashion, whereas units which are different will respond differently. A process of internal 'selection' or 'segregation' of specialized parts will be set afoot.

'If,' wrote Spencer, 'in an aggregate containing two or more orders of mixed units, those of the same order will be moved in the same way, and in a way that differs from that in which units of other orders are moved, the respective orders must segregate... the mixed units must undergo a simultaneous selection and separation.'

The movement from homogeneous to heterogeneous, with the increasing rapidity and complexity of differentiation attendant upon the multiplicity of effects, will therefore not be arbitrary. A pattern of specialized differentiation is likely to occur. This will be better clarified when we consider Spencer's sociological examples.

(d) Equilibration

A fourth element of explanation is the outcome of Spencer's consideration of the *limits* of heterogeneity, differentiation, and complexity in the transformations of phenomena. Are the kinds and degrees and paces of evolutionary change in nature unlimited, unbounded, uncircumscribed? They most certainly are not, said Spencer.

There is, of course, or so it seems in all natural phenomena, the ultimate of dissolution. But, a long way before that, and all the way before that, the changes of all phenomena are bounded by the conditions of their environments. Their nature is constrained by their environments both in the sense that changes in them cannot go beyond certain limiting conditions in their environments, and in the sense that they cannot avoid responding in some appropriate way to forces imposed upon them by their environments. They are constrained, that is to say, to establish some manageable 'equilibrium'.

All phenomena are in a process of adjustment and accommodation until a 'moving equilibrium' is reached; a situation in which the 'ensemble' of its parts and their total functioning is nicely adjusted to the interplay of forces in the environment; and the limitations of change and differentiation will be when such an equilibrium is reached.

'Every evolving aggregate', wrote Spencer, 'must go on changing until a moving equilibrium is established...

'Respecting the Structural state simultaneously reached, it must obviously be one presenting an arrangement of forces that counterbalance all the forces to which the aggregate is subject. So long as there remains a residual force in any direction–be it excess of a force exercised by the aggregate on its environment, or of a force exercised by its environment on the aggregate, equilibrium does not exist; and therefore the re-distribution of matter must continue. Whence it follows that the limit of heterogeneity towards which every aggregate progresses, is the formation of as many specializations and combinations of parts, as there are specialized and combined forces to be met.'

This fourth principle, therefore, according to Spencer, means that the explanation of the nature and limitations which any phenomenon undergoes in its 'evolution'; in its movement from simplicity to complex differentiation, from homogeneity to heterogeneity and the like; can be sought and uncovered in an 'equilibrium–dis-equilibrium' analysis.

(e) Dissolution

A fifth and final aspect of explanations is rooted in the process of 'dissolution', to which, ultimately, every phenomenon must submit. 'Evolution' is a process whereby elements are brought together in a certain form of growth and organisation. 'Dissolution' is the *reverse* process: of the *undoing* of these forms, and the disengagement and dissipation of the elements of which they consist. Dissolution is the undoing of evolved forms.

Spencer, it is important to notice, does not regard 'evolution' and 'dissolution' as two totally separable 'stages'. On the contrary, he insists that, in the 'equilibrium–dis-equilibrium' adjustments to internal and environmental forces in which any phenomenon is continuously engaged, forces making *both* for integration *and* disintegration are always involved, and what happens is always a *resultant* of these forces.

Spencer put it in this way:

'...neither of these two antagonistic processes goes on unqualified by the other, and a movement towards either is a differential result of the conflict between them...'

In any evolving aggregate:

'...after the integrative changes have ceased to predominate, the reception of motion...constantly tends to produce a reverse transformation, and eventually does produce it. When Evolution has run its course–when an aggregate has reached that equilibrium in which its changes end, it thereafter remains subject to all actions in its environment which may increase the quantity of motion it contains, and which in course of time are sure, either slowly or suddenly, to give its parts such excess of motion as will cause disintegration. According as its size, its nature, and its conditions determine, its dissolution may come quickly or may be indefinitely delayed–may occur in a few days or may be postponed for billions of years. But exposed as it is to the contingencies, not simply of its immediate neighbourhood but of a Universe everywhere in motion, the time must at last come when, either alone or in company with surrounding aggregates, it has its parts dispersed.'

One part of the 'explanation' of any phenomenon, then–in its origins, growth, change and disintegration–will be the uncovering of those forces which lead to its dissolution; those factors which lead to the undoing of its nature, the decline of the equilibrium situation which it had attained, and the dispersal of those parts and elements which had been bound together, in organized fashion, within it. Again, it will be best to leave any illustration of this until we come to look at Spencer's suggestions when considering the dissolution of *societies* especially.

There is no doubt whatever, then, that Spencer provided not only a 'descriptive generalization' of 'evolution', but also a systematic approach to the *analysis* and *explanation* of it; and this will be seen to be quite vital in his system of sociology.

It is well worth emphasizing, too, before leaving this point, that Spencer, in proposing this scheme of knowledge which was focused upon the unifying concept of 'evolution', was *not* guilty of a 'naive' inductivism' any more than Comte and Mill had been before him.

Throughtout, he sought hypotheses and deductive support for the empirical generalizations (the 'inductions') gleaned from experience.

Having clarified this pattern or evolutionary change, and having maintained that it applied to all phenomena, Spencer then proceeded to test his law, by empirical observation, in the sphere of each science. We are only concerned here with what he had to say about society, but before turning to this, let us simply note that Spencer was quite clear in his mind about the method he was pursuing. He had clarified his supposition that the pattern of 'evolution' was central to all natural processes; derived a set of hypotheses as to the explanation of this from the fundamental laws of physics; made deductions from them as to what the behaviour of other, and more complicated phenomena in nature would be, and, following that, he wrote:

'Deduction has now to be verified by induction.'

There was clearly no lack of clarity with regard to inference and method here.

If all that I have said it true, however–and it is; the question arises: why has Spencer been thought to have been guilty of borrowing the evolutionary explanations of *biology,* in particular, and applying them inappropriately in sociology? The answer lies in a central feature of Spencer's treatment: the considerable (some would say the inordinate) use he made of the analogy between the nature of a biological organism and the nature of a society.

The analogy between a society and an organism

Spencer used this analogy to make it perfectly clear what he meant by analysing a society in terms of 'structure' and 'function', and the 'functional interdependence' of parts in the social system as a whole. It may be true that Spencer used this analogy in much greater detail than most other thinkers. In fairness, however, it must be insisted that Spencer was always quite explictly aware that he was dealing with an analogy only. He *never* believed that societies *were* organisms, that organism *were* societies. He *never* believed that the relationship between the two was homologous rather than analogous, and later we shall see exactly what he said about this.

Even at the start of his argument, however, he took care to point out that when discussing the 'evolution' of human societies he was *not* thinking of this in terms of *organic* evolution, but what he called *super-organic* evolution. Human societies, though having some characteristics similar to those possessed by organisms, were something *more* that biological organisms as such. They consisted of forms of social organisation which were *other* than the characteristics of biological organisms; and any change that took place in them was therefore a kind of change over and above organic change proper. Hence his term '*super-organic evolution*': a kind of evolutionary change which occurred in addition to, and over and above, the changes peculiar to biological organisms.

Let us look at the nature of the analogy which he drew, and, in order to be as clear as possible, elucidate first the *similarities,* and then the *differences* between societies and organisms to which he drew attention.

(a) Similarities

Societies and organisms are *similar,* Spencer maintained, in the following ways:

1. They both differ from inorganic phenomena in that they *grow* in size.
2. As they grow in size, so there takes place, in both, a differentiation of internal elements of structure, and their total internal organisation becomes more complicated.
3. In both, this differentiation of structurer is concomitant with a differentiation of functions. The internal specialization of structures and functions develops together.
4. In both–and this is an important point for Spencer–the differences in size, structure, and functions brought about by evolutionary change are not *arbitrary.* They are *definitely related* differences resulting from adjustments to environmental factors. Both organisms and societies encounter environmental problems, environmental challenges, and the changes of size, structure and function which come into being are not *arbitrary* changes, but a definite outcome of adaptations to these problems.
5. Even though their whole unity, as such, may be destroyed, the individual parts–in both–may continue to live for some time afterwards. The parts of both possess a certain independence and continuity. For example, when an organism dies, certain parts continue to grow even though they no longer perform their appropriate function in the life of the organism as a whole. Similarly,

> if a human society is destroyed as a total independent entity–by conquest, earthquake, economic absorption into a larger power, or some other disaster–nonetheless, even in this context of overall disorganisation, certain parts and components of the society may continue to function. For example, family groups may continue to exist, some local communities may retain their entity, religious practices may survive, and so on.

(b) Differences

Having outlined these similarities in much detail, Spencer then, however, spent a good deal of effort in pointing out the very important ways in which societies and organisms *differed* from each other. There were three chief differences which he emphasized. We may note before glancing at these, that Spencer pointed them out very carefully, because he was clearly aware of the *dangers* that could attend the analogy between societies and organisms when used irresponsibly by philosophers or statesmen of authoritarian persuasions.

Societies and organisms are *different,* Spencer argued, in the following ways:

1. In an organism, the parts, the internal units, form–together–a united living whole; a concrete physical entity. The parts are bound together in actual physical connection with each other. In a society, however, the parts are separated and dispersed. For example, families are disconnected from each other and widely dispersed throughout a country. Similarly, schools, industrial firms, political parties, and other groups and institutions, though all interrelated, are nonetheless all distinct and separate entities, whereas, in an organism, the brain, the lungs, the heart, are actually in physical interconnection with each other.

2. In an organism, the internal differentiation of structures and functions results in the fact that particular functions are fulfilled by specific organs alone, and by no other. For example, the brain may be said to be the 'organ of thought', and no other organ in the body can fulfil that function. Similarly, the stomach may be said to perform certain specific functions of digestion. Other parts of the organism do not have these special functions at all, and are, in these particular respects, insensitive. This,

Spencer emphasizes, is *not* true of a human society. It is *not* the case that the government of a society is the sole 'organ of thought' or the sole 'seat of authority', or that the religion of a society, for example, is the sole 'seat of feeling of belief'. *All* human beings in a society, and as members of *all* institutions, to some extent share *all* these functions amongst each other. Specialization occurs among forms of social organisation, but the specialisation is different in kind from that which takes place among the parts of an organism.

In making this point, Spencer was emphasizing very carefully that he did *not* believe (as certain other thinkers had believed) that, in a society, there was such a thing as a *group mind* (one of the dangers of this analogy which has given rise to a great deal of criticism).

3. In an organism, Spencer maintained, the parts function with regard to the good of the whole, whereas, in a society, the entire 'ensemble' of institutions, exists only for the good of its parts–its individual members. In this point, too, Spencer wished to make it perfectly clear that his use of this analogy did *not* entail the idea that the individual was subordinated to the state.

It is surely perfectly clear–beyond all doubt whatever–that, having taken the differences, as well as the similarities, of the analogy into account:

(a) Spencer was perfectly clear that he was drawing *an analogy only,* and
(b) he specifically rejected those aspects of the analogy which might possibly carry unwarranted implications of totalitarianism.

It is true, however, that Spencer employed this analogy on almost every page of his treatise on social institutions. It is as though he felt compelled by the demands of systematization–having given an account of the way in which social institutions in certain types of society had developed–to illustrate this, in much detail, with reference to similar organic changes in particular biological species. This was done so frequently, and in such great detail, that it is perfectly understandable that many people should think he was interpreting social institutions and their changes in terms of biological evolution. Nonetheless, it is clear that this is an incorrect interpretation. Certainly the elaborate use of this analogy gave a decided biological flavour to Spencer's treatment. But we have seen perfectly clearly, that the fundamental 'law' of evolution which formed the basis of all his discussion was rooted not in biology but in the more fundamental (as he thought them) laws of physics.

Actually, however clumsy and unnecessary we may now judge this element of Spencer's treatment to have been, it was the employment of this analogy between a society and an organism which enabled him to give what was undoubtedly the clearest 'structural-functional' account of society that had been produced up to his day.

It was not totally new. Comte had used the same analogy extensively, and had also offered a 'structural-functional' analysis of the 'consensus' of institutions in the total social system. But Spencer's analysis of the process of differentiation of structures and functions in the pattern of evolutionary change gave his account a far greater clarity. It also enabled him to construct very clear models of certain *types* of society, and thus to make very clear indeed what he meant by the process of social evolution.

Just as the evolution of forms of organic life is characterized by the emergence of *species* which have a greater differentiation of structure and function, and are thus better fitted to survive in their natural environments, so the evolution of societies is characterized by the emergence of new *types* of *social system* which have a greater differentiation of structure and function and are thus better fitted to survive in their natural and social environment. Spencer's notion of social evolution, then, was that of an ongoing pattern of change in the structure and functions of social institutions which emerged to deal with newly encountered conditions and problems, and came to form distinctive 'types' of society. These changes, and these 'types', he claimed, were no more *arbitrary* than those which occurred in the evolution of biological species. They were distinctive and determinate social forms quite definitely related to particular problems and particular sets of environmental circumstances.

'The many facts contemplated,' Spencer wrote 'unite in proving that social evolution forms a part of evolution at large. Like evolving aggregates in general, societies show *integration,* both by simply increase of mass and by coalescence and by re-coalescence of masses. The change from *homogeneity* to *heterogeneity* is multitudinously exemplified up from the simple tribe alike in all its parts to the civilized nation full of structural, functional unlikenesses. With progressing integration and heterogeneity goes, increasing *coherence*. We see the wandering group dispersing, dividing, held together by no bonds, the tribe with parts made more coherent by subordination to a dominant man, the cluster of tribes united in a political plexus under a chief with sub-chiefs, and so on up to the civilized nation, consolidated enough to hold together for a thousand years or more. Simultaneously comes increasing *definiteness*. Social organisation is at first vague. Advance brings settled arrangements which grow slowly more precise. Customs pass into laws which, while gaining fixity, also become more specific and their applications to varieties of actions and all institutions at first confusedly intermingled slowly separate, at the same time each within itself marks off more distinctly its component structures, thus in all respects is fulfilled the formula of evolution. There is progress towards greater size, coherence, multiformity and definiteness.

'The inductions arrived at,' he claimed, 'thus constituting in rude outline an empirical sociology, show that in social phenomena there is a general order of co-existence and sequence and that, therefore, social phenomena form the subject matter of a science reducible in some measure at least to the deductive form.

'Guided then by the law of evolution in general and in subordination to it, guided by the foregoing inductions, we are prepared for following out the synthesis of social phenomena.'*

It is quite plain, then, how and why Spencer used the analogy between an organism and a society, and we are now in a position to see what exactly this analogy led him to say about the nature of a society and the processes of social evolution. Before moving on to this, however, I think it is worthwhile to make it clear beyond doubt that *this is not simply my own interpretation* of Spencer. It must be insisted that *this is his own view* which he himself makes quite plain for all who will read him. Let us see what Spencer said about this analogy towards the end of the second section of Volume 1 in *The Principles of sociology,* in which he discussed this matter. Having pointed out the inadequate uses of the analogy in the work of some earlier thinkers, such as Plato and Hobbes, he went on to say:

'Here let it once more be distinctly asserted that there exist no analogies between the body politic and the living body save those necessitated by that mutual dependence or parts which they display in common. Though in foregoing chapeters, sundry comparisons of social structures and functions to structures and functions in the human body have been made, they have been made only because structures and functions in the human body furnish familiar illustrations of structures and functions in general...'

'But now,' he says, 'let us drop this alleged Parallelism between individual organisations and social organisation. I have used the analogies elaborated, but as a scaffolding to help in building up a coherent body of sociological inductions. Let us take away the scaffolding, the inductions will stand by themselves.'

Nothing, surely, could be clearer than this. All those who criticise Spencer on this count can clearly be seen to be wrong.

In the same way, it may be worthwhile to see how Spencer himself thought of 'Evolution' as a universal process of transformation, of which social transformations were an example and a part, rather than as essentially a *biological* theory which could be applied in sociology.

'While we think of Evolution', he wrote, 'as divided into astronomic, geologic, biologic, psychologic, sociologic, etc., it may seem to some extent a coincidence that the same law of metamorphosis holds throughout all its divisions. But when we recognize these divisions as mere conventional groupings, made to facilitate the arrangement and acquisition of knowledge –when we remember that the different existences with which they severally deal are component parts of one Cosmos; we see at once that there are not several kinds of Evolution having certain traits in common, but one Evolution going on everywhere after the same manner.

'So understood, Evolution becomes not one in principle only, but one in fact. There are not many metamorphoses similarly carried on, but there is a single metamorphosis universally progressing, wherever the reverse metamorphosis has not set in...

'...In any locality, great or small, when the occupying matter acquired an appreciable individuality, or distinguishableness from other matter, there Evolution goes on, or rather, the acquirement of this appreciable individuality is the commencement of Evolution. And this holds regardless of the size of the aggregate and regardless of its inclusion in other aggregates...'

Having made Spencer's position clear beyond question, let us now examine his conception of the nature of a society, and the nature of social evolution, which he illuminated by this analogy, because on these matters too he has been very strangely and falsely criticized.

The nature of a society

Following upon the discussion of his analogy, and his conclusion that there is something of an 'organic' nature about a society, Spencer quite decisively rejected two ideas. He quite explicitly insisted that 'a society', as an entity, is something more than, and other than, an 'organism', even though human 'organisms' (individuals) are members of it. It is a total system of elements of social organisation and their interdependent functions within which individuals pursue their courses of social action. It is a *super-organic* entity; an *organizational entity* over and above the level of the 'organism'.

Also, Spencer just as emphatically rejected the idea that a 'society' was no more than a collective name for a number of individuals.

The nature of a 'whole', he maintained, was quite distinguishable from a mere collection of its parts, or its elements, by virtue of 'the permanence of relations among its component parts'. Thus, a house is not only a collective name for a heap of bricks, wood, stones, and other bits and pieces–it is a certain ordering and connecting of these parts in a distinctive total form.

Similarly, he wrote:

'We consistently regard a society as an entity, because, though formed of discrete units, a certain concreteness in the aggregate of them is implied by the general persistence of the arrangements among them throughout the areas occupied. And it is this trait which yields our idea of a society. Withholding the name from an ever-changing cluster...(of individuals)...we apply it only where some constancy in the distribution of parts has resulted from settled life.'

When clarifying the 'scope of sociology' as a scientific study of 'societies', Spencer was also meticulously clear in specifying what the parts of a 'society' were.

First of all, there was the family and kinship system, whereby 'successive generations are produced, reared, and fitted for co-operation.' Secondly, there were the many aspects of the political organisation–central and local; military (for offence and defence); regulatory over internal aspects of social organisation; and the relations between all these and such other aspects of authority as the law and ecclesiastical institutions and other aspects of social co-ordination, such as 'communications'. Thirdly, there was religion itself: its doctrines and rituals and its ecclesiastical organisation. Fourthly, there were all aspects of social control: law, custom, morality, and all the many symbols and insignia of ceremonial connected with them. Fifthly, there were the several distinctive aspects of the economic system: the organisation of production, distribution, and of the procedures of industrial arbitration. Sixthly, there were the distinctive social classes which were attendant upon this entire division of functions. And seventhly, there were all the determinate aspects of the social life of the people within this complex of institutions: their language, knowledge and education, art and entertainment, and morals.

A 'society' was an organizational entity consisting of these parts in interrelationship, and an analysis of a 'society' would consist of a clear description of them. But it would *not,* said Spencer, consist of a description of each part in isolation from the others.

'We have,' he wrote, 'to consider that inter-dependence of structures, and functions, and products, taken in their *totality.* Among these many groups of phenomena there is a *consensus;* and the highest achievement in Sociology is so to grasp the vast heterogeneous aggregate, as to see how the character of each group at each stage is determined partly by its own antecedents and partly by the past and present actions of the rest upon it.'

Spencer's conception of a 'society', and of the nature of the 'Sociological analysis' of a total society was perfectly clear; but his discussion of the 'organic' analogy enabled him to go even further. It is not to our purpose to explore the analogy itself, but the points which Spencer drew from it are important.

Of all the totality of parts in a society, he claimed, it was possible to distinguish three clear 'systems'. All societies had to deal with their physical and social environments, and during the course of this, three major differentiations took place. In order to organize a society for effective conflict with the environment, groups especially responsible for authoritative control–both with regard to the regulation and co-ordination of internal resources and with regard to the organisation of military offence and defence–came to be differentiated from groups chiefly responsible for economic productivity. Spencer spoke of the differentiation, sometimes, as being one between responsibility for 'Outer' protection and security, and 'Inner' sustenance. A 'Regulating System' was clearly differentiated from the 'Sustaining System' of societies, and this was a fundamental differentiation of functions and appropriate structures. These two systems, however, especially as they became larger in scale and more complex, had to be linked together by an efficient network of communications and a determinate distribution of resources. This third differentiation of functions and structures gave rise to the 'Distributive System'.

Spencer analysed each society, then, into all its specific elements of social structure; all its 'organs' of social organisation; but he then emphasized especially these differentiations of the 'Regulating', 'Sustaining', and 'Distributive' systems, and examined the nature of societies in terms of the relative preponderance of each.

All the major aspects of 'evolutionary' change–of growth in size; of structural-functional differentiation; of the change from the homogeneous to the heterogeneous, from the indefinite to the definite, from the incoherent to the coherent, and in various conditions of 'equilibrium'–were then studied with the use of this analytical model. And this lead us to consider how Spencer went about the comparative study of societies in order to establish a body of descriptive knowledge about them.

Before leaving this pint, however, let us simply note that when a modern American sociologist writes: 'Superorganic evolution is a beautiful term, but it has meaning only if it denotes a clear conception of the nature of society–a matter that unfortunately Spencer never clarified'–he is writing sheer stuff and nonsense. As we have seen, Spencer was completely clear about his conception of the nature of society, the parts of which it was composed, and what constituted a 'sociological analysis' of it. It is also important, in readiness for criticisms which will arise much later to note that in this 'structural-functional' analysis of a 'society', Spencer was quite clear that the elements of structure to which he referred were organizations of the '*combined actions*' of men in their associations with each other. In short, Spencer was quite clearly analysing the '*social action*' of men in his '*structural-functional*' analysis of '*social systems*'. The reason why this should be borne clearly and emphatically in mind will be seen later.

However, having clarified the nature of societies as entities, Spencer then argued:

'But now before trying to *explain* these most: involved phenomena, we must learn by inspection the relations of co-existence and sequence in which they stand to one another. By comparing societies of different kinds, and societies in different stages, we must ascertain what traits of size, structure, function, etc., are associated. In other words, before deductive interpretation of the general truths, there must come inductive establishment of them.'

It can be seen that Spencer followed the comparative and historical method in the way advocated by Comte and Mill, and–like Mill especially here–thought it of primary importance to *undertake empirical studies of societies;* to establish *empirical generalizations* about them. Adequate explanations could then be considered. And it is interesting to notice that such empirical generalizations about societies and the 'consensus' of parts within them, were, according to Spencer, 'relations of co-existence and sequence'. Here again, we see the strand of empirical, causal analysis which had continued from Hume onwards. And here again, too, we see Spencer's way of employing the kind of distinction which Comte had called 'Statics' and 'Dynamics'. Spencer's conceptual analysis of the nature of society as one kind of consensus of facts in our experience–his 'Social Statics' was based upon his conception of 'Evolution'. With this analysis, he then approached the study of the many varieties of societies in the world in order to establish empirical knowledge about them and the ways in which they changed: his 'Social Dynamics'.

Types of society: classification and comparison

His clear conception of the nature of a society enabled Spencer to construct very clear models for the classification and comparison of societies. Two methods arose quite directly from his analysis.

First: his evolutionary 'law' suggested that societies would change in terms of growth, aggregation, and an increasing differentiation of institutions. Small, simple aggregates became 'clustered' or 'compounded'–as a result of many factors–into larger, more complex aggregates. Societies could be classified, then, on the basis of their *'degree of composition'*.

Secondly, however, the actual and detailed processes of this aggregation' might be illuminated by a supplementary method of classification: the method of constructing 'models' or 'types' of societies in terms of the relative preponderance of one or other of the 'Regulating', 'Sustaining' and 'Distributive' systems. A society which subordinated its entire pattern of life to its 'Military' security would have a very different 'consensus' of institutions from one which subordinated his entire social life to the extension of wealth and welfare by developing its 'sustaining' (economic) system. And the patterns of aggregation which societies have undergone in historical change might prove to be significantly related to the changing pre-dominance of one or other of these 'systems'. 'Models' of this kind would therefore provide another dimension of interpretation and understanding.

It is very important to notice two things about Spencer's methods of classification. Firstly, the two methods are quite different. The classification according to the 'degree of composition' rests upon an *empirically determinate set of characteristics of social organization* which can be *observed*. It can be *seen* whether the society one is studying is a 'tribe', or a 'confederation of tribes', or a 'confederation of nations'; and societies of the same level of aggregation can be grouped together accordingly. The classification according to 'typologies' or 'models' does *not* rest upon empirically determinate facts–though it *refers* to them in attempting *interpretation.* These 'types' or 'models' are hypothetical constructs. Spencer does not claim, or wish to claim, that societies *actually exist* in the extreme form which his models may take. All societies will have *some* blend of the 'Regulating, Sustaining, and Distributive systems' and our understanding of *this actual blend* may be aided by our construction of analytical extremes. We shall see what Spencer had to say about the specific 'types' which he constructed in a moment.

The second point to notice here is that Spencer quite clearly introduced into comparative sociology this method of the construction of 'types' of society: which were 'structural-functional' models of societies in which certain predominant traits were assumed, and emphasized, in such a way as to give a total picture of the pattern of social action in that society, and to provide an understanding of it (including the close relationship between the institutional structure of the social order and the pattern of life and character of its individual members). All this we shall come back to again, but this insight and this method of Spencer's must be noted and emphasized now, because later we shall see that some modern critics argue as though the subjective understanding of social *action,* and the construction of 'types' for this purpose, had been absent from sociology until very recently–whereas, as we can see, they had been firmly incorporated into sociology during the nineteenth century.

(a) Classification by 'degree of composition'.

Spencer's first method of classification can best be made clear by referring to the following diagrams which he provided.

Simple Societies

Headless	*Nomadic:* (hunting) Fuegians, some Australians, Wood-Veddahs, Bushmen, Chepangs and Kusundas of Nepal. *Semi-settled:* most Esquimaux. *Settled:* Arafuras, Land Dyaks of Upper Sarawak River.

Occassional Headship	*Nomadic:* (hunting) some Australians, Tasmanians. *Semi-settled:* some Caribs. *Settled:* some Uaupes of the upper Rio Negro.
Vague And Unstable Headship.	*Nomadic:* (hunting) Andamanese, Abipones, Snakes. Chippewayans. (pastoral) some Bedouins. *Semi-settled:* some Esquimaux, Chinooks, Chippewas (at present), some Kamschadales, Village Veddahs, Bodo and Dhimals. *Settled:* Guiana tribes, Mandans, Coroados, New Guinea people, Tannese, Vateans, Dyaks, Todas, Nagas, Karens, Santals.
Stable Headship.	*Nomadic:* *Semi-settled:* some Caribs, Patagonians, New Caledonians, Kaffirs. *Settled:* Guaranis, Pueblos.

(II) Compound Societies

Occasional Headship	*Nomadic:* (pastoral) some Bedouins. *Semi-settled:* Tannese. *Settled:*
Unstable Headship.	*Nomadic:* (hunting) Dacotahs, (hunting and pastoral) Comanches, (pastoral) Kalmucks. *Semi-settled:* Ostyaks, Beluchis, Kookies, Bhils, Congo-people (passing into doubly compound), Teutons before 5th century. *Settled:* Chippewas (in past times), Creeks, Mundrucus, Tupis, Khonds, some New Guinea people, Sumatrans, Malagasy (till recently), Coast Negroes, Inland Negroes, some Abyssinians, Homeric Greeks, Kingdoms of the Heptarchy, Teutons in 5th century, Fiefs of 10th century.

Stable Headship.	*Nomadic:* (pastroal) Kirghiz. *Semi-settled:* Bechuanas, Zulus. *Settled:* Uaupes, Fijians (when first visited), New Zealanders, Sandwhich Islanders (in Cook's time), Javans, Hottentots, Dahomans, Ashantees, some Abyssinians, Ancient Yucatanese, New Grandà people, Honduras people, Chibchas, some town Arabs.

(III) Double Compound Societies

Occasional Headship.	*Semi*-settled: *Settled:* Samoans.
Unstable Headship..	*Semi-settled* *Settled:* Tahitains, Tongans, Javans (occassionally), Fijians (since fire-arms), Malagasy (in recent times), Athenian Confederacy, Spartan Confederacy, Teutonic Kingdoms from 6th to 9th centuries, Greater Fiefs in France of the 13th century.
Stable Headship.	*Semi-settled:* *Settled:* Iroquois, Aracucanians, Sandwich Islanders (since Cook's time), Ancient Vera Paz and Bogota peoples, Guatemalans, Ancient Peruvians, Wahhabees (Arab), Oman (Arab), Ancient Egyptian Kingdom, England after the 10th century.

(IV) Civilized Nations

'There remain to be added the great civilized nations which need no tabular form, since they mostly fall under one head–trebly compound. Ancient Mexico the Assyrian Empire, the Egyptian Empire, the Roman Empire, Great Britain. France, Germany, Italy, Russia, may severally be regarded as having reached this stage of composition, or perhaps, in some cases, a still higher stage. Only in respect of the stabilities of their governments may they possibly require classing apart–not their political stabilities in the ordinary sense, but their stabilities in the sense of continuing to be the supreme centres of these great aggregates. So defining this trait, the ancient trebly-compound societies have mostly to be classed as unstable; and of the modern, the Kingdom of Italy and the German Empire have to be tested by time.

'As already indicated,' Spencer insisted, 'this classification must not be taken as more than an approximation to the truth.'

It will be readily seen that this is a clear, systematic, and comprehensive scheme of classification within which all societies known to us can be compared.

The 'degrees of composition' are defined quite clearly. Simple societies, Spencer wrote, are those 'which form simple working wholes unsubjected to any other and of which the parts co-operate with or without a regulating centre for certain public ends'.' 'Compound societies are those in which the simple groups of which they are compounded have their own respective chiefs under a supreme chief.' 'Doubly compounded societies are those formed by the federation of these compound groups, giving rise to more settled complex forms of social organisation with stable and more elaborate forms of government.' And trebly compounded societies are all the 'great civilized nations' and large-scale empires or federations of nations, whether of ancient or modern times.

It will be noticed, too, that Spencer introduced two subsidiary categories of classification into this scheme–namely that of stable or unstable 'headship' and whether the society was 'nomadic, semi-settled, or settled'; but these do not require particular comment. Two or three other points, however, deserve brief emphasis.

Firstly–it will be seen that the societies drawn together under these categories are *both* histrical *and* contemporary. In short, this is a *classificatory scheme* into which *all* societies of which we have knowledge can be manageably drawn. Secondly, its objective is no more than to *arrange* empirical knowledge of societies under certain headings so that further, detailed comparative study can be undertaken, and so that, as an outcome, generalized (systematic) knowledge can be arrived at about the 'consensus' of institutions in each category and the pattern of institutional change which characterizes the development of one 'consensus' out of another. Uniformities of co-existence and sequence can be established. This classification of knowledge does not, of itself, *explain* social order or social change, it is simply a way of *gaining* and *extending* systematic (descriptive) knowledge, which we shall then *seek* to explain; and this is exactly how Spencer regarded it.

Thirdly, however, it is worth noting that Spencer put his scheme forward *tentatively* rather *dogmatically*. It was the best he felt able to do given the basis of the evolutionary conception and the 'status' of the empirical knowledge he had at his disposal.

'This classification', he wrote, 'must not be taken as more than an approximation to the truth. In some cases the data furnished by travellers and others are inadequate, in some cases their accounts are conflicting; in some cases the (degree of) composition is so far transitional that it is difficult to say under which of two heads it should come.

But still, he argued, this was the best scheme of classification available, and it rested upon, and revealed, certain generalizations which could be quite safely accepted. Spencer also poured scorn on those critics who with glib and Oxford-historian-like facility, made much of the uncertainty of his data, and the fact that much was drawn from 'travellers' tales'.

'I am aware', he wrote, 'that in the eyes of most, antiquity gives sacredness to testimony and that so, what were "travellers tales" when they were written in Roman days have come in our days, to be regarded as of higher authority than like tales written by recent or living travellers. I see, however, no reason to ascribe to the second-hand statements of Tacitus a trustworthiness which I do not ascribe to the first-hand statements of modern explores; many of them scientifically educated–Barrow, Barth, Galton, Burton, Livingstone, Seeman, Darwin, Wallace, Humboldt, Burckhardt, and others too numerous to set down...'

Spencer was very well aware–indeed, much better aware than his critics–of the limitations of the data at his disposal.

(b) Classification by the construction of 'types'.

Using the second of his two methods, Spencer thought it most useful to construct two extremely dissimilar types–*so* dissimilar as to constitute a 'polarity'–the 'Militant' and the

'Industrial'. The first was a type in which the 'Regulating System' was dominant over all other aspects of society. The second was one in which the 'Sustaining System' was emphasized, and all other aspects of society were subordinated to its service. The 'Distributing System' was, of course, significantly different in the differing 'consensus' of the two types.

Here again it is necessary to insist how clear Spencer was in the *tentative* nature of his approach. He was quite clear that, excepting for some of the simplest societies which occupied territories where they were quite safe from invasion, *both* regulating *and* sustaining systems always existed in some conjunction; *both* militant *and* industrial aspects existed in some combination in *all* societies.

'But,' he wrote, 'while the two systems in social organisms co-exist in all but the rudimentary forms, they vary immensely in the ratios they bear to one another. In some cases the structures carrying on external actions are largely developed; the sustaining system exists solely for their benefit; and the activities are militant. In other cases there is predominance of the structures carrying on sustentaton; offensive and defensive structures are maintained only to protect them; and the activities are industrial.'

'Much less definite (i.e., than that based upon degree of composition) is the division to be made among societies according as one or other of the great systems of organs is supreme.

'Nevertheless, as the militant type, characterized by predominance of the one, is framed on the principle of *compulsory co-operation,* while the industrial type, characterized by predominance of the other, is framed on the principle of *voluntary co-operation,* the two types, when severally evolved to their extreme forms, are diametrically opposed; and the contrasts between their traits are among the most important with which Sociology has to deal.'

This was therefore a construction of two polar 'types' for the sake of a clearer understanding of societies which possessed a relative preponderance of one or other of the two systems. It is interesting to notice that, in his conviction that the exploration of the contrasts between these two types is possibly the most important task for Sociology, Spencer was again very much in agreement with Comte. Spencer's distinction between the

'Militant' and 'Industrial' types of society was, really, the same as Comte's distinction between the 'Theological' and the 'Positive' types; and the agreement between these two men–and others to be mentioned later–points to the crucial distinction we have already touched upon between the 'Traditional' societies of the past and the 'Modern Industrial' societies which have developed since the French Revolution. We shall see that this is the central, continual, preoccupation of Sociology.

Spencer described his two 'types' of society as follows:

(I) The Militant Society

The militant society is a type in which organisation for offensive and defensive military action is predominant. It is one, said Spencer, 'in which the army is the nation mobilized and the nation is the quiescent army' and, consequently, in which the entire structure of society is closely moulded about its military structure, reflecting its military organisation.

Such a society has the following marked characteristics:

There is firstly, a highly centralized pattern of authority and social control. The military head is also the political head, and he has a despotic power over the life and property of all his subjects. The absolute control of the ruler makes necessary a clear, precise, and rigid hierarchy of power throughout society, in which each level of officials has to be completely subservient to that above, and completely in power over those below. 'All are slaves', wrote Spencer 'to those above and despots to those below.' And this rigid hierarchy of power necessarily involves a precise and rigid grading of social status and social ranking and thus gives rise to rigid social classes in economic life. The distribution of property, the distribution of material rewards in society, is meticulously linked with the order of social ranks.

But this authoritarian and hierarchical nature of the society is also reflected in the prevailing system of ideas and beliefs. There exists also a set of doctrines, myths, and attendant rituals which portrays a similar form or supernatural authority and government. The gods themselves, and their divine agencies, are pictured in terms of a hierarchy of power, and as being closely concerned with the destiny of society. 'Ever in antagonism with other societies,' Spencer said, 'the life is a life of enmity and the religion a religion of enmity.'

This hierarchical power of the gods as pictured in doctrine and myth is also reflected, indeed embodied, in the hierarchical form of the actual ecclesiastical organisation. The religion itself is a hierarchical organisation, and the Ecclesiastical Head himself possesses supreme, despotic authority. Furthermore, in such a society, the despotic head is, at one and the same time, not only the Military and Political, but also the Ecclesiastical head. His central power over government, army, and all civil and economic affairs, is sanctified and given justification by religion.

It follows that the whole tenor of life in such a society is characterized by rigorous discipline and by a close identity between private and public life. No element of the private life of the citizen is closed to the state. The state can invade and interfere in the private lives of citizens whenever it is felt necessary or desirable to do so. Indeed, the word 'citizens' is hardly appropriate. The great majority of the population are completely subjected to the regulatory purposes of the central authority. And this lack of individual rights in the relationship between individual and state is supported by the belief 'that its members exist for the benefit of the whole and not the whole for the benefit of its members. The loyalty of the individual to the state has to be unquestioning.'

'Human relationship', said Spencer, 'are characterized in this kind of society by a state of "*compulsory co-operation*".'

Clearly (without elaborating this point here) Spencer's Militant 'type' of society is applicable, as a basis of interpretation, not only to the despotic societies of antiquity, but also to totalitarian societies in the contemporary world. It is intriguing to consider his analysis in relation to the Soviet Union, or China, Nazi Germany, or Fascist Italy. As a 'type,' the 'militant society' can be seen to be of wide use for the purpose of comparative studies, being relevant to societies of both the past and the present.

(II) The Industrial Society

Spencer's 'Industrial Type' of society is one in which military activity and organisation, though it still exists, is carried on at an increasing distance from the civilian life and concerns of the community. It takes place on the periphery of the society; and the greater part of social organisation is peaceful, concentrating upon the increase and improvement of all aspects of human production and welfare; upon economic and civil activities.

The characteristics of such a society contrast strongly with those of the 'militant' type.

First of all, there is a clear and firm recognition, on the part of all its members, of *personal rights,* which they hold as citizens of the community. On this basis there is a continual exercise of the making of mutual claims and counter-claims, and a voluntary submission on the part of individuals to impartial procedures for the resolution of them. There is also an active concern for the maintenance of these rights by an insistence upon effective means of representative government.

In this society, too, the 'sustaining system' possesses a large degree of freedom, a large degree of disengagement, from the 'regulatory system'. The control and government of economic affairs is largely and deliberately divorced from the political government. It is, indeed, assumed by the government, as well as by everyone else in society, that intelligent individuals concerned with their own economic activities will be better capable of making their own decisions than remote administrative officials. And, indeed, they are not only *allowed,* they are actively *encouraged*, to do so.

With the growing complexity of agriculture, commerce and industrial manufacture, within the peaceful context of an area bounded, at the distant periphery, by military security, there is therefore a growth of free associations and institutions. In all such forms of association, there comes to be a growth of *committee* procedures for the government of affairs, and, within this context, the appointment of officers by *election.* These factors bring about a much less rigid and less tyrannical class structure, which rests increasingly upon human relationships which are contractual and free, and in which gradations of status and rank are less precisely marked. There is a growth, as Spencer put it, or combinations of workmen and employers' to resolve particular disputes, quite separately from central authority and law.

Similarly, religious organisation and religious beliefs lose their hierarchical structure and absolute power. Individual faith, individual and sectarian discrimination, enters into religion. In place of the doctrine that the members of society exist for the good of the state, emerges the idea that it is the will and the well-being of the individual citizens which is of supreme importance in society, and that the organ of government, and, indeed, all forms of organisational control, exist merely to manifest their wishes and to serve them.

In such a society, then, it is not only thought that despotic government is wrong; it becomes a positive duty on the part of citizens to *resist* irresponsible government. There is always a tendency to *disobedience* amongst minorities and individuals, and such a critical tendency is positively encouraged. Human relationships in the industrial society are, therefore, wholly different from those in the militant society. Free, responsible, contractual relationships between individuals require *voluntary co-operation,* not the compulsory co-operation which characterizes relationships in the militant type.

It must be emphasized again that Spencer did not believe that societies actually existed in the world with the sharp clarity of distinction that he described in drawing up these two 'models'. He merely thought that comparison between these two specially constructed types was useful in conjunction with his other mode of classification (on the basis of degrees of composition) in order to interpret and understand some of the crucially important trends of social evolution, and, especially, those trends which were of importance as traditional societies were being radically transformed by the processes of industrialization.

Having provided these modes of classifying societies, Spencer then undertook a very detailed comparative study of each major social institution within each 'type' of society; arranging an enormous range of descriptive facts into this classificatory framework in order to establish the main characteristics and trends of social evolution. This gave him a picture of what, in the whole field of social institutions had actually occurred in the past, and what was happening in the present.

This comparative study was carried out with meticulous clarity and consistency. Each chief element of social structure, and each of the major 'systems' of institutions in society–

Domestic, Ecclesiastical, Political, Industrial institutions–were studied in turn, and the nature of these was examined firstly in societies according to their 'degrees of composition' and secondly in accordance with their contrasting nature in societies which approximated to the 'militant' or 'industrial' types. In each case, too, Spencer summarized his findings in a section in 'Retrospect and Prospect' so that a clear perspective of contemporary changes in society was provided. A remarkably systematic and well-ordered body of knowledge about the nature of societies; about the 'consensus' of institutions in each type, and the patterns of change which they experienced in coming to terms with different situations; was thus provided. And this, it must be noted, was not only an ordered body of descriptive knowledge (though it *was* that), but also a system of knowledge resting upon certain *explanations* deductively derived from an analysis of 'systems' within their context of 'evolutionary transformation', and utilized to provide certain *interpretations* of the structures of social action in societies of different types.

Spencer's contribution to the making of sociology was a remarkable achievement. He has been much criticized for using library materials and documentary data, and having other people carry out researches for him; but on what other sources of materials could Spencer have drawn in his time? And, in any case, Spencer was chiefly concerned to achieve a clear scientific fabric within which *any* relevant data could be most reliably studied. As we have seen, he was well aware of the limitations of much of the material on which he could lay his hands. Furthermore, the data which Spencer amassed is still extremely useful, and much knowledge and illumination is still to be gained from a reading of the volumes of the *Principles of Sociology*.

However, the outcome of Spencer's efforts in these wide comparative studies was the provision of a very clear picture of the nature of social evolution as he saw it. And it would be a pity to leave Spencer having pointed out only the methodological and theoretical schema which he created, and not the substantive knowledge in which his methods resulted. Also, I would like especially to demonstrate the way in which Spencer was attempting to *explain* the several aspects of social evolution, because I believe he is very much underrated, misunderstood, and misrepresented in this, and his ideas really deserve much critical attention. Let us look, then, at the picture of social evolution which Spencer's studies provide–as briefly as is commensurate with sufficiency for purposes of understanding.

The nature of Social Evolution

No summary statement of Spencer's over-all picture of the facts of social evolution could be better than that which he himself provided.

'Societies,' he wrote, 'are aggregates which grow. In the various types of them there are great varieties in the growths reached. Types of successively larger sizes result from the aggregation and re-aggregation of those of smaller sizes; and this increase by coalescence, joined with interstitial increase, is the process through which have been formed the vast civilized nations.

'Along with increase of size in societies goes increase of structure. Primitive hordes are without established distinctions of parts. With growth of them into tribes habitually come some unlikeness; both in the powers and occupations of their members. Unions of tribes are followed by more unlikenesses, governmental and industrial--social grades running through the whole mass, and contrasts between the differently-occupied parts in different localities. Such differentiations multiply as the compounding progresses. They proceed from the general to the special. First the broad division between ruling and ruled; then within the ruling part divisions into political, religious, military, and within the ruled part divisions into food-producing classes and handicraftsmen; then within each of these divisions minor ones, and so on.

'Passing from the structural aspect to the functional aspect, we note that so long as all parts of a society have like natures and activities, there is hardly any mutual dependence, and the aggregate scarcely forms a vital whole. As its parts assume different functions they become dependent on one another, so that injury to one hurts others; until, in highly-evolved societies, general perturbation is caused by derangement of any portion. This contrast between undeveloped and developed societies, arises from the fact that with increasing specialization of functions comes increasing inability in each part to perform the functions of other parts.

'The organisation of every society begins with a contrast between the division which carries on relations, habitually hostile, with environing societies, and the division which is devoted to procuring necessaries of life; and during the earlier stages of development these two divisions constitute the whole. Eventually there arises an intermediate division serving to transfer products and influences from part to part. And in all subsequent stages, evolution of the two earlier systems of structures depends on evolution of this additional system.

'While the society as a whole has the character of its sustaining system determined by the character of its environment, inorganic and organic, the respective parts of this system differentiate in adaptation to local circumstances; and, after primary industries have been thus localized and specialized, secondary industries dependent on them arise in conformity with the same principle. Further, as fast as societies become compounded and re-compounded, and the distributing system develops, the parts devoted to each kind of industry, originally scattered, aggregate in the most favourable localities; and the localized industrial structures, unlike the governmental structures, grow regardless of the original lines of division.

'Increase of size, resulting from the massing of groups, necessitates means of communication; both for achieving combined offensive and defensive actions, and for exchange of products. Faint tracks, then paths, rude roads, finished roads, successively arise; and as fast as intercourse is thus facilitated, there is a transition from direct barter to trading carried on by a separate class; out of which evolves a complex mercantile agency of wholesale and retail distributors. The movement of commodities effected by this agency, beginning as a slow flux to and re-flux from certain places at long intervals, passes into rhythmical, regular, rapid currents; and materials for sustentation distributed hither and thither, from being few and crude become numerous and elaborated. Growing efficiency of transfer with greater variety of transferred products, increases the mutual dependence of parts at the same time that it enables each part to fulfil its function better.

'Unlike the sustaining system, evolved by converse with the organic and inorganic environments, the regulating system is evolved by converse, offensive and defensive, with environing societies. In primitive headless groups temporary chieftainship results from temporary war; chronic hostilities generate permanent chieftainship; and gradually from the military control results the civil control. Habitual war, requiring prompt combination in the actions of parts, necessitates subordination. Societies in which there is little subordination disappear, and leave outstanding those in which subordination is great; and so there are produced, societies in which the habit fostered by war and surviving in peace, brings about permanent submission to a government. The centralized regulating system thus evolved, is in early stages the sole regulating system. But in large societies which have become predominantly industrial, there is added a de-centralized regulating system for the industrial structures; and this, at first subject in every way to the original system, acquires at length substantial independence. Finally there arises for the distributing structures also, an independent controlling agency.

'Societies fall firstly into the classes of simple, compound, doubly-compound, trebly-compound; and from the lowest the transition to the highest is through these stages. Otherwise, though less definitely, societies may be grouped as militant and industrial; of which the one type in its developed form is organized on the principle of compulsory co-operation, while the other in its developed form is organized on the principle of voluntary co-operation. The one is characterized not only by a despotic central power, but also by unlimited political control of personal conduct; while the other is characterized not only by a democratic or representative central power, but also by limitation of political control over personal conduct.

'Lastly we noted the corollary that change in the predominant social activities brings metamorphosis. If, where the militant type has not elaborated into so rigid a form as to prevent change, a considerable industrial system arises, there come mitigations of the coercive restraints characterizing the militant type, and weakening of its structures. Conversely, where an industrial system largely developed has established freer social forms, resumption of offensive and defensive activities causes reversion towards the militant type.'

It is worthwhile to notice, before leaving this, that Spencer did *not* predict that industrial societies would inevitably be *peaceful.*

It can be seen in the last paragraph above that Spencer saw quite clearly that even when industrialization was extensively developed, an involvement in military activities would bring about some degree of 'reversion' towards an authoritarian social structure. We shall return to this point later. However, just as Spencer's over-all summary of the *facts* of social evolution is admirably clear, so also is his summary statement of how these facts can be seen to be in accordance with the general principles of evolutionary transformation which he had outlined earlier. He wrote as follows:

'The many facts contemplated unite in proving that social evolution forms a part of evolution at large. Like evolving aggregates in general, societies show *integration,* both by simple increase of mass and by coalescence and re-coalescence of masses. The change from *homogeneity* to *heterogeneity* is multitudinously exemplified; up from the simple tribe, alike in all its parts, to the civilized nation, full of structural and functional unlikenesses. With progressing integration and heterogeneity goes increasing *coherence.* We see the wandering group dispersing, dividing, held together by no bonds; the tribe with parts made more coherent by subordination to a dominant man; the cluster of tribes united in a political plexus under a chief with sub-chiefs; and so on up to the civilized nation, consolidated enough to hold together for a thousand years or more. Simultaneously comes increasing *definiteness.* Social organization is at first vague; advance brings settled arrangements which grow slowly more precise; customs pass into laws which, while gaining fixity, also become more specific in their application to varieties of actions; and all institutions, at first confusedly intermingled, slowly separate, at the same time that each within itself marks off more distinctly its component structures. Thus in all respects is fulfilled the formula of evolution. There is progress towards greater size, coherence, multiformity, and definiteness.

'Besides these general truths, a number of special truths have been disclosed by our survey. Comparisons of societies in their ascending grades, have made manifest certain cardinal facts respecting their growths, structures, and functions–facts respecting the systems of structures, sustaining,. distributing, regulating, of which they are composed: respecting the relations of these structures to the surrounding conditions and the dominant forms of social activities entailed; and respecting the metamorphoses of types caused by changes in the activities. The inductions arrived at, thus constituting in rude outline an Empirical Sociology, show that in social phenomena there is a general order of co-existence and sequence; and that therefore social phenomena form the subject-matter of a science reducible, in some measure at least, to the deductive form.

Nothing could be clearer than these statements. What I would now like to do, however, is to take certain elements of the *explanations* of evolution which we clarified earlier, and show as clearly as possible how Spencer thought of these as possible *explanations* of *social* evolution. I do not want to claim too much for Spencer here, but it is of the utmost importance to see that his scheme of analysis resting upon the concept of 'Evolution' *did* contain definite elements and dimensions of *explanation,* and that these were not all nebulous and vague. I will take some of the more important of these in turn.

Explanations of Social Evolution

(a) Society is a co-ordinated system of institutions going beyond individuals, but always exists within a determinate physical context.

The first source of explanation of the changes which occur to a society is that of the variations in the physical resources from which the society draws its sustenance. A society comes to assume a form which goes beyond particular individuals, and exercises a vast system of control over the physical environment in which it exists. But this control is never complete, and changes in the nature of the social system can sometimes be accounted for in terms of the consequences of changes in this environment. Spencer wrote as follows:

'Whatever takes place in a society results either from the undirected physical energies around, from these energies as directed by men, or from the energies of the man themselves.

'While, as among primitive tribes, men's actions are mainly independent of one another, social with forces can scarcely be said to exist: they come into existence along with co-operation. The effects which can be achieved only by the joint actions of many, we may distinguish as social. At first these are obviously due to accumulated individual efforts, but as fast as societies become large and highly organized, they acquire such separateness from individual efforts as to give them a character of their own. The network of roads and railways and telegraph wires–agencies in the formation of which individual labours were so merged as to be practically lost–serve to carry on a social life that is no longer thought of as caused by the independent goings of citizens. The prices of stocks, the rates of discount, the reported demand for this or that commodity, and the currents of men and things setting to and from various localities, show us large movements and changes scarcely at all affected by the lives and deaths and deeds of persons. But these and multitudinous social activities displayed in the growth of towns, the streams of traffic in their streets, the daily issue and distribution of newspapers, the delivery of food at people's doors, etc., are unquestionably transformed individual energies, and have the same source as these energies–the food which the population consumes.

'The correlation of the social with the physical forces through the intermediation of the vital ones, is, however, best shown in the different amounts of activity displayed by the same society according as its members are supplied with different amounts of force from the external world. A very bad harvest is followed by a diminution of business. Factories are worked half-time; railway traffic fails; retailers find their sales lessened; and if the scarcity rises to famine, a thinning of the population still more diminishes the industrial vivacity. Conversely, an unusually abundant supply of food occurring under conditions not otherwise unfavourble, both excites the old producing and distributing agencies and sets up new ones. The surplus social energy finds vent in speculative enterprises. Labour is expended in opening new channels of communication. There is increased encouragement to those who furnish the luxuries of life and minister to the aesthetic faculties. There are more marriages, and a greater rate of increase in population. Thus the society grows larger, more complex, and more active. When the whole of the materials for subsistence are not drawn from the area inhabited, but are partly imported, the people are still supported by certain harvests elsewhere grown at the expense of certain physical forces, and the energies they expend originate from them.'

This is an element of explanation stemming from Spencer's general principle of the 'Equivalence of Forces.'

(b) Social growth and its directions

It would be too long a task to show in substantive detail how Spencer described the processes of the *growth* of society in such a way as to demonstrate that it was accompanied by the other characteristics of evolution: integration, differentiation and specialization, definiteness, coherence, and the like; but it is worthwhile to see in some detail how Spencer thought the *directions* of social growth could be *explained* by the principle that, following upon the 'equivalence of forces', changes 'took the direction in which they encountered least resistance'.

The *direction* of a society's growth, wrote Spencer, was that 'in which the aggregate of opposing forces is least':

'Its units have energies to be expended in self-maintenance and reproduction. These energies are met by various antagonistic energies–those of geologic origin, those of climate, of wild animals, of other human races with whom there is enmity or competition. And the tracts the society spreads over are those in which there is the smallest total of antagonism while they yield the best supply of food and other materials which further the genesis of energies. For these reasons it happens that fertile valleys where water and vegetal products abound, are early peopled. Sea-shores, too, supplying much easily-gathered food, are lines along which mankind have commonly spread. The general fact that, so farms we can judge from the traces left by them, large societies first appeared in those warm regions where the fruits of the earth are obtainable with comparatively little exertion, and where the cost of maintaining bodily heat is but slight, is a fact of like meaning. And to these instances may be added the allied one daily furnished by emigration, which we see going on towards countries presenting the fewest obstacles to the self-preservation of individuals, and therefore to national growth.

'Similarly with that resistance to the movements of a society which neighbouring societies offer. Each of the tribes or nations inhabiting any region, increases in numbers until it outgrows its means of subsistence. In each there is thus a force ever pressing outwards on to adjacent areas–a force antagonized by like forces in the tribes or nations occupying those areas. And the wars that result–the conquests of weaker tribes or nations, and the overrunning of their territories by the victors, are instances of social movements taking place in the directions of least resistance. Nor do the conquered peoples, when they escape extermination or enslavement, fail to show us movements which are similarly determined. For, migrating as they do to less fertile regions–taking refuge in deserts or among mountains–moving in directions where the resistances to social growth are comparatively great; they still do this only under an excess of pressure in all other directions: the physical obstacles to self-preservation they encounter, being really less than the obstacles offered by the enemies from whom they fly.

Internal social movements also may be thus interpreted. Localities naturally fitted for producing particular commodities–that is, localities in which such commodities are got at the least cost of energy...become localities devoted to the obtainment of these commodities. Where soil and climate render wheat a profitable crop... the growth of wheat becomes a dominant industry. Where wheat cannot be economically produces, oats, or rye, or maize, or potatoes, or rice, is the agricultural staple. Along sea-shores men support themselves with least effort by catching fish, and hence fishing becomes the occupation. And in places which are rich in coal or metallic ores, the population, finding that labour expended in raising these materials brings a larger return of food and clothing than when otherwise expended, becomes a population of miners.

'This last instance introduces us to the phenomena of exchange, which equally illustrate the general law. For the practice of barter begins, as soon as it facilitated the fulfilment of men's desires, by diminishing the exertion needed to reach the objects of those desires. When instead of growing his own corn, weaving his own cloth, sewing his own shoes, each man began to confine himself to farming, or weaving, or shoemaking; it was because each found it more laborious to make everything he wanted, than to make a great quantity of one thing and barter the surplus for other things...

'The process of transfer which commerce presupposes, supplies another series of examples. So long as the forces to be overcome in procuring any necessary of life in the district where it is consumed a less than the forces to be overcome in procuring it from an adjacent district, exchange does not take place. But when the adjacent district produces it with an economy that is not outbalanced by cost of transit...transfer commences.

'Movement in the direction of least resistance is also seen in the establishment of the channels along which intercourse takes place. At the outset, when goods are carried on the backs of men and horses, the paths chosen are those which combine shortness with levelness and freedom from obstacles–those which are achieved with the smallest exertion. And in the subsequent formation of each highway, the course taken is that which deviates horizontally from a straight line so far only as is needful to avoid vertical deviations entailing greater labour in draught. The smallest total of obstructive forces determines the route, even in seemingly exceptional cases; as where a detour is made to avoid the opposition of a landowner. All subsequent improvements, ending in macadamized roads, canals, and railways, which reduce the antagonism of friction and gravity to a minimum, exemplify the same truth. After there comes to be a choice of roads between one point and another, we still see that the road chosen is that along which the cost of transit is the least: cost being the measure of resistance.

'When there arises a marked localization of industries, the relative growths of the populations devoted to them may be interpreted on the same principle. The influx of people to each industrial centre is determined by the payment for labour–that is, by the quantity of commodities which a given amount of effort will obtain. To say that artisans flock to places where, in consequence of facilities for production, an extra proportion of produce can be given in the shape of wages, is to say that they flock to places where three are the smallest obstacles to the support of themselves and families; and so growth of the social organism takes place where the resistance is least.

'Nor is the law less clearly to be traced in those functional changes daily going on. The flow of capital into businesses yielding the largest returns, the buying in the cheapest market and selling in the dearest, the introduction of more economical modes of manufacture, the development of better agencies for distribution, exhibit movements taking place in directions where they are met by the smallest totals of opposing forces. For if we analyse each of these changes...we see that all these commercial phenomena imply complicated motions set up along lines of least resistance.'

The *explanation* of certain social changes and social developments may also be sought, in part, then, in the analysis of the forces and circumstance which the society, or the group within society, faces. This was part and parcel of Spencer's conviction that the transformations of a society will be explicable in terms of its process of 'adaptation' to its environmental circumstances, and we may note that this element of explanation is applicable *both* to societies as total entities *and* to *parts* of societies.

(c) The instability of the homogeneous

We might ask, however, what initiates this vast process of social growth, complexity, specialization in the first place? Why do not small simple groups of men stay as they are? Why do societies tend to grow into large, different systems of complex institutions, which, though containing more highly specialized parts are nonetheless more integrated and coherent in their articulation?

It is here that Spencer emphasized the 'instability of the homogeneous' as an explanatory principle. It is, he argued, well-nigh impossible for a large number of very similar units to *remain* very similar. For their reactions to each other *give rise to differences* among them, which tend to be perpetuated, and, in any case, some may be exposed to different sets of circumstances, which, again, may produce differences among them.

Spencer emphasized five different factors which must tend to initiate and develop differences among men who, in their simple groups, are originally relatively similar to each other.

First: men have to act in relation to each other in their various activities, and this must give rise to struggles between them. In this, some differences of 'supremacy and subordination' must come to be established.

'So long as men are constituted to act on one another, either by physical force or by force of character, the struggles for suremacy must finally be decided in favour of some class or some one; and the difference once commenced must tend to become ever more marked. Its unstable equilibrium being destroyed, the uniform must gravitate with increasing rapidity into the multiform. And so supremacy and subordination must establish themselves, as we see they do, throughout the whole structure of a society, from the great class-divisions pervading its entire body, down to village cliques, and even down to every posse of school-boys.'

Secondly, though men may be very similar, their modes of life, circumstances and experience are bound to encounter and therefore to engender differences.

'...an aggregation of men *absolutely* alike *in their endowments,* would eventually undergo a similar transformation. For in the absence of uniformity in the lives severally led by them–in their occupations, physical conditions, domestic relations, and trains of thought and feeling--there must arise differences among them; and these must eventually initiate social differentiations.'

Thirdly, even completely accidental circumstances are likely to bring about differences.

'Even inequalities of health caused by accidents will, by entailing inequalities of physical and mental power, disturb the exact balance of mutual influences among the units; and the balance once disturbed, will inevitably be lost.'

Fourthly, though men may be similar, they are likely to have different aptitudes and desires, and to develop different interests and abilities–which is likely to give rise to some differences of specialization. But these:

Fifthly, will be much emphasized when, as a people inhabit an ever more extensive area, quite different local and regional conditions and circumstances come to play upon them. Different occupations and different problems will be forced upon them.

'A community' Spencer wrote, 'which, by conquest, or otherwise, has overspread a large tract, and has become so far settled that its members live and die in their respective districts, keeps its several sections in different circumstances; and then they no longer remain alike in their occupations. Those who live dispersed continue to hunt or cultivate the earth; those who spread to the sea-shore fall into maritime occupations; while the inhabitants of some spot chosen, perhaps for its centrality, as one of periodic assemblage, become traders, and a town springs up. In the adaptations of these social units to their respective functions, we see a progress from uniformity to multiformity caused by unlike incidence of forces. Later in the process of social evolution these local adaptations are greatly multiplied. Differences in soil and climate, cause the rural inhabitants in different parts of the kingdom to have their occupations partially specialized, and to become known as chiefly producing cattle, or sheep, or wheat, or oats, or hops, or fruit. People living where coal-fields are discovered are transformed into colliers; Cornishmen take to mining because Cornwall is metalliferous; and iron-manufacture is the dominant industry where ironstone is plentiful. Liverpool has taken to importing cotton, because of its proximity to the district where cotton-goods are made; and for analogous reasons Hull has become the chief port at which foreign wools are brought in. Thus in general and in detail, industrial heterogeneities of the social organism primarily depend on local influences.'*

There are several factors in the 'instability of the homogeneous', then, which ar *explanations* of the beginnings of social change and differentiation.

(d) The multiplication of effects

All these initial tendencies to differentiation are then *reinforced* in various ways. Once differences exist they breed *more* differences of stimulus and response, and cumulative experience in relation to diversities of environments. Social differences feed upon themselves. so to speak, and tend to be ever more rapid and extensive in their developments. Again Spencer gave specific examples.

First of all, the specialization of skills and occupation, once it has emerged, tends to establish itself.

'Consider the growth of industrial organisation. When some individual of a tribe displays unusual aptitude for making weapons, which were before made by each man for himself, there arises a tendency towards the differentiation of that individual into a maker of weapons. His companions, warriors and hunters all of them, severally wishing to have the best weapons that can be made, are certain to offer strong inducements to this skilled individual to make weapons for them. He, on the other hand, having both an unusual faculty, and an unusual liking, for making weapons (capacity and desire being commonly associated), is predisposed to fulfil these commissions on the offer of adequate rewards: especially as his love of distinction is also gratified. This first specialization of functions, once commenced, tends ever to become more decided. On the side of the weapon-maker, continued practice gives increased skill. On the side of his clients, cessation of practice entails decreased skill. Thus this social movement tends to become more decided in the direction in which it was first set up; and the incipient heterogeneity is, on the average of cases, likely to become permanent for that generation, if no longer.'

Secondly, this relatively simple specialization implies a system of barter and exchange, so that a wider impetus is given to additional specializations.

This extension of specialization is accentuated, thirdly, by the increase of population, which again is a cumulative process.

'An *addition* to the number of citizens', Spencer wrote, 'involving a greater demand for every commodity, intensifies the functional activity of each specialized person or class; and this renders the specialization more definite where it exists, and establishes it where it is nascent. By increasing the pressure on the means of subsistence, a larger population again augments these results; since every individual is forced more and more to confine himself to that which he can do best, and by which he can gain most. And this industrial progress opens the way for further growth of population which reacts as before.'

The extraordinary ramifications which such specialization ultimately comes to have for the entire structure of a complicated society is very colourfully given by Spencer's illustration of the effects of the invention of the 'locomotive engine'.

'Let us confine ourselves to the latest embodiment of steam-power–the locomotive engine. This, as the proximate cause of our railway-system, has changed the face of the country, the course of trade, and the habits of the people. Consider, first, the complicated sets of changes that precede the making of every railway–the provisional arrangements, the meetings, the registration, the trial-section, the parliamentary survey, the lithographed plans, the books of reference, the local deposits and notices, the application to Parliament, the passing Standing-Orders Committee, the first, second, and third readings: each of which brief heads indicates a multiplicity of transactions, and a further development of sundry occupations, (as those of engineers, surveyors, lithographers, parliamentary agents, share-brokers), and the creation of sundry others (as those of traffic-takers, reference-makers). Consider, next, the yet more marked changes implied in railway construction–the cuttings, embankings, tunnellings, diversions of roads; the building of bridges, viaducts, and stations; the laying down of ballast, sleepers, and rails; the making of engines, tenders, carriages, and wagons: which processes, acting upon numerous trades, increase the importation of timber, the quarrying of stone, the manufacture of iron, the mining of coal, the burning of bricks; institute a variety of special manufacturers weekly advertised in the *Railway Times;* and call into being some new classes of workers–drivers, stokers, cleaners, plate-layers, signalmen. Then come the changes, more numerous and involved still, which railways in action produce on the community at large. The organization of every business is modified. Ease of communication makes it better to do directly what was before done by proxy; agencies are established where previously they would not have paid; goods are obtained from remote wholesale houses instead of near retail ones; and commodities are used which distance once rendered inaccessible. Rapidity and economy of carriage tend to specialize more then ever the industries of different districts–to confine each manufacture to the parts in which, from local advantages, it can be best carried on. Cheap distribution equalizes prices, and also, on the average, lowers prices: thus bringing divers articles within the reach to those before unable to buy them. At the same time the practice of travelling is immensely extended. People who before could not afford it, take annual trips to the sea, visit their distant relations, make tours, and so are benefited in body, feelings, and intellect. The prompter transmission of letters and of news produces further changes–makes the pulse of the nation faster. Yet more, there arises a wise dissemination of cheap literature through railway book-stalls, and of advertisements in railway carriages: both of them aiding ulterior progress. So that beyond imagination are the changes, thus briefly indicated, consequent on the invention of the locomotive engine.'

Here again, then, Spencer sought to provide *explanatory* principles in his elaboration of the 'Multiplication of Effects'.

(e) Segregation

Once these differences have been established, a certain 'selectivity' also takes place in the ways in which they will develop. A certain 'segregation' of specialist groups and classes and organized associations takes place, and here Spencer attempted to introduce certain factors which could explain the 'composition' of society, or the 'distribution' or 'localization' within it of particular groups. To some extent these elements of explanation were further aspects of his earlier discussion of the 'direction of social growth'.

Firstly, Spencer argued that geographical factors determined a certain 'segregation' of mankind in the world.

'Of the forces which effect and maintain the segregations of mankind, may first be named those external ones classed as physical conditions. The climate and food which are favourable to an indigenous people, are more or less detrimental to an alien people of different bodily constitution. In tropical regions the northern races cannot permanently exist: if not killed off in the first generation, they are so in the second, and, as in India, can maintain their footing only by the artificial process of continuous immigration and emigration. That is to say, the external forces acting equally on the inhabitants of a given locality, tend to expel all who are not of a certain type, and thus to keep up the integration of those who are of that type.'

Secondly, however, these kinds of groupings tended to give rise to 'segregations' *within* any particular society in which they might reside.

'The other forces conspiring to produce these national segregations, are those mental ones shown in the affinities of men for others like themselves. Units of one society who are obliged to reside in another, generally form colonies in the midst of that other–small societies of their own. Races which have been artificially severed, show tendencies to re-unite... The feelings characterizing a member of a given race, rare feelings which get complete satisfaction only among other members of that race–a satisfaction partly derived from sympathy with those having like feelings, but mainly derived from the adapted social conditions which grow up where such feelings prevail.

Thirdly, similar 'segregations' arose from specialist groups and classes within each society.

'During the development of each society we see analogous segregations caused in analogous ways... Those most important ones which constitute political and industrial organisations, result from the union of men in whom similarities have been produced by training. Men brought up to bodily labour are men who have had wrought in them a certain likeness–a likeness which, in respect of their powers of action, obscures and subordinates their natural difference. Those trained to brain-work have acquired a certain other community of character which makes them, as social units, more like one another than like those trained to manual occupations. And there arise class-segregations answering to these super induced likenesses. More definite segregations take place among the more definitely assimilated members of any class who are brought up to the same calling. Even where the necessities of their work forbid concentration in one locality, as among artisans happens with masons and bricklayers, and among traders happens with the retail distributors, and among professionals happens with the medical men, there are not wanting Operative Builders' Unions, and Grocers', and Medical Associations, implying a process of sifting out and grouping. And where, as among the manufacturing classes, the functions discharged do not require the dispersion of citizens who are artificially assimilated, there is an aggregation of them in special localities, and a consequent increase in the definiteness of industrial divisions.'

And fourthly, particular local conditions in a large society–the existence of resources suitable to the pursuit of a certain trade, for example–led to a 'localization' of industries and the 'clustering' of distinctive communities.

'If there be any locality which, either by its physical peculiarities or by peculiarities wrought on it during social evolution, is rendered a place where a certain kind of industrial action meets with less resistance than elsewhere, it follows from the law of direction of motion that those social units who have been moulded to this kind of industrial action, will be segregated by moving towards this place. If, for instance, the proximity of coal and iron mines to a navigable river, gives the Glasgow an advantage in the building of iron-ships--if the total labour required to produce a given vessel, and get its equivalent in food and clothing, is less there than elsewhere; there is caused a concentration of iron-shipbuilders at Glasgow, either by detention of the population born to iron-ship building or by immigration of those elsewhere engaged in it, or by both. The principle equally holds where the occupation is mercantile instead of manufacturing. Stock-brokers cluster where the amount of effort to be severally gone through by them in discharging their functions, and obtaining their profits, is less than elsewhere. A local exchange having once been established, becomes a place where the resistance to be overcome by each is smaller than in any other place; and, being like units under stress of common desires, pursuit of the course of least resistance by each involves their aggregation around this place.'

(f) Equilibration

Spencer also introduced the tracing of cause and effect relationships in the changing nature of societies in his 'equilibrium–disequilibrium' analysis. The structural-functional pattern of institutions which constituted a society would change in accordance with changes encountered in its total external environment, and with changes in its internal conditions. There would be a changing disposition of the parts of a society until some appropriate 'equilibrium' was reached. A few of the factors discussed by Spencer can be briefly mentioned.

First of all, he argued that the population of a society was continuously in process of adapting itself to its material subsistence.

'Each society,' he wrote, 'displays the process of equilibration in the continuous adjustment of its population to its means of subsistence. A tribe of men living on wild animals and fruits, is manifestly, like every tribe of inferior creatures, always oscillating from side to side of that average number which the locality can support. Though, by artificial production unceasingly improved, a superior race continually alters the limit which external conditions put to population; yet there is ever a checking of population at the temporary limit reached.'

Secondly, he discussed the many ways in which the many aspects of the economic, or industrial system, of a society are continuously adjusting themselves to the forces of 'supply and demand'. In this the 'equilibrium' analysis of economics is seen as part of a wider sociological explanation. This is clear enough, but Spencer had interesting things to say about the changing nature of such economic 'equilibrium situations' as a society developed towards the maximal use of its known resources. One example might be given.

'During early stages of social evolution, while the resources of the locality inhabited are unexplored and the arts of production undeveloped, there is never anything more than a temporary and partial balancing of such actions. But when a society approaches the maturity of that type on which it is organized, the various industrial activities settle down into a comparatively constant state. Moreover, advance in organisation, as well as advance in growth, is conducive to a better equilibrium of industrial functions. While the diffusion of mercantile information is slow and the means of transport deficient, the adjustment of supply to demand is very imperfect. Great over-production of a commodity is followed by great under-production, and there results a rhythm having extremes that depart widely from the mean state in which demand and supply are equilibrated. But when good roads are made and there is a rapid diffusion of printed or written intelligence, and still more when railways and telegraphs come into existence–when the periodical fairs of early days grow into weekly markets, and these into daily markets, there is gradually produced a better balance of production and consumption: the rapid oscillations of price within narrow limits on either side of a comparatively uniform mean, indicate a near approach to equilibrium.'

Thirdly, Spencer discussed political institutions in 'equilibrium-disequilibrium' terms in a very interesting way, and in a way remarkably reminiscent of Kant's principle of the 'Unsociable-Sociability of man'.

'On the one hand,' he wrote, 'there is in each man more or less of resistance against restraints imposed on his actions by other men–a resistance which, tending ever to widen each man's sphere of action, and reciprocally to limit the spheres of action of other men, constitutes a repulsive force mutually exercised by the members of a social aggregate. On the other hand, the general sympathy of man for man and the more special sympathy of each variety of man for others of the same variety, together with allied feelings which the social stage gratifies, act as an attractive force, tending ever to keep united those who have a common ancestry. And since the resistances to be overcome in satisfying the totality of their desires when living separately, are greater than the resistances to be overcome in satisfyingly the totality of their desires when living together, there is a residuary force that prevents separation. Like other opposing forces, those exerted by citizens on one another produce alternating movements which, at first extreme, undergo gradual diminution on the way to ultimate equilibrium.'

Again, Spencer had interesting things to say about the gradual development of institutions in dealing with such 'oppositions' in society, and his view was that a 'moving equilibrium' can be reached when political institutions reflect these oppositions so effectively as to make necessary adjustments ever more marginal.

'Each primitive nation,' he wrote. 'exhibits wide oscillations between an extreme in which the subjects are under rigid restraint, and an extreme in which the restraint fails to prevent rebellion and disintegration. In more advanced nations of like type, we always find violent actions and reactions of the same essential nature. "despotism tempered by assassination", characterizing a political state in which unbearable repression from time to time brings about a bursting of bonds. Among ourselves the conflicts between Conservatism (which stands for the restraints of society over the individual) and Reform (which stands for the liberty of the individual against society), fall within slowly approximating limits; so that this temporary predominance of either produces a less marked deviation from the medium state–a smaller disturbance of the moving equilibrium.'

The close approximation between many of the policies of the 'opposed' political parties in contemporary Britain is a good example of what Spencer had in mind.

Societies as total entities, then, and the parts of any society in their interrelationships, could be analysed in relation to environmental conditions, and changes in them could, in part, be *explained* by 'equilibrium–disequilibrium' adjustments.

(g) Dissolution

Sometimes, however, societies are overcome by conditions which destroy them. Sometimes, the power of the forces making for 'disequilibrium' is such that there is a failure to adapt to them. Then there follows an 'undoing' of the coherent, definite, integrated pattern of institutions which had existed, and a sequence of incoherence, indefiniteness, and disintegration follows in its place. Even this process of *dissolution,* however, Spencer argued, can be systematically analysed and *explained.*

'...social disorder,' he wrote, 'however caused, entails a decrease of integrated movements and an increase of disintegrated movements. As the disorder progresses the political actions previously combined become uncombined: there arise the antagonistic actions of riot or revolt. Simultaneously, the industrial and commercial processes that were co-ordinated throughout the body politic, are broken up; and only the local, or small, trading transactions continue. And each further disorganizing change diminishes the joint operations by which men satisfy their wants, and leaves them to satisfy their wants, as best they can by separate operations.'

Sometimes, this disorder may be brought about by direct conquest; but sometimes it is an outcome of being drawn suddenly under the influence of quite different environmental circumstances and pressures. Spencer gave the highly interesting example of Japanese society, and we might note that this written in 1867.

'Of the way in which such disintegrations are set up in a society that has evolved to the limit of its type, and reached a state of moving equilibrium, a good illustration is furnished by Japan. The finished fabric into which its people had organized themselves, maintained an almost constant state so long as it was preserved from fresh external forces. But as soon as it received an impact from European civilization, partly by armed aggression, partly by commercial impulse, partly by the influence of ideas, this fabric began to fall to pieces. There is now in progress a political dissolution. Probably a political reorganization will follow; but, be this as it may, the change thus far produced by an outer action is a change towards dissolution--a change from integrated motions to disintegrated motions.'

In general, however, a developed society can become so rigid as not to be able to accommodate itself with sufficient flexibility and speed to new competitive pressures from outside, and then, too, gradual decline and disintegration can occur.

'Decline of numbers is, in such case, brought about partly by emigration; for a society having the fixed structure in which evolution ends, is one that will not yield and modify under pressure of population: so long as its structure is plastic it is still evolving. Hence the surplus population is continually dispersed: the influences brought to bear on the citizens by other societies cause their detachment, and there is an increase of the uncombined motions of units instead of an increase of combined motions. Gradually as the society becomes still less capable of changing into the form required for successful competition with more plastic societies, the number of citizens who can live within its unyielding framework becomes positively smaller. Hence it dwindles both through continued emigration and through the diminished multiplication that follows innutrition.'

Even, then, when societies *fail* to come to terms with their environments and are either gradually or suddenly dissolved, grounds of *explanation* can be given within Spencer's conceptual scheme of the 'evolution' of 'systems' in the contexts of their environments.

It is totally beyond doubt, then, that Spencer's elaborate account of social evaluation was one of systematic *explanation* as well as one of detailed *description.* A few special points in connection with this deserve quite firm and distinctive emphasis, but these can be delayed for a moment in order to note the kind of thing Spencer had to say about *particular* social institutions within his *general* scheme of comparative study.

Specific Institutions: Examples

We have already seen quite clearly that, within his classificatory, schema, Spencer studied each major social institution (each 'part' of society) and each major 'system' of institutions ('regulating', 'sustaining', etc.,) in detail: examining the nature and functions of such in each 'type' of society (*both* in terms of social 'composition' *and* in terms of whether they approximated to the Militant or Industrial types) and clarifying the changes which characterized the 'transformations' from one type to another–especially the changes attendant upon industrialization. It is important to emphasize how *consistent* Spencer was in this. Every element of social structure was dealt with in turn according to his schema, and no study could have been carried out more systematically than his. This, again, needs emphasis because of much misleading criticism to the contrary.

What I think it important to do, however, is to give at least some indication of the kinds of comments his studies led him to make about just one or two particular institutions. This will give at least some impression of the quality of his observations and insights and the value of his analysis in providing a perspective within which the contemporary changes of institutions can be judged. Here, I select some of Spencer's comments on 'Domestic Institutions' and 'Ecclesiastical Institutions,' but equally telling comments could be selected from every institutional field.

(a) The Family and Marriage in society

Here are a few of Spencer's *predictions* about the changes in the nature of marriage and of the relations between parents and children in the family which are attendant, in his view, upon the processes of industrialization and the many social conditions–of scientific knowledge, urbanization, etc., which go with it.

(i) Firstly, he maintained that as the conditions of industrialization spread throughout the world, there would be a spread of 'monogamy'. Furthermore, the growth of disapproval of many earlier practices–of the abduction of women, the practice of marriage for money, or status, other arrangement of marriage by elders, and the like–could be expected, he said, to 'purify' the monogamous marriage by making it, in all *cases, real*–a *chosen* union between two parties of equal status, and resting upon personal affection–rather than, in many cases, nominal.

(ii) Secondly, he wrote:

'As monogamy is likely to be raised in character by a public sentiment requiring that the legal bond shall not be entered into unless it represents the natural bond, so perhaps it may be that maintenance of the legal bond will come to be held improper if the natural bond ceases. Already, increased facilities for divorce point to the probability that whereas, while permanent monogamy was being evolved, the union by law was regarded as the essential part of marriage, and the union by affection as non-essential, and whereas at present the union by law is thought the more important and the union by affection the less important, there will come a time when the union by affection will be held of primary moment, and the union by law as of secondary moment, whence reprobation of marital relations in which the union by affection has dissolved.'

When making this point, Spencer was by no means under any illusion that it would be understood, popular, or well-received.

'That this conclusion will be at present unacceptable,' he said, 'is likely, I may say certain.'

(iii) This view did not lead Spencer to think pessimistically about any decline in the stability of marriage or the family. He wrote:

'those higher sentiments accompanying union of the sexes, which do not exist among primitive men, and were less developed in earlier European times than now, may be expected to develop still more as decline of militancy and of industrialism foster altruism, for sympathy which is the root of altruism is a chief element in these sentiments. Moreover, with an increase of altruism must go a decrease of domestic dissension, whence, simultaneously, a strengthening of the moral bond and a weakening of the forces tending to destroy, it, so that the changes which may further facilitate divorce under certain conditions are changes which will make those conditions more and more rare.'

(iv) Spencer also said that a strengthening of the bond between husband and wife resting upon their joint interest in their children might be anticipated. This factor, he said, must become stronger as the solicitude for the care and education of children becomes greater and more prolonged, as we have seen that it does with progressing industrial civilization, and will doubtless continue to do. The implication, he maintained, was that 'welfare of offspring must hereafter determine the course of domestic evolution.'

(v) Concerning the status of women, he said that a

continual movement towards the equality of status between the sexes would take place. With the development of industrialism, with a decrease of compulsory co-operation and an increase of voluntary co-operation, with a strengthening sense of personal rights and an accompanying sympathetic regard for the personal rights of others, there must go, he thought, a diminution of the political and domestic disabilities of women until there would remain only those resting on differences of personal constitution.

'That in time to come,' he said, 'the political status of women may be raised to something like equality with that of men, seems a deduction naturally accompanying the preceding ones.'

(vi) Having considered the changing nature of parental authority, which was resting increasingly upon responsible concern, Spencer also concluded that relationships between parents and children would come into being which would need no external control to ensure their sensitive, reciprocal concern and their good working.

These predictions, made in 1879 require, I think, no detailed comment. The qualities of Spencer's analysis are borne out by their aptness. Every one is sound. Every one has occurred as he supposed. Indeed, the judgments underlying them are more acute and advanced than many people in our own day are capable of. The new Divorce Law Reform Bill (1968) and the new 'Family Law' proposals (1969) rest exactly upon the judgements Spencer made clear, and the arguments advanced by opponents of these reforms of the law rest upon assessments of social change which have still not caught up with the contributions of Spencer's analysis. At least *some* of the Great Victorians, a hundred years ago, possessed a social knowledge and a progressive judgement which was for more soundly based than those of many politicians, churchmen, and administrators in the nineteen-sixties.

(b) Religion in society

The same aptness can be demonstrated in what Spencer had to say about the nature, functions and development of religion in society.

In his study of 'Ecclesiastical Institutions', Spencer offered a far more detailed analysis of the effects of industrialization upon the nature, organization, and changing functions of religion than anyone before him, and, indeed, a more comprehensive analysis than that offered by Durkheim a good deal later, (and Durkheim is, according to some, the scholar of greatest originality in the sociological analysis of religion).

Spencer offered a theory of the 'origins' of religion in 'ancestorworship'; in the fear and love felt by the living for the dead, (and hence accounted for the 'compound' emotion of 'awe' which was at the heart of religion). But also, going for beyond this, he discussed the distinction between magic and religion, the tendencies to move from polytheism to monotheism with the growth of knowledge and, especially, the emergence and nature of 'ecclesiastical hierarchies' and the social functions which they–in conjunction with the doctrines and rituals they served–performed. In short, he studied the *organization* of religions, and traced their connection with political, military, judicial, and other organisation in society. His was, in fact, a truly *sociological* analysis of religion.

In all this, he analysed religion as a 'supplementary regulatory' system, reinforcing the political and judicial systems, and as a system of doctrines and rituals insisting on obedience to authority and reinforcing the 'social bond' in society. He clarified the ways in which 'ecclesiastical hierarchies' had been involved in military, political and judicial authority and its maintenance; how, in educative functions, they were important elements in instilling 'socializing disciplines'; how they were essentially conservative in their social influences: preserving 'verities', defending the 'cult' and 'institutionalized religion', sustaining reverence for existing authority, upholding the existing nature of 'property', and engendering appropriate sentiments by their modes of collective worship. His analysis was detailed and his comparative study was very wide in its range.

Again, however, we might best gain an impression of the quality of his treatment by considering what he had to say about religion in modern industrial society, and what the tendencies of development were.

Spencer thought that although Ecclesiastical Institutions held a less important place in industrial societies than in traditional societies of a simpler kind, they were not likely to disappear, but to change.

First of all, he thought that the tendency towards the separation of ecclesiastical institutions from the political institutions with which they had been initially fused would, in industrial society, become complete. There would be a very considerable extension os secularization. Spencer thought, as part of this tendency in Britain, for example, that there would be a growing pressure towards the disestablishment of the Church of England. Religion and priests would lose their earlier 'coercive' authority.

Secondly, he thought that with the growth of knowledge and critical reflection upon earlier dogmas, there would be an increase in the *number* of religious bodies, independent of the State, with respective differences of belief and practice. There would tend to be a growth of 'sects' in society; a multiplicity of points of view in religious belief and behaviour.

Thirdly he thought that within the government and organisation of the larger churches and religious bodies there would be a strong tendency for *central* power and authority to decline; and for the relative autonomy of local groups and individuals (priests or lay members) to increase. This would be a continuity of a marked trend towards the 'relinquishment' of central priestly (or ecclesiastical) power which was already considerably advanced among the 'Dissenters'.

However, Spencer did not think this 'de-centralization' *inevitable*. If there was a 'recrudescence of militancy'–which he thought might well be the case–then there could also be a simultaneous reversal of this tendency.

In all this, too, Spencer thought that there would be a marked shift of emphasis in the functions of the churches and priests in society.

In the past, the chief priestly duty was that of 'officiating' in modes of worship, and the insisting on rules of conduct was related to this. With the development of a scientific, industrial, secular society the first function, Spencer said, would become of much diminished importance, and the second–the detailed concern about morality in society–would greatly increase.

'The insistence on duty...' Spencer wrote, 'may be expected to assume a marked predominance and a wider range. The conduct of life, parts of which are already the subject-matters of sermons, may hereafter, probably be taken as subject-matter throughout its entire range. The ideas of right and wrong, now regarded as applying only to actions of certain kinds, will be regarded as having applications coextensive with actions of every kind. All matters concerning individual and social welfare will come to be dealt with; and a chief function of one who stands in the place of a minister, will be not so much that of emphasizing precepts already accepted, as that of developing men's judgments and sentiments in relation to those more difficult questions of conduct arising from the ever-increasing complexity of social life.'

The concern for morality in all directions of personal life and social welfare would therefore come to supersede the emphasis upon modes of ritual and worship, and the emphasis upon doctrines about the nature of God and theological 'truths' as such.

Spencer, then, had much of interest to say about the fate of the religious *doctrines* of the past, and the effects of scientific ways of thinking and knowing upon the nature of the 'religious consciousness'.

On the one hand he thought there was no doubt whatever that the specific religious theories or doctrines of the past were doomed. The growing sophistication of thought would increasingly show the 'anthropomorphic' nature of earlier doctrines. Higher moral sentiments would make it increasingly repugnant to continue to attribute to God motives which no decent human being ought to be guilty of. And, in general, these early doctrines would be revealed as the relatively crude pictures of reality which they really were.

Notions of original sin, atonement, hell and damnation, in Christianity, for example, would be rejected as men came to see the crudity and injustice of the old orthodox story.

'The visiting on Adam's descendants,' Spencer wrote, 'through hundreds of generations, of dreadful penalties for a small transgression which they did not commit; the damning of all men who do not avail themselves of an alleged mode of obtaining forgiveness, which most men have never heard of; and the effecting a reconciliation by sacrificing a son who was perfectly innocent, to satisfy the assumed necessity for a propitiatory victim; are modes of action which, ascribed to a human ruler, would call forth expressions of abhorrence; and the ascription of them to the Ultimate Cause of things, even now felt to be full of difficulties, must become impossible.

So, too, must die out the belief that a Power present in innumerable worlds throughout infinite space, and who during millions of years of the Earth's earlier existence needed no honouring by its inhabitants, should be seized with a craving for praise; and having created mankind, should be angry with them if they do not perpetually tell him how great he is. As fast as men escape from that glamour of early impressions which prevents them from thinking, they will refuse to imply a trait of character which is the reverse of worshipful.'

The new methods and knowledge of science would properly move men away from such doctrines to a responsible 'agnosticism', Spencer thought. At the same time this did not mean that men would cease to feel the 'religious consciousness'; would cease to be perplexed and moved by the enigma of the world; would cease to feel wonder at the very existence of things., On the contrary--and this is a very important point which Spencer rightly emphasized--the scientific picture of the world is such, really, as to *increase* man's sense of amazement. The man of science, far *more* than the untutored man, realizes the complex nature of the world; he realizes much more profoundly, too, the *limitations* of his knowledge. Science therefore *enlarges* rather than *reduces* the range of the 'religious consciousness'; it is only the dogmas about it that it can no longer accept. Indeed, it cannot accept these dogmas *because* of an enlarged consciousness of the nature of things. It is religious men, one might almost say, who most emphatically reject religions.

Even within religious bodies, and among priests, this element of sustaining the religious consciousness will therefore remain, despite absence of convincing dogma.

'...it does not follow,' said Spencer, 'that there will lapse all observances tending to keep alive a consciousness of the relation in which we stand to the Unknown Cause, and tending to give expression to the sentiment accompanying that consciousness. There will remain a need for qualifying that too prosaic and material form of life which tends to result from absorption in daily work, and there will ever be a sphere for those who are able to impress their hearers with a due sense of the Mystery in which the origin and meaning of the Universe are shrouded. It may be anticipated, too, that musical expression to the sentiment accompanying this sense will not only survive but undergo further development. Already protestant cathedral music, more impersonal than any other, serves not unfitly to express feelings suggested by the thought of a transitory life, alike of the individual and of the race–a life which is but an infinitestimal product of Power without any bounds we can find or imagine; and hereafter such music may still better express these feelings.'

Both the sense of wonder and the sense of moral duty which mankind possesses are therefore likely to be increased and to become more sophisticated in modern scientific society, but man's ability to be *certain* about matters of spiritual and metaphysical dogma will necessarily be much diminished, and honesty and integrity demand that this should be recognized. No harm is necessarily done by this. We can do nothing better than to devote ourselves, with careful scepticism, to a pursuit of the truth. 'The highest truth he sees,' said Spencer (about 'modern main') 'he will fearlessly utter, knowing that, let what may come of it, he is thus playing his right part in the world knowing that if he can effect the change he aims at–well; if not–well also; though not so well.'

But Spencer wanted to emphasize that, quite beyond religious organisations as such, the religious consciousness could be enlarged, not diminished, by science.

'Those who think,' he wrote, 'that science is dissipating religious beliefs and sentiments seem unaware that whatever of mystery is taken from the old interpretation, is added to the new. Or rather, we may say that transference from the one to the other is accompanied by increase; since, for an explanation which has a seeming feasibility, science substitutes an explanation which, carrying us back only a certain distance, there leaves us in presence of the avowedly inexplicable.

'Under one of its aspects, scientific progress is a gradual transfiguration of nature. Where ordinary perception saw perfect simplicity. It reveals great complexity; where there seemed absolute inertness, it discloses intense activity; and in what appears mere vacancy it finds a marvellous play of forces.'

'This awareness, he said, 'possesses:..an accompanying

feeling as much beyond that of the present cultured man as his feeling is beyond that of the savage. And this feeling is not likely to be decreased, but to be increased by that analysis of knowledge which, while forcing him to agnosticism, yet continually prompts time to imagine some solution of the Great Engima which he knows cannot be solved. Especially must this be so when he remembers that the very notions, origin, cause and purpose, are relative notions belonging to human thought, which are probably irrelevant; and when, though suspecting that explanation is a word without meaning when applied to this Ultimate Reality, he yet feels compelled to think that there must be an explanation.

'But one truth must grow ever clearer–the truth that there is an Inscrutable Existence everywhere manifested to which he can neither find nor conceive either beginning or end. Amid the mysteries which become the more mysterious the more they are thought about, there will remain the one absolute certainty, that he is ever in presence of an Infinite and Eternal Energy from which all things proceed.'

Again, everything that Spencer said about the changing nature of religion in industrial society can be seen to be most apt with regard to what has happened since his day, and, indeed, with regard to what is happening *now*. Modern theological writings such as those–to take one example–of the Bishop of Woolwich bear out all the tendencies of doctrine to which Spencer pointed. And the tensions within even the Roman Catholic Church over the matter of birth control is evidence of the increasing pressures against central power and authority and towards the discrimination of individual priests and lay members.

These two examples, at any rate–on the Family and Religion in society–substantiate the modernity of Spencer, and the continued utility and validity of much that he had to say about specific social institutions.

Points of special emphasis

There remain a number of points about Spencer's entire system of analysis which need special emphasis with regard to our central concern to clarify the making of sociology.

(a) Spencer and Comte: the similarity of concern

The over-all similarity between Comte and Spencer in terms of their conceptions of scientific knowledge and 'laws'; their conceptions of societies, the parts of which they consisted, the classificatory, comparative and historical methods by which they should be studied, and the like, are already so apparent as to need no further elaboration: excepting simply to note this strong continuity in the making of the subject.

One element of their treatment does, however, deserve special remark–and that is the same persuasion and concern which is apparent in there classification of 'types of society'. To be brief, Comte's 'Theological' and 'Positive' types are almost exactly the same as Spencer's 'Militant' and 'Industrial' types (it being remembered that, for Comte, the 'Metaphysical' type was a 'Transitional' and not a stable type between the Theological and the Positive). And this similarity not only refers to a substantive agreement about the historical transition of human society–which is very important, and which, as we shall see, is borne out in the work of many other scholars–but also to a shared concern: the concern, that is, for understanding the recent and present transition from traditional agrarian to modern industrial society in such a way as to make political action as wise and effective as is possible in dealing with its many complex problems.

The crucial concern of both men was that a transition of unprecedented scale and dimension had overtaken mankind, and that a new systematic *knowledge* of society was necessary in order to deal with it.

(b) Spencer and Comte: the Future

This central agreement can be reinforced further by a brief indication of a third 'type' of society which Spencer only mentioned, but then put aside because it was really only a possibility for the future.

It will be remembered that Comte envisaged a global unity of mankind, as all societies, of all levels of development, were drawn together by the connecting influences of industrialization. Also, that he elaborated a 'Council of Europe' which would assist undeveloped countries in coming to achieve and enjoy the new and shared level of material and moral civilization in the world. In a very similar way, Spencer, too, foresaw a global drawing together of societies–not, by any means, in any simple-minded, jejune way, as we shall see later–and the possibility of what he called in 'Ethical' type of society.

The spreading interconnections of industrialization, he thought, would lead to wider areas of social co-operation; going beyond nation states to federations of states, for example. And as basic economic and political problems were dealt with in an ever more satisfactory way, men would be able to concern themselves increasingly with cultural activities–with the more refined arts of living.

'Were this the fit place,' he wrote, 'some pages might be added respecting a possible future social type, differing as much from the industrial as this does from the militant, a type which having a sustaining system more fully developed than any we know at present, will use the products of industry neither for maintaining a militant organisation, nor exclusively for material aggrandizement, but will devote them to the carrying on of higher activities. As the contrast between the militant and the industrial types is indicated by inversion of the belief that individuals exist for the benefit of the state into the belief that the state exists for the benefit of individuals, so the contrast between the industrial type and the type likely to be evolved from it, is indicated by inversion of the belief that life is for work into the belief that work is for life.'

With characteristic realism, however, Spencer went on,

'But we are here concerned with inductions derived from societies that *have been* and *are* and cannot enter into speculations respecting societies that may be.'

This is all that Spencer had to say about the ethical type of society, but it is enough to see that his analysis of social evolution did not pretend to finality, and that it led him to a consideration of a kind of social life which, he thought, was possibly on the point of coming into being after the full development of industrialization, when a level of productivity of wealth had been achieved far greater than that possible in the society of his own time. And this was very similar both to the vision of Comte before him, and to the vision of Marx whose ideas we shall be considering shortly.

(c) The increase of Functional Coherence in society

A further agreement of substance and emphasis between Comte and Spencer is also worth noting, as it is one of the central points of all the major theories of society during the nineteenth century, and, as we shall see, is now receiving renewed emphasis in contemporary sociology. Spencer's system of analysis and explanation led him to full agreement with Comte that the more societies developed in their structural-functional complexity, and the more that all societies became drawn together in economic, political, and cultural involvement in common problems and concerns, the more *coherent* and *definite* they became, and–therefore–the more *predictable*. The more differentiated societies became in their global interdependency, the more they moved towards a similarity and predictability of institutionalization. Paradoxical though it may sound, then, both writers maintained that sociological analysis yielded *more precise* descriptions and explanations when studying more complex but more highly articulated social systems that it could when studying a multitude of simple but homogeneous groups.

Properly understood, this point if of great importance, because it is a telling argument against the criticism that sociology must grow more and more incapable of managing its subject-matter as societies become more complex. Both Comte and Spencer agreed in arguing that the reverse was the case.

In Spencer, of course, this point took the form of demonstrating the greater *functional coherence* of the interdependent parts of society as structural and functional differentiation took place, and as this proceeded between and among, as well as within, societies as wholes.

Concerning political interdependency, Spencer wrote:

'Of the European nations it may be remarked that in the tendency to form alliances, in the restraining influences exercised by governments over one another, in the system of settling international arrangements by congresses, as well as in the weakening of commercial barriers and the increasing facilities of communication, we see the beginnings of a European federation–a still larger integration than any now established.'

And this extension of political interconnection would grow, he thought, throughout the world. And of functional differentiation and 'segregation' among all societies of the world, he wrote:

'...beginning with a primitive tribe, almost if not quite homogeneous in the functions of its members, the progress has been, and still is, towards an economic aggregation of the whole human race; growing ever more heterogeneous in respect of the separate functions assumed by separate nations, the separate functions assumed by the local sections of each nation, the separate function assumed by the many kinds of producers in each place, and the separate functions assumed by the workers united in growing or making each commodity...'

In short, all societies in the world were moving towards as increasing degree of interdependence–taking the form of a vast network of functional differentiation embracing them all. And the more this developed, the more definite the sociological analysis and knowledge of them could be.

This is a point of considerable interest which tends, firstly, to be borne out, in the sense that modern sociologists now draw up many of their generalizations in terms of the correlates of industrialization: 'education in an industrial society,' 'the family in an industrial society', 'law in an industrial society', and so on. There is a wide agreement that the process of modern industrialization has certain predictable institutional concomitants, no matter what the nature of the traditional society in which it develops, and which it transforms. Indeed, many contemporary generalizations about social change are focused upon the transition brought about in 'Traditional' societies by the process of 'industrialization', and, more recently, 'modernization'. But secondly, it is an encouraging point, in the sense that it allows us to expect, not purely in terms of optimistic desire, but on reasonably firm intellectual grounds, that we may be able to establish a body of reliable knowledge about the regularities of our institutions and problems in the context of industrialization, and thus be able to deal adequately and effectively with them.

(d) Spencer's account of Evolution not unilinear or inevitable or of total uniformity

These first three points of emphasis have immediately, however, to be qualified by, and seen within the context of a fourth, which is, perhaps, the most important point of all.

Spencer has been massively and militantly criticized on certain supposed aspects of his theory of evolution. He has been criticized for advancing a *unilinear* theory of social evolution: that the line of evolution is always in the one direction from simplicity to complexity, from homogeneity to heterogeneity, and the like. He has been criticized for claiming that this *unilinear* direction of evolution was *inevitable,* and, on the grounds of this inevitability, for '*prophesying*' what, in future, it would be like, and for being inconsistent in–at one and the same time–predicting the *inevitable* course of change and proposing that statesmanship was able to do something responsibly to *qualify* it. He has been criticized for claiming that all societies, in this unilinear evolution, must inevitably pass through the same determinate *stages*, or '*types,*' and must move from the 'militant' to the 'industrial'. And, sometimes he has been thought guilty of claiming an ultimate *uniformity* of social institutions throughout the world as the ultimate pattern of differentiation and coherence comes to be achieved.

Now a detailed reading of Spencer will show that he was open to *none* of these criticisms; that his fundamental position was quite different from that suggested in them; and that his statements on all these matters were far more qualified and careful than they suggest.

It is true, as we have seen, that Spencer described a certain process of evolutionary change which characterized all the kinds of 'aggregates' known in nature–from planetary systems to societies; and it is also true that he maintained that the directions and the extent of this process (of increasing differentiation, definiteness, coherence, etc.) in any aggregate would accord with the extent of environmental influences, and would pass through a certain sequence in its adjustment to an 'equilibrium' situation within the context of these influences. He did not think, for example, that a simple social aggregate of clans within a tribe would be likely to become a highly industrialized society–manufacturing aeroplanes and locomotives–over-night. He thought a certain sequence of social, intellectual, economic, political development was necessary between the two kinds of 'social aggregation', and, in fact, that all developed societies in the world bore evidence of this.

But–Spencer's position did not at all entail all these other supposed errors with which he has been charged. Let us dispense with them in turn.

Firstly, Spencer distinctly did *not* couch these ideas in terms of a *prophecy* of a *unilinear* pattern of change which *all* societies would in fact undergo. He simply maintained that societies, like all other kinds of aggregates in nature, assumed a nature as they encountered and dealt with environmental problems. He clarified a system of analysing and explaining the nature of 'social systems' in this process of adaptation; and this gave a basis of *scientific prediction* (as *distinct* from prophecy). His analysis allowed him to make propositions of the kind: '*IF* the conditions and circumstances of a society (or a part of a society) are such and such...THEN, in accordance with such and such 'sociological law' (i.e., an explanatory hypothesis so far borne out by empirical generalizations) such and such is likely to be the case.' And all the procedures of inference and method and the truth or falsity of the actual predictions could be submitted to test. But Spencer did *not* maintain that *all* societies would undergo the entire sequence of evolutionary change his analysis provided.

On the contrary, he quite explicitly held that each society would change only according to some equilibrium position appropriate to its own environmental conditions. So that some societies might forever be simple aggregates of clans or tribes.

Right at the end of the *Principles of Sociology,* for example, Spencer wrote.

'The cosmic process brings about retrogression as well as progression, where the conditions favour it. Only amid an infinity of modifications, adjusted to an infinity of changes of circumstances, do there now and then occur some which constitute an advance: other changes meanwhile caused in other organisms, usually not constituting forward steps in organisation, and often constituting steps backwards. Evolution does not imply a latent tendency to improve, everywhere in operation. There is no uniform ascent from lower to higher, but only an occasional production of a form which, in virtue of greater fitness for more complex conditions, becomes capable of a longer life of a more varied kind. And while such higher type begins to dominate over lower types and to spread at their expense, the lower types survive in habitats or modes of life that are not usurped, or are thrust into inferior habitats or modes of life in which they retrogress.'

What holds for evolution in general, also holds, Spencer argued, for types of society.

'Social evolution throughout the future, like social evolution throughout the past, must, while producing step after step higher societies, leave outstanding many lower. Varieties of men adapted here to inclement regions, there to regions that are barren, and elsewhere to regions unfitted, by ruggedness of surface or insalubrity, for supporting large populations, will, in all probability, continue to form small communities of simple structures. Moreover, during future competitions among the higher races there will probably be left, in the less desirable regions, minor nations formed of men inferior to the highest: at the same time that the highest overspread all the great areas which are desirable in climate and fertility.'

It is also perfectly clear, of course, that in introducing his analysis of 'Dissolution'–the undoing of social systems which failed to come to terms with their environmental problems–Spencer quite consciously drew attention to the fact that societies could *decline* as well as develop; *cease* to be, as well as come into being. And between large-scale development manifesting *all* his characteristics of evolutionary change and the disaster of final dissolution and destruction–was a wide gamut of societies evolving to this or that degree, in accordance with this or that set of circumstances.

The idea of a definite, unilinear evolution of societies through which all must inevitably pass is therefore foreign to Spencer's system. And the idea of *prophesying* some *inevitable* course of social change is also foreign to him. He provided a schema for the description, analysis and explanation of social systems, and his supposed 'prophecies' were tentative 'predictions' of an 'IF...THEN...' nature.

A second point to insist upon is that although Spencer thought that each society would undergo a certain sequence of change in accordance with its circumstances (e.g., the 'primitive society' would not jump to becoming an 'industrialized society' overnight), he was not so foolish, of course, to suggest that *all* societies would go through *all* the *same* stages in their own pattern of development. He was well aware that a simpler society could be absorbed by conquest into a larger one; that a society with rude techniques could suddenly encounter a society with advanced technological skills and so be rapidly and radically changed by it; and also, indeed, that once a certain sequence of development had occurred, it could well be consciously introduced by men in other parts of society, as in other parts of the world, *in the reverse order!* To think that Spencer was guilty of such an inflexible view with regard to the sequence of stages for *all* societies is really to attribute to him a degree of idiocy that he was very far from possessing. Indeed, all such criciticms are almost beyond academic belief. Spencer's only insistence here, or course, was that the 'jumping' or various stages of differentiation on the part of such societies was possible only because they had encountered societies which had already experienced and assimilated these sequences of change themselves.

A third, and similar, and attendant point is that though Spencer thought that the spread of industrialization throughout the larger societies in the world would bring about an increasing 'functional coherence' and a growing similarity in *cardinal* aspects of institutionalization–he very explicitly did *not* maintain that all societies would become *uniform*. On the contrary, he argued that in this coming to terms with a common interdependency, each society would make *cardinal* adjustments–in political constitutions, in economic organization, etc.–but would obviously have to do this by altering its *existing* pattern of institutions, so that variety would still, nonetheless, remain. Here, I will give only one example–but a completely clear one–from what Spencer had to say about the adjustment of political constitutions to the conditions of industrialization Spencer wrote:

'It seems likely that hereafter, as heretofore, the details of constitutional forms in each society, will not be determined on a *prior* grounds, or will be but partially so determined. We may conclude that they will be determined in large measure by the antecedents of the society; and that between societies of the industrial type, there will be differences of political organisation consequent on genealogical differences. Recognizing the analogies furnished by individual organizations, which everywhere show us that structures evolved during the earlier stages, of a type for functions then requisite, usually do not disappear at later stages, but become remolded in adaptation to functions more or less different; we may suspect that the political institutions appropriate to the industrial type, will, in each society, continue to bear traces of the earlier political institutions evolved for other purposes; as we see that even now the new societies growing up in colonies, tend thus to preserve marks of earlier stages passed through by ancestral societies. Hence we may infer that societies which, in the future, have alike become completely industrial, will not present indentical political forms; but that to the various possible forms appropriate to the type, they will present approximations determined partly by their own structures in the past and partly by the structures of the societies from which they have been derived.'

Nothing, surely, could be clearer than that. It is worthwhile to notice, to make a fourth important point, that Spencer followed this passage by saying:

'Recognizing this probability, let us now ask by what changes our own political constitution may be brought into congruity with the requirements.'

And two points may be seen with complete clarity in this:– first, that Spencer analysed this tendency as a *probability* (not as an *inevitability* or as a *prophecy*), and secondly, that, following it, he was concerned to ask *what the members of society could do, and should do to amend their institutions in such a way as to make them 'congruous' with 'constraining requirements'*. There is nothing of the brash 'historicist' or 'determinist' here; and no inconsistency whatever in these attempts to foresee the probable exigencies attendant upon certain constraining tendencies in such a way as to be able to act wisely in relation to them.

Whenever Spencer attempted to 'foresee the future'–which he certainly did try to do–it was always tentatively in terms of the 'IF...THEN...' grounds of prediction of his system of analysis; always in terms of carefully qualified 'probabilities'; and always with reference to understanding society for the pressing purposes of wise political deliberation and action.

It is of the utmost importance, too, on this point, to realize that Spencer's emphasis in the sphere of statesmanship was always, and very powerfully, to *understand* BEFORE *acting,* and–very frequently–in terms of this understanding, *not to act at all.* Very unlike the other great sociologists of the nineteenth century, Spencer was on the side on an extreme liberalism. I do not want, here, to enter into any ethical consideration as to whether this position was right or wrong, good or bad, defensible or indefensible. It is only necessary here to see that Spencer most definitely and powerfully believed that men, by study, deliberation, and wise action, could affect the changes to which their societies and institutions were constrained by changing pressures and circumstances. As John Stuart Mill would have put it: there was no misconceived 'necessitarianism' in Spencer's conception of the 'cause and effect' analysis of things; of scientific knowledge and its application to the affairs of society.

As to the 'inevitability' of the 'industrial type' of society and its corollary of 'peacefulness'–on which Spencer has been so strongly denounced for being in error; a *reading* of Spencer will show that he not only maintained that conditions of increased militancy might lead to the growth of new totalitarian powers of a collectivist kind in highly industrial societies, but also actively feared that such totalitarian forms of authority and power were actually taking place in his time. Again, it was a matter of an 'IF...THEN...' prediction, and a detailed reading of Spencer will show how astonishingly correct his prediction was.

If ever there was a stark and true warning against the powers and dangers of modern bureaucracy, of modern totalitarianism and its ramifications throughout all the institutions of society, it was that delivered by Herbert Spencer, and I can only say that, for my part, his analysis and the insights it contains seem to have become more rather than less relevant as the political experience of the twentieth century has worn on. The various kinds of 'collectivism' proposed, were, Spencer thought, all modes of replacing the social system resting increasingly on 'contract' by an earlier kind of social system resting on 'status'. They were likely to produce complex systems of power in which: 'The individual withers and the State is more and more.'

'There seems no avoiding the conclusion,' he wrote, 'that these conspiring causes must presently bring about that lapse of self-ownership into ownership by the community, which is partially implied by collectivism and completely by communism...

'In what way the coming transformation will be effected is of course uncertain. A sudden substitution of the *regime* proposed for the *regime* which exists, as intended by bearers of the red flag, seems less likely than a progressive metamorphosis. To bring about the change it needs but gradually to extend State-regulation and restrain individual action. If the central administration and the multiplying local administrations go on adding function to function: if year after year more things are done by public agency, and fewer things left to be done by private agency; if the businesses of companies are one after another taken over by the State or the municipality, while the businesses of individuals are progressively trenched upon by official competitors; then, in no long time, the present voluntary industrial organisation will have its place entirely usurped by compulsory industrial organisation.'

'As shown in multitudinous ways throughout this work, a society organized for coercive action against other societies, must subject its members to coercion. In proportion as men's claims are trampled upon by it externally, will men's claims be trampled upon by it internally. History has familiarized the truth that tyrant and slave are men of the same kind differently placed.'

'Men thus constituted cannot maintain free institutions. They must live under some system of coercive government; and when old forms of it lose their strength must generate new forms...'

'Instead of restraints and dictations of the old kinds, new kinds of restraints and dictations are being gradually imposed. Instead of the rule of powerful political classes, men are elaborating for themselves a rule of official classes, which will become equally powerful or probably more powerful–classes eventually differing from those which socialist theories contemplate, as much as the rich and proud ecclesiastical hierarchy of the middle ages differed from the group of poor and humble missionaries out of which it grew.'

However, far from regarding this as inevitable, Spencer powerfully argued for ways of preventing it, and advocated a struggle on the basis of a modestly conceived optimism for the maintenance and extension of such freedoms as man had achieved within the context of industrial society.

'The function of Liberalism in the past,' he wrote, 'was that of putting a limit to the powers of kings. The function of true Liberalism in the future will be that of putting a limit to the powers of Parliaments.'

And, contemplating the large variety of societies drawn together in the modern world, and their functional diversities, he wrote also:

'While the entire assemblage of societies thus fulfils the law of evolution by increase of heterogeneity–while within each of them contrasts of structure, caused by differences of environments and entailed occupations, cause unlikenesses implying further heterogeneity; we may infer that the primary process of evolution–integration–which up to the present time has been displayed in the formation of larger and larger nations, will eventually reach a still higher stage and bring yet greater benefits. As, when small tribes were welded into great tribes, the head chief stopped inter-tribal warfare; as, when small feudal governments became subject to a king, feudal wars were prevented by him; so, in time to come, a federation of the highest nations, exercising supreme authority (already foreshadowed by occasional agreements among "the Powers"), may, by forbidding wars between any of its constituent nations, put an end to the re-barbarization which is continually undoing civilization.'

All his own efforts and desires were towards the formation of 'this peace-maintaining federation.'

These several criticisms of Spencer's position are therefore simply not true, and I can only hope that, during the course of this discussion, the true nature of Spencer's scientific analysis and explanation of social systems has been made completely clear. As we shall see, it is most important to have a correct appreciation of this when we come to consider and judge the so-called 'systems analysis' of our day.

A few remaining points of emphasis can very rapidly be made.

(e) Spencer did not use only Ethnographic data

It must be emphasized again, in defence of Spencer's classificatory and comparative studies, that it is simply not true that he used only, or even chiefly, ethnographic data. He did, in fact, draw on a very wide range of historical and contemporary material drawn from societies of all types. His studies were not in this way 'slanted' in any one direction, therefore, as has been suggested.

(f) The nature of Spencer's 'types' of society

It is necessary for future reference, simply to note that Spencer's 'Militant' and 'Industrial' *types* of society were constructed in terms of *(a)* the total 'structural-functional' pattern of institutions *(b)* the 'social psychological' aspects of the relationship between the institutional structure of society and the concomitant qualities of personality and character required in its individual members, and *(c) an understanding* of all this in terms of *a system of social action*–both at the collective and at the individual level. It will be seen that this 'typological' method is closely in accord with Comte's types–constructed in terms of institutional patterns of thinking, feeling, and acting; and with Mill's conceptions of the three levels of 'social structure', 'social psychology,' and 'individual psychology', and, in all this, the exercise of deliberate choice in individual and social action. But it will also be seen later, that it is also in accord with the construction of 'types' for the interpretation of social change through different levels of social complexity by all subsequent important scholars in sociology–Tonnies, Durkheim, Weber, and others up to the most recent theorists such as Becker, Parsons and others.

(g) Spencer's basis of 'Materialism'

A final point of emphasis is that Spencer's entire system of analysis rested upon a 'materialistic' basis. This is not all to say that Spencer was a 'materialist' in any metaphysical sense; indeed he explicitly was not. Neither is it to say that he 'reduced' his explanations of all levels of phenomena to 'materialistic' terms; again he explicitly did not. And in these and similar ways he was more properly qualified in his thinking than Marx–and others–who held a 'materialist' position. But it is *just because of this,* that this point needs emphasis, and again it is a point on which both Comte and Spencer were agreed.

Spencer insisted that all 'aggregates' in nature were indeed material aggregates (whatever other emergent qualities they possessed) and therefore had to be understood and explained in the context of their relationship with their material environment–consisting of other aggregates of many kinds. Furthermore, he insisted that all this was a *process*. No phenomenon could be understood or explained as an *object* in isolation; every phenomenon in our experience was itself a PROCESS *of transformation assuming a certain form in relation to internal accommodation to external* PROCESSES. What this really amounts to is that Spencer was as good a '*dialectical materialist*' as you are likely to find, BUT that his system did NOT suffer from any naive historicism or from any metaphysical dogma and reductionism.

At the end of this entire section on 'The Foundations of Sociology' I will try, by way of both substantiation and summary, to bring together some of the statements of Comte, Spencer and Marx on this subject, in such a way as to show how much error has crept into it by some curious insistence that Marx was the most important exponent of it. In fact, Marx was by far the *least* adequately qualified in his handling of the *material basis* or the *material aspects* of human society among all the three of them. But here this may be simply entered and emphasized as a point to be noted.

Some Criticisms

Many criticisms of Spencer's system of sociology have been raised and dealt with as we have clarified each point in his argument. In order to be as complete as possible in our present assessment of his contribution to the making of sociology, however, a few others must be mentioned.

(a) Criticisms of the concept of evolution

These need not be elaborated as they have been sufficiently dealt with. We might simply note, however, that we have demonstrated:

(i) That Spencer's 'law' of evolution was *not* only a descriptive generalization but also a system of *explanation,*

(ii) That it was *not* an application of the *biological* theory of evolution in the field of sociology, but something much more than this,

(iii) That Spencer was quite clear and consistent in his use of the analogy between an organism and a society; that he did not misunderstand it; and, indeed, that he dispensed with it when he thought fit: i.e., when he thought his meaning had been made sufficiently clear,

(iv) That it was not a *unilinear* theory of evolution,

(v) Nor *inevitable,*

(vi) Nor inconsistent with the advocating of positive political deliberation and action,

(vii) That it did not imply that all societies passed through identical determinate stages,

(viii) And that it did not specify any ultimate uniformity.

And these are really quite a lot of points to be getting on with. Other attendant criticisms, however, have also been made.

(b) Criticism of the range of relevance of the concept of Evolution Going beyond the concept of evolution itself and its utility in sociology, many critics have claimed that Spencer was at fault in thinking that it could be relevant to all phenomena– astronomical, physical, chemical, biological, psychological, sociological, and all else. Such a view, they claim, could not nowadays be advanced.

I do not wish to deal with this criticism exhaustively here, but will be content simply to raise a question about it. On what evidence, one wonders, do the critics make this claim? For in all fields of science the concept of evolution still seems quite central.

Consider cosmology. Professor Fred Hoyle writes as follows:

'Let me tell you a few words about what we mean by stellar evolution. A star does not stay the same all the time. It changes and the reason why it changes is because nuclear processes take place within its interior...

'Many starts have grown very much brighter than they originally were: they not only grow brighter but they change their size, their physical dimensions, and when we look in these clusters we can see stars at all stages of this evolutionary development. Notice particularly that we do not see them actually evolve, because to do that you would have to live for thousands of millions of years actually to see the evolution taking place. Perhaps I can give you a simple analogy here that may be helpful. Suppose you went into a factory and you saw a motor car being assembled, or rather you saw an assembly line in a motor car factory. You might see if you looked along the line, all the stages through which a car is assembled, and it would be quite clear to you from what you saw, just how a car is put together. This would be so even if you did not see a single operation actually take place, as long as you saw all the stages of development laid out one by one before you, and this is the situation for the astronomer in these clusters. He sees the evolution laid out before him at all its stages.

'This again is a development of very recent times, indeed of the last five years. It is only within five years that observational astronomers, particularly at the Mount Wilson and Palomar Observatories, have been able to measure and to determine these various evolutionary states with great precision. The observations do not in themselves reveal how fast the stars pass from one evolutionary stage to another. They simply tell us what these evolutionary stages are, but they do not tell us how fast the star passes through those stages. This last piece of information can, however, be supplied by calculation. Knowing the evolutionary stages and knowing how fast they pass along them it is possible whenever we see one of these groups, these clusters of stars, to give some sort of an estimate of how old that particular cluster is. So far, neither the observations nor the calculations have been or are anything like complete, but a very good beginning has been made.'

And, it seems, this picture of the 'evolution' of stars holds good whatever theory one may hold about the *origins* of the stars.

In the study of astronomical phenomena then–of stars and planetary systems–and of the physical and chemical processes involved, 'evolution' still seems a central concept. In biology it goes without saying that evolution is still quite fundamental, and it is increasingly relevant in the connected studies of the behaviour of organisms and comparative psychology. Thus the classification of 'behaviour patterns' characterizing particular species is now as definite a matter as the classification of anatomical and physiological details, and the explanation of all the genetic and environmental processes involved is still rooted in the fundamental concept of evolution.

Within sociology, too,'evolution' is far from being as redundant a concept as some very myopic critics appear to think.

Here, I will give only a curious example.

In relatively recent times, the supposed 'school' of Functionalism has been thought by some to dispense with the concept of evolution, and, indeed, not to concern itself with 'social change' at all. And one of the most eminent 'founders' of 'Functionalism' was Radeliffe-Brown. But what do we find Radcliffe Brown himself saying about 'social evolution'? We find him saying this:

'Evolution, as I understand the term, refers specifically to a process of emergence of new forms of structure. Organic evolution has two important features: (1) in the course of it a small number of kinds of organisms have given rise to a very much larger number of kinds: (2) more complex forms of organic structure have come into existence by development out of simpler forms. While I am unable to attach any definite meaning to such phrases as the evolution of culture or the evolution of language, I think that social evolution is a reality which the social anthropologist should recognize and study. Like organic evolution, it can be defined by two features. There has been a process by which, from a small number of forms of social structure, many different forms have arisen in the course of history; that is, there has been a process of diversification. Secondly, throughout this process more complex forms of social structures have developed out of or replaced, simpler forms.

'Just how structural systems are to be classified with reference to their greater or less complexity is a problem requiring investigation. But there is evidence of a fairly close correlation between complexity and another feature of structural systems, namely the extent of the field of social relations. In a structural system with a narrow total social field, an average or typical person is brought into direct and indirect social relations with only a small number of other persons. In systems of this type we may find that the linguistic community–the body of persons who speak one language–numbers from 250 to 500, while the political community is even smaller, and economic relations by the exchange of goods and services extend only over a very narrow range. Apart from the differentiation by sex and age, there is very little differentiation of social role between persons or classes. We can contrast with this the systems of social structure that we observe today in England or the United States. Thus the process of human history to which I think the term social evolution may be appropriately applied might be defined as the process by which wide-range systems of social structure have grown out of, or replace, narrow-range systems. Whether this view is acceptable or not, I suggest that the concept of social evolution is one which requires to be defined in terms of social structure.'

Such are the curiosities of fashion in academic thought! One's only possible conclusion is that critics do not *read*! There is no other explanation. Even so, it is very odd to find Radcliffe-Brown writing like this, because one would suppose, on reading him, that no work whatever had been done on the 'classification of structural systems' with reference to their 'greater or lesser complexity', whereas Spencer had produced several very clearly written volumes on the subject, as had Comte and Mill before him.

At any rate–I have said enough to question the assertions of the critics. Evolution *does* still seem a concept central to all processes of change, rather as Spencer conceived it to be. The critics, then, may well be wrong.

On final and very curious work which might be mentioned in considering the supposed redundancy of Spencer's ideas is *the Phenomenon of Man* by Teilhard de Chardin, (who was a French Roman Catholic thinker). In this book, which was given an excellent reception by the press only a few years ago, and has since been very influential and highly thought of, all the main-propositions of Spencer are somberly laid out and clothed with a fantastic kind of mystical philosophizing. Herbert Spencer, in short, has almost been taken to Church. Almost, but not quite–since Chardin himself was not accepted. But in this book there is scarcely anything about the theory of evolution which Spencer had not already laid down and, indeed, said much better. It is one of the curiosities of our time that some people are criticized for being outmoded, their ideas thought dead and buried, whilst at the self-same time, new thinkers are thought to be making a great contribution to scholarship by reiterating the self same ideas! Herbert Spencer's ideas are dead for many people. Yet, trailing clouds of obscurantist, theological glory, they are greeted with enthusiasm in the work of Chardin. The modern intellectual scene is very strange indeed.

(c) The illustration rather than the testing of hypotheses

A further criticism is that though Spencer's methods of classification and comparison, of hypotheses and deduction to explain empirical generalization, seemed, logically speaking, acceptable, and though they had the *appearance* of science, they were not *really* scientific at all. Spencer *began* (it is said) with his conviction as to the trends of social evolution. His 'Law of Evolution' was an 'a priori' generalization. He then gathered (or had gathered for him) an enormous amount of documentary evidence, and proceeded to *select* those elements of this evidence which *illustrated* and *supported* his presupposed laws. This criticism, though it requires a more careful statement than this, has a degree of weight.

There is nothing illegitimate, scientifically speaking, about having a hypotheses in mind before approaching the study of data. Indeed, it is now thought that any study, even the most simple observation or description of data, involves *some* selective hypothesis–implicit or explicit. In science, however, the crucial thing is that the hypotheses should be made both clear *and vulnerable* in the sense of exposing it to test under certain specifies conditions. And though Spencer does speak as though he is *testing* his hypotheses and deductions (against empirical generalizations) it must be conceded that he does not anywhere prescribe precise conditions under which his hypotheses could be subjected to crucial test. Within his work there is no clear way of checking whether or not he has *illustrated* his hypotheses by *selecting* from all the available data those examples which will support it. Spencer is, therefore, open to criticism on these grounds.

How serious a criticism this is, however, it is difficult to decide. My own judgement is that, firstly, though not providing a procedure of crucial experiment (remembering Mill's arguments, it is questionable whether this is possible), Spencer did nonetheless set up a clear schema of classification and comparison within which empirical generalizations could be gathered, arranged, explored, and explained; and within this framework itself, the adequacy of Spencer's own propositions can be checked. It is possible for the student to place specific societies within Spencer's classificatory scheme and to see whether or not the 'consensus' of its institutions accords with that which he proposed. Putting this in another way: given the difficulty of crucial experiment in sociology (perhaps, even, its impossibility) Spencer's methods of classification and comparative study must be critically assessed in terms of whether they are the most satisfactory *alternative methods of testing* generalizations and hypotheses that can be achieved. It is not enough simply to say that they do not constitute crucial experiment.

The second point, also, is that there is no doubt whatever that Spencer did survey the facts he could assemble with a critical eye. Indeed, he would have liked to have provided more data in relation to his many points than it seemed feasible to publish. And, in fact, he deleted much empirical detail from his chapters–some of which were first printed in the *Fortnightly Review*–when he came to publish them in *The Principle of Sociology*. This was to meet some criticism as to the 'readability' of his work. However, he did not cut material unduly. He wrote in a preface:

'That with a view to improved effect I have not suppressed a large number of illustrations, is due to the fact that scientific proof, rather than artistic merit, is the end to be here achieved. If sociological generalizations are to pass out of the stage of opinion into the stage of established truth, it can only be through extensive accumulations of instances: the inductions must be wide if the conclusions are to be accepted as valid. Especially while there continues the belief that social phenomena are not the subject-matter of a Science, it is requisite that the correlations among them should be shown to hold in multitudinous cases. Evidence furnished by various races in various parts of the world, must be given before there can be rebutted the allegation that the inferences drawn are not true, or are but partially true. Indeed, of social phenomena more than all other phenomena, it must, because of their complexity, hold that only by comparisons of many examples can fundamental relations be distinguished from superficial relations.'

There is no doubt that 'scientific proof' was the end that Spencer kept continuously before him.

(d) Evolution and Progress; ethical ambiguities

A final criticism of a Spencer is that he was unclear and, indeed, ambiguous in what he had to say about the *facts* of evolution and the grounds of his *ethical* judgements of them.

He spoke of the 'progress' of evolution; of 'higher' and 'lower' types of social evolution; sometimes in a purely technical sense but sometimes, also, in an ethical senser. And, clearly, to speak of the 'advance' of social evolution simply in the sense of moving through certain sequences of differentiation and complexity is a very different thing from judging the 'more developed' societies as being 'better' in a moral sense than the less developed.

There is nothing wrong or incorrect in exercising ethical judgements about the facts of social evolution *so long as the two processes of thought and judgement* (i.e., the scientific study of facts and the philosophical clarification of ethical principles) *are clearly distinguished and studied appropriately and sufficiently*. But *it is* incorrect to assume that ethical principles can simply be drawn from the facts; or to confuse propositions about facts with propositions about evaluative judgements.

It can be readily agreed that Spencer was ambiguous about these matters, and that he did not sufficiently clarify them. This problem was one left over for later scholars, and we shall see that to deal more successfully with it was an important part of the contribution of L. T. Hobhouse. And we might also notice that Spencer seemed to slip unwittingly into a mixture of fact and value in some of his work. For example, we have seen that he feared the 'recrudescence' of militancy among industrial societies which, he thought, would bring about a 'reversion' to a 'militant' type of society. Now we may well share his fears and his moral judgements here–for it is clear that his ethical principles rest firmly upon the maximization of individual liberty within the state–but, even so, in terms of the *facts* of social change, why should he not think that some degree of collectivization in the nature of industrial societies was one more evolutionary change as such societies adapted themselves to qualitatively new and different environmental conditions? And indeed–to be extreme–if totalitarian societies are better fitted to survive in the process of adaptation to these changed conditions, what is wrong with that *in terms of the scientific analysis of social change clone?*

I hope it is clear that I myself do not accept any reliance upon scientific analysis alone. My concern here is only to point out the difficulties in the problem, and the kind of ambiguity in which Spencer was involved.

This criticism of Spencer, then, is a correct one.

At the same time, it is worth our while to note that there is something in Spencer's view which deserves a good deal of thought. The differentiation of institutions in societies, he maintained, were not arbitrary. They were causally related to newly emergent social and environmental problems. They were an embodiment of the greater ability, on the part of man, to exercise effective control over nature and over the organisation of society. And within this context, the development of moral ideas may not have been arbitrary either. Men may have been constrained to consider, unravel, clarify, their moral issues as their societies and the nature of their social problems changed. In this sense, moral ideas and the direction of philosophical reflection concerning them, may have been intimately connected with these new problems. Morality and moral progress, like other aspects of human endeavour, may have been more closely connected with necessity than we commonly think. Necessity may have been the mother of ethical concern, acuteness, and heart-searching deliberation, just as it has been the mother of thought, discovery, and action in other spheres. In it *possible* then, that the actual historical growth of civilization has been accompanied, factually, by a more elaborate and progressive consideration of the moral problems attendant upon them, and by a progressive clarification of moral criteria. Certain directions of social change *may,* therefore, have been morally progressive. Though recognizing completely that ethical criteria cannot be simply drawn from a survey of facts, it is, nonetheless, not self-evident in any easy sense that Spencer is altogether wrong. There is a difficult problem here.

I think it is worthwhile to point out, too, that Spencer was more aware of the moral 'malaise' attendant upon the rapid transitions of society from a 'traditional' to a scientific, technological and industrialized condition than many other thinkers. He saw the 'anomie' which Durkheim later emphasized with great clarity and concern. He wrote, for example:

'The growth and spread of exact knowledge, changing as it is now doing men's ideas of the Universe and of the Power manifested through it, must increasingly modify the regulative action of ecclesiastical institutions. A necessary concomitant is the waning authority of the associated system of morals, now having an alleged supernatural sanction; and before there is accepted in its place a scientifically-based ethics, there may result a disastrous relaxation of restraints. Simultaneously with progression towards more enlightened conceptions, we see going on retrogression towards old religious beliefs, and a strengthening of the sacerdotal influences associated with them. The immediate issues of these conflicting processes appear incalculable. Meanwhile men's natures are subjected to various disciplines, and are undergoing various kinds of alterations. The baser instincts, which dominated during the long ages of savage warfare, are being invigorated by revived militancy; while the many beneficent activities distinguishing our age, imply a fostering of the higher sentiments. There is a moral struggle of which the average effect cannot be estimated.'

However, it still remains perfectly true that before we can reliably judge all questions of an evaluative kind, we have to possess criteria of moral judgement, ethical standards, which are themselves philosophically clarified and justifiable, and which are not simply 'taken' from a study of facts, and this Spencer did not sufficiently make clear.

These then are the more important criticisms of Spencer, and though some of them can be seen to have grounds which must be considered seriously, others rest on misconceptions or an insufficient knowledge of what he said. None of them is seriously damaging with regard to the over-all system of sociological analysis which Spencer contributed to the making of the subject.

Spencer's work, of course, has dimensions of interest which go far beyond his contributions to sociological theory. His essay on 'Education' is still a remarkably modern and valuable piece of work. His essays on political philosophy, though framed in terms of nineteenth century Liberalism, are still exciting and highly relevant to contemporary political life, no matter what the extent to which one agrees or disagrees with him. His comments on may slight and incidental issues in the social life of his own day, particularly in the latter half of the nineteenth century, also make fascinating reading now. However, our concern here must be centrally with his contribution to the making of sociology as a science, and his clarification of elements of theory and method.

In this, as we have seen, he made a very considerable contribution which added much to the work of Comte and Mill.

Within the changed perspectives of the knowledge of his time; the new perspectives brought about by the upsurge of science and its extended application to all aspects of human experience; he did indeed produce a new systematic approach to knowledge which provided a new picture of 'Man's place in Nature'. And, as with Comte and Mill, this system of knowledge was consciously seen as a necessary foundation for deliberation and action as society encountered the grave and complex problems attendant upon the rapid transformations of industrialization.

He carried the analysis of social systems, the comparative study of societies within a classificatory scheme, and the outline of a systematic approach to the explanation of them, to a greater level of clarity, precision, and detail than Comte, Mill, or any of the earlier philosophers of history and historians had achieved before him. Also, by his enormous collection of data on every kind of social institution in all kinds of human society, he brought together, in a systematic way, a far greater amount of information than had been gathered together hitherto within the context of sociological analysis, and, in so doing, emphasized the fundamental importance of *empiricism.* His contribution was very great indeed, and his influences, during the latter half of the nineteenth century, was equal to that of Comte.

I cannot withhold a final remark that Spencer was well aware, at the end of his life, of the criticisms, and in some cases, the misrepresentations of his ideas, and also of the wide reputation he had of being a 'theoretician', and that he regarded the all with a certain balanced humour and cynicism.

When writing of an afternoon visit to T. H. Huxley, for example, he said that Huxley had greeted him with the words.

'..."Come upstairs; I want to show you something which will delight you–a fact that goes slick through a great generalization!" His inonical expression (Spencer continued) was prompted by his consciousness that being so much given to generalizing I should be disconcerted."

And when explaining, in a prefect to *First Principles* (in 1880) that his theory of evolution was *not* derived from Darwin, and that it had, in fact, been stated in his writing *before* Darwin's publication of the *Origin of Species,* Spencer nonetheless resignedly wrote:

'I do not make this explanation in the belief that the prevailing misapprehension will thereby soon be rectified; for I am conscious that, once having become current, misapprehensions of this kind long persist–all disproofs notwithstanding. Nevertheless, I yield to the suggestion that unless I state the facts as they stand, I shall continue to countenance the wrong conviction now entertained, and cannot expect it to cease.'

Spencer had obviously learned a lot in a long life, but, come what may, correctness would be insisted upon and observed. Spencer was great, consistent, and indefatigable scholar, and his system of sociology, his contribution to the making of sociology, was one of the greatest to be produced during the nineteenth century, or indeed, at any time.

Summary

The great similarities and agreements between the ideas of Comte and Mill and those of Spencer are already quite plain. However, with our ultimate objective in mind of seeing the interrelationship between all their contributions with complete clarity, let us briefly summarize the main elements of Spencer's system.

(a) Scientific knowledge: a clear delimitation

(I)THE LIMITATIONS OF SCIENTIFIC KNOWLEDGE

Like Comte, Spencer insisted that science was productive of knowledge exactly because of its very careful and precise delimitation. Reality no doubt had many dimensions going beyond our awareness, but we could achieve and intellectually justified position of clear agnosticism. Scientific knowledge was the establishing of testable 'laws' about the interconnections of *the facts of our experience.* It explicitly *confined* itself to stating regularities of *phenomena;* propositions about the interrelations among elements of the world *as we experienced them.* This was knowledge; *this* could be clear; whatever the riddles of reality which might lie beyond.

(II) SCIENTIFIC LAWS

Scientific 'laws' were such statements of interconnection: 'uniformities of co-existence and succession'; and there again, Spencer was in agreement with Hume, Kant, Comte and Mill.

Explanation was a matter of stating hypotheses and deductions which provided a satisfactory (testable) account of empirical generalizations.

(III) SCIENCE ROOTED IN COMMON SENSE, AND PHILOSOPHY ROOTED IN SCIENCE

Science sprang, by critical reflection, from the insufficiencies of common sense–which was *un-unified* knowledge. The many special sciences were systems of *partially-unified* knowledge. But all these could be brought together in an entirety of *completely-unified* knowledge–and, for Spencer, this latter was the task of philosophy. For Spencer, as for Comte, then, all the sciences could be brought together to provide a unity of knowledge.

(IV) SCIENCE A BASIS FOR FORESIGNT AND ACTION

As with Comte and Mill too, Spencer maintained that scientific knowledge alone provided a reliable basis for prediction, and therefore for sound judgement and effective action in relation to both nature and society.

(b) Evolution: a central guiding concept

(I) EVOLUTION: A UNIFYING CONCEPTION

The unity of science, the relatedness of its findings in *all* fields, and the clarification of its appropriate methods in *each* field, could be centrally illuminated, Spencer held, by the concept of 'evolution'. Evolution was a universal process. Nature consisted of a multiplicity of finite living forms in a continuous process of transformation. All these forms manifested definite regularities and definite relationships with the elements of their environments in the context of which they came into existence, grew, developed, and went out of existence. Change in all these forms was a re-ordering of elements in a necessary adjustment to seek equilibrium in the context of constraining forces. The course of evolutionary change manifested a certain pattern: from indefiniteness of definiteness; from simplicity and sameness, through a differentiation of parts and functions, to complexity and difference; but also from incoherence and simple connectedness of parts, to a complex coherence of organisation (or articulation) of parts. All forms in nature permitted of clear scientific analysis in these terms.

(II) EVOLUTION: GROUNDS FOR EXPLANATION

The concept of evolution was not only a unifying *description:* an empirical generalization; it also provided clear grounds for systematic *explanation.* Such grounds were: the instability of the homogeneous; the multiplicity of effects–once differentiation had begun; factors making for specialization and segregation of parts; adjustments to achieve equilibrium; factors making for destruction and dissolution. A 'schema' of *both* analysis *and* explanation was therefore provided by the concept of 'evolution'.

(III) EVOLUTION: APPLICABLE TO 'SOCIETIES'

Evolution could also prove a unifying concept in the making of *Sociology*–for *societies* were forms in nature, organisational systems, which were shaped, and which grew and developed, in the process of coming to terms with constraining and challenging environmental factors. Societies, therefore could be systematically studied in accordance with the same 'schema' of analysis and explanation. A science of society was possible, and its nature and methods could be made perfectly clear.

(c) Sociology: statical analysis: the nature of a society

(I) SOCIETY: AN ENTITY: AN ORGANIZATIONAL SYSTEM

Societies, Spencer held, were definite organizational entities, institutional systems which had specifiable and determinate, attributes just as clearly as had any other forms in nature. They were 'superorganic' systems. They did not exist independently of individuals: they did not obliterate individuals; they did not compound individuals into some new metaphysical 'collective entity'; but they were *systems of institutions* which were something *more* than, and *other* than individuals, possessing clearly discernible attributes. Sociology was, therefore, *the scientific study of such social systems.*

(II) STRUCTURAL–FUNCTIONAL ANALYSIS

Societies, like all other forms, could be analysed into their component parts and the functions they fulfilled in relation to the whole. Institutions possessed discernible *structures* of organization, and they fulfilled discernible *functions:* both in dealing with a specific social task, a specific set of social problems and in operating interdependently with other institutions in the entire society. The structures and functions of institutions should therefore be explored in relation to their place in the 'totality' of the social system.

(III) A 'CONSENSUS' OF INSTITUTIONS

This structural-functional interdependence of the institutions of a society meant a certain 'consensus', a determinate inter-connectedness of all the parts of the society as a whole, which could be uncovered by study. The 'consensus' of institutions, the kind of inter-connectedness among them, would be different in societies of different types. These similarities and differences could also be uncovered and made clear by careful study.

(IV) THE NATURE OF A SOCIAL SYSTEM TO BE ANALYSED AND EXPLAINED IN TERMS OF ITS HISTORY AND ITS ACCOMMODATION TO ENVIRONMENTAL PROBLEMS

Like all other forms, societies too were essentially *processes,* continuously involved in the transformations of elements, energies and resources, and continuously constrained by environmental conditions. The patterns of change, growth, and development–or change, diminution and dissolution; the differentiations of structures and functions which characterized them could be analysed and explained in terms of their historical accommodation to the conditions and challenges they had experienced. *Structural-Functional analysis* would therefore, simultaneously, be an analysis of *social and historical change.*

(V) SIGNIFICANT GROUPINGS OF INSTITUTIONS

In addition to the analysis of structure, functions, and their patterns of change as outlined so far, Spencer also maintained that institutions could be significantly *grouped* with regard to the *predominant* social functions which they *shared*. Regulative, Sustaining and Distributive groups of institutions could be distinguished, and the kind of *consensus* existing in a society at a particular period of its history could be illuminated and explained by the relative dominance of one or other of these groups. Sometimes the Sustaining (Economic) institutions might be predominant; sometimes the Regulative (Political and

Military). This grouping of institutions therefore provided a basis for the analytical construction of 'types' of society.

(d) Sociology: Dynamics: the empirical study of societies

This statical (in Comte's terms) analysis of the nature and components of social systems could then be consistently applied in the empirical study of the actual variety of societies in the world in order to achieve substantive, testable knowledge, and specific testable theories, about them.

(I) OBSERVATION, CLASSIFICATION, COMPARISON, AND HISTORICAL STUDIES TO ESTABLISH DESCRIPTIVE KNOWLEDGE

The methods of *observation;* of the *classification* of *types* of society (on the observable basis of the degree of social aggregation, or on the basis of the theoretical construction of 'models'); of careful *comparison;* and *of historical* study were all proposed, and held to be necessary by Spencer–as they had been by Comte and Mill–in the undertaking of satisfactory empirical studies. It is unnecessary to elaborate again each one of these methods–though each one is of vital importance.

Spencer insisted that all these methods were necessary even to establish–in a systematic, satisfactory, and manageable form–a body of *descriptive* knowledge about societies. But this was not the *end* of empirical studies. The aim of science, and of sociology, was to establish *explanatory theories.*

(II) GROUNDS OF EXPLANATION

The analysis of social systems derived from the concept of 'evolution' could also be applied in seeking the *explanation* of the *descriptive generalizations* about specific societies, their similarities, their differences, their institutions, the 'consensus' of institutions appropriate to particular types, the sequences of structural-functional differentiation discovered in them, and, in short, all the known or supposed 'uniformities of co-existence and succession' which descriptive studies had provided.

These grounds of explanation were, again, the consideration of societies always in relation to the constraining conditions of their environments; the unstable condition of the homogeneous'–exposed, in different settings, to different conditions and influences; the multiplicity of effects once differential change had begun; the factors making for specialization and segregation of parts in the development of differentiation; the struggle of adaptation in relation to 'equilibrium-disequilibrium' stresses; and the factors making for disintegration and dissolution if the environmental conditions could not be met.

Spencer's system therefore specified a schema for the stating of specific *explanatory theories* about the many aspects of the nature of social order and social change; it was by no means the simple 'blanket-like' dogma of uniliner and uniform evolution as has been commonly supposed.

Sociology, then, in Spencer's conception, was a completely clear science of society, of social systems, which provided a meticulously clear analysis of the nature of its subject-matter, and an equally clear set of methods and directive whereby, within the context of this over-all analysis, specific empirical studies and theoretical explanations could be pursued.

Other things could be said by way of summary: Spencer's agreement with Comte and Mill on many other important points–the prospect of a future in which men could eliminate gross economic problems and devote themselves more freely to improved ethical and cultural qualities of living; the persuasion that the increasing functional coherence of human societies on a global scale would make sociological generalizations and understanding *more* rather than *less* possible; the conviction that sociology could provide men with a basis for sounder judgement and more responsible and effective action; and the like. But here, it is best to concentrate only upon the major conceptions which Spencer put forward for the making of sociology, and in which his agreement with Comte and Mill was so clearly apparent.

We turn now to a man whose theory has often–and very militantly–been thought to offer a theory of society and social change vastly *different* from those we have considered so far: a quite distinctive theory of *revolutionary,* not *evolutionary,* change; of *conflict* and violent antagonism in the relationships of society, not of consensus and order. But we shall see that, like most other simple juxta-positions and exaggerations, these, too, are no more than a kind of hectically coloured vapour.

5

Karl Marx: Economy, Class, and Social Revolution

I have chosen to follow our discussion of Comte, Mill, and Spencer with a study of the work of Marx for a number of quite definite reasons. Marx was, of course, one other of the great Victorian thinkers who was dedicated the making of an adequate science of society for the purpose of changing and improving the society he saw about him. For many reasons, however, he has come to be thought a *heretic* among intellectuals: a heretic among economists, a heretic among philosophers, a heretic in politics...in short, just about the most conspicuous and disastrous 'enfant terrible' of the nineteenth century; and one who has sown more trouble than any other single figure for the twentieth. In terms of the political upheavals which followed in his train, there are, no doubt, understandable grounds for this reputation, but in what follows I hope to show that, when the polemical cloud that hangs about him is cleared, and even when quite basis disagreements with him are clearly stated, his conception of the science of man and society was, in very large part, the same as that of others who were engaged in the making of sociology, if not presented with anywhere near the same clarity.

Our concern here, of course, is not to accomplish a definitive assessment of the work of Marx, or of 'Marxism', in all its aspects but essentially *only to clarify Marx's contribution to the making of a science of society;* and this must be strongly borne in mind. Even so, a proper estimation of Marx (that is, an assessment in which one can be thoroughly satisfied that one has done him justice) is very difficult to achieve, and I would like to explore these difficulties a little in stating, in an introductory way, why I have chosen to attempt a study of him here.

Like all the other men we have considered. Marx was far from being only a 'scholar', and was certainly most not a 'professional scholar. His intellectual efforts sprang from a deeply and genuinely felt humanity, and his entire work was the outcome of a complete and unswerving moral commitment to all those qualities that add up to the freedom and dignity of the human person. His social science was undertaken for humanitarian purposes, and many things are connected with this emphasis. The first thing, however, that must be said is that Marx was thoroughly likeable and admirable as a man in this fundamental respect. He was devoted to his intellectual and political causes, but all these were rooted in a sensitive concern for people at the *personal* level. We have seen that Comte, Mill, and Spencer also had this fundamental concern for humanity and for those standards of material well-being, social and cultural enrichment, and political liberty which would do most to ensure individual fulfilment, but it is worth remarking that in certain ways Marx had a more immediate and personal humanity than them all. This is not to derogate *them,* by any means, but only to say that Marx's humanitaria-nism had essentially *personal* qualities which were different, and which must not be forgotten. Whatever one may come to think about his ideas, or about the uses to which they have been put, this fundamental fact of his sensitive and staunch humanity must be appreciated and cannot be denied. Whatever one's intellectual disagreements with him, this firm moral stand for certain qualities of humanity and human dignity, and his insistent efforts to achieve them in the day-today relations of society, must be admired.

Later we shall emphasize the particular quality which this humanity lent to this interpretation of 'materialism' and other elements of his system which it is all too easy to caricature, and thus improperly estimate. For now, however, it is enough to note that, though always involved in intellectual work and political agitation on a broad cosmopolitan scale, he was always, also, a man of warm personal relationships–as husband and father in his family, and as friend and colleague with all those among whom he worked.

'I make bold to say,' said Engels at his graveside, 'that though he may have many opponents he has hardly one personal enemy.'

Also–when attacking, with a passionate disgust and anger, the harshness of the treatment and conditions of wage-earning people in the context of industrial capitalism, it was always the very concrete examples of savagely over-worked children, women, and men to which he referred; it was always the humiliations, the indignities to which individuals were subjected, as well as the gross physical poverty, toil, illness, and ugliness which they suffered, against which he protested. And when he advocated freedom, he thought firstly, and always very practically, of such measures as the shortening of the working day. Contrary to many present-day conceptions of him, Marx was in fact opposed to a vulgar notion of 'Communism' in which public ownership might simply bring a certain equality in '*having*' things, and, instead, desired the creation of '*human*' society in which the qualities of creative social life among *persons* could, at fast, be achieved.

Let me stress again, to prevent any misunderstanding, that this insistence upon the quality of Marx's humanitarianism is far from being a kind of litany of his virtues for its own sake. Besides this–important in itself–this quality has a quite basic relevance for correct appreciation of many of his ideas.

A second important point on which his persuasions were in considerable agreement with the other thinkers we have discussed was that his concern was centrally upon the problems of *industrial* society. Like them, he was convinced not only that the vast social transformations brought about by science, technology and manufacturing industry constituted a radical movement from traditional agrarian society to something qualitatively new in human history, but also that–when its turmoils were over–it would provide the basis for a new and improved condition of human life such as had not been experienced before.

Like other thinkers too, he believed that the efforts to understand the social processes which were afoot, and the political efforts to create such a society, required a rigorous *scientific* study of man and society.

His central desire to *change* society rather than simply to *understand* it, led to what is one of the greatest complicating factors for the study of Marx–namely, that he was a journalist and committed political agitator; very much an activist in his writing and organizing; and *not* only concerned to work out a satisfactory intellectual system. Indeed, he failed to complete a systematic account of his ideas. Of all the thinkers we have mentioned so far, Marx is the *least* satisfactory in this respect. Furthermore, the scope and quality of his writing is very variable: depending on whether he was really working out his reflections or whether he was writing a manifesto for the guidance of political action. Some of his writing in the *Economic and Philosophical Manuscripts of 1844* is the outcome of genuine, exploratory, profound study and thought, and is most compelling–again, despite disagreements–and there is brilliance in his essays of a historical nature–as, for example, in *The Eighteenth Brumaire of Louis Bonaparte,* whereas the *Communist Manifesto* and similar writing contains the most insufficiently worked out notions, the most sweeping and unqualified statements; whilst sections of *Das Capital* contain the most fantastically *over*-worked notions which do not carry any conviction whatever. But a greater complication is attendant upon this.

Because Marx did not complete much of his work, and because many of his ideas were not developed beyond a certain point; because, too, he was involved with colleagues in his political activities; the fact is that many of his ideas came to be argued through, and even prepared for publication, by others. During, and immediately after, his won lifetime, it was Engels who most contributed to this 'supplementary' argumentation and explanation. Since then, however, the process has been never-ending. Lenin undertook extensive works of 'interpretation' of Marx's ideas, and of the application of them in a new situation of 'socialist' power. And this was followed to a lesser, but still important extent, by the writings of Stalin and others. It therefore becomes very difficult to disentangle Marx's notion of (let us say) 'materialism' and its application to the study of history, from the interconnected ideas of Engels, and, later, of Lenin and Stalin. And this, again, is not necessarily to *derogate* the writing of these other authors. Stalin, for example, was a much better and clearer thinker and writer than is commonly thought, and showed himself very painstaking and systematic in endeavouring to present the ideas of Marx and Engels in a compact and coherent form. It is simply that it is difficult always to know whether one is interpreting Marx (himself) aright, or whether one is attributing to *him* an emphasis which was introduced or pressed by others. However, one can only do one's best to be accurate in this, and the problem is, after all, not of such grave consequence for us, since our concern is chiefly to become clear as to how Marx went about the making of a science of society, not to chase all the ambiguities of his political propositions.

Despite this, however, this is a point on which *much* care must be exercised. Engles, for example, in both good ways and bad, was (it seems to me) much more of variable and 'opportunist' polemicist than Marx, and one can never be quite sure whether he qualified Marx too far, or, sometimes, interpreted him too narrowly, Though both writers vouched for a good deal of agreement between themselves, Marx's writing on the nature of 'materialism', for example, was distinctively different from that of Engels: being couched in much less orthodox philosophical language, and much less philosophically 'pedantic'. It seems to me to claim much *less,* philosophically, than did the argument of Engels. Yet both treatments, both sets of arguments, form part of the theory of 'dialectical materiaslim' and 'historical materialism' which is central for the Marxian explanation of the nature of society and social change. So there are real problems here. Engels, too, tended on some occasions to use the techniques and standards of a platform-orator in his writing, which sometimes gave a decided bias and flavour to his judgments without advancing substantive *arguments.* For example, he praised Feurebach (as did Marx) for being the first great writer since Hegel to demolish 'idealism' and to achieve a convincing statement of 'materialism' but–in then criticizing what he thought were limitations of Feuerbach–he went on to speak of the '*rank* materialism' of Feuerbach as against that of Marx; and elements of derisiveness creep into his attack. The clarification of the serious elements in the writing of Marx and Engels has therefore to grapple with this task of distinguishing and casting aside much of a spcious polemical nature.

It is the same with regard to the question of 'economic determinism' in the explanation of social change. Engels so qualified the determining influence of the 'economic basis', or the 'productive forces', of society upon the nature of all other social institutions as to seem to strip the 'hypothesis' of any distinction, of any 'cutting edge' for purposes of analysis, whatever. And yet he wished to *retain* it as the distinguishing feature of the Marxian system of social explanation. How far Marx was in agreement with the extent of such qualifications is very difficult to decide.

We are, in short, faced with a body of ideas riddled with ambiguities, intensified by the excitement of polemics and political practice, and vexed by a multiplicy of interchanges of argument coming from many–and equally dogmatic–sources. So problems–in plenty–confront us.

An immediate question which arises is: is this tangle of ideas and ambiguities really worth bothering with? If Marx, Engels, and many of their followers chose to stride round Europe declaiming vehemently about this and that; asserting themselves over all other notable thinkers in history; all well and good. But if the intellectual wares they were selling comprised a bundle of ill-assorted and insufficiently connected bits of brash and arrogant nonsense...which were politically dangerous in the highest degree: why bother to give them serious consideration? Why not drop them into the waste-paper basket where they belong, and get on with something serious? And this leads to another group of very important reasons why we should try, in this place, properly to estimate the nature and value of Marx's 'system' among all other contributions to the making of sociology.

The most immediate and obvious reason why we cannot leave Marx and his ideas unexamined is that, whether rightly or wrongly, justifiably or unjustifiably, they have come to form the basis of the largest and most radical political movement in the modern world. The *importance* of these ideas for what is happening in social science and the 'understanding' of the nature and destiny of man, and what is happening on the world's vast stage of political power, can neither be denied nor escaped. Furthermore, even if we come to decide that these ideas are wrong, incorrect, and must be rejected, we are still left with the fact that, over great stretches of human society throughout the world, they have clearly been thought to be relevant to the economic, social and political struggles attendant upon the transforming influences of industrialization, and they have, without any doubt whatever, become the effective focus for political effort and political organisation. Why is this? Even if the ideas of Marx themselves are insufficient on various clear intellectual grounds, they may well be rooted in some very important and significant ways with the conditions of rapidly changing industrial society. They may–almost in Marx's own terms–be functioning as a powerful 'ideology' in modern society, even if they are something of a 'false consciousness' and intellectual error underlies them; and, if this is so, then this is a fact of great importance both for social science and for our estimation of concrete political events in the world.

Given this great prominence of Marx's 'system' in the prevailing struggle for power and the re-shaping of societies, it is also of the greatest importance that we gain a *true* and satisfactory understanding of this system. If there are dimensions of truth in it, then we must accept them. If there are grave errors in it, then we must *know clearly* what they are, and be able to demonstrate them. It is not enough–whether in *support* of the ideas of Marx or *against* them–simply to vituperate. It behoves everyone to seek clear knowledge and known grounds of judgement in an area of thought on which so much now hangs.

But a further aspect of this point is one on which I have come to feel very powerfully indeed. It is this. In the developing of these several approaches to the study of society, for the purpose of understanding and governing society, the all-pervading tendency has seemed, and still seems to be one of emphasizing *differences*. Everybody has wanted, and still wants, to set up a *new* theory. And, furthermore, everybody wants–in setting up their *own* theory–to denounce (critically) all others. Everybody wants their own theory to be *the* theory which supersedes all others. So that there appears to be a continuous fight between diametrically opposed theories: 'dialectical materialist' against 'metaphysical'; 'revolutionary' against 'evolutionary'; 'functionalist' against 'evolutionary'; and so on. Now by and large these antitheses are *bogus*! And I want especially to show that this it true concerning Marxism and its relations with other nineteenth-century theories. The titles given to this chapter and the last: 'Structure, Function, and Evolution' with regard to Spencer, and 'Economy, Class, and Revolution' with regard to Marx, point to the *marked distinction* which is commonly thought to differentiate the two kinds of theoretical positions. Now, I want to demonstrate beyond doubt that this is a false appraisal of the development of sociological theory, I want to show that Marx, like Spencer, provides a structural-functional model of society for the analysis of both social order and social change, and that his theory is one of social *evolution,* completely the sane, in form, as that of Spencer, and, indeed, as that of Comte. It is, in my view, most important to see that the supposed 'dichotomies' between these theories are false, and, especially, that all these thinkers, despite differences of emphasis *within* their scheme of description, analysis, and explanation, nonetheless adopted the *same kind of scheme.* In the making of sociology they all agreed as to the over-all framework and components of the science they were so concerned to construct and use.

Marx did *not* offer a qualitatively different science of society from that which we have seen taking shape at the hands of others. He was subject to the same intellectual influences which had played upon others in his time–the emergence of the scientific method and the new perspectives resulting from the work of the natural sciences; the new perspective (especially) of evolution; the insufficiencies of moral and political philosophy, the philosophy of history, and the like–and he made his scientific study of man out of the stuff of these same influences. He was aware of the same historical juncture in human society which had dominated the concerns of others: the crucial turning point of technological and industrial change; and confronted these dilemmas constructively and creatively as others had done. He was couched within the same context of thought and action–and was by no means the isolated heretic he is sometimes thought to be. But this raises a final source of difficulty we might note.

Like other theorists, Marx brought together many strands of earlier thought and worked them into a new synthesis. One's estimation of him depends to quite a large extent upon which of these influences and which element of this syntesis one considers to have been the most important. The position I shall adopt here is quite clear. There is no doubt, it seems to me, that there were two main roots in Marx's thinking. First, he was a scholar of the philosophy of history, and his central orientation here was a critique of the 'Idealist' philosophy of history of Hegel and the replacement of it by a 'materialist' philosophy stimulated in very large part by the work of Feuerbach. Marx was rooted firmly in Hegel; his way towards a science of society was that by way of a critical amendment of the philosophy of history; and he cannot be understood apart from this. Second, he was a scholar of political economy, and his study of Adam Smith, Ricardo, Jean-Baptiste Say, and others, led him into a detailed analysis of the relationships involved in industrial capitalism. It was this root of thought which led him to set 'labour' and 'capital' against each other as the chief source of class conflict and the main lever of social and political change. And Marx, in bringing together his philosophy of history and his analysis of the fundamental economic relationships of capitalism, created a *sociology*. He produced, without any doubt, a scientific study of societies as wholes–a theory of the nature of social order and of social change. And this is the pattern of ideas which we shall trace here.

It is true that a third source of influences was the large and varied body of writings of the French 'socialists'; and these ideas were obviously at work in influencing the way in which he brought together the philosophy of history and his analysis of industrial capitalism. However, it is these two latter components which, together, formed his system of analysis, and, in his hands, they were fused to create a sociology–a systematic science of society.

Bearing in mind these several important introductory points, and the difficulties they entail, let us now try to clarify, in turn, each component of Marx's sociological system.

Remembering our brief analysis of Hegel's system, it may be helpful, for purposes of complete clarity, to attempt a condensed diagrammatic summary of Marx's ideas along the same lines. As the text proceeds, it will gradually fill in and elaborate each specific item; but a study of the diagram itself may prove useful as an initial guide.

The necessity and the nature of science in the study of Man

In the first place it is worthwhile to establish the fact that Marx and his several 'interpreters' were quite emphatic about their theory of knowledge, and their persuasion that scientific methods were the *only* methods productive of testable knowledge. But the position adopted has certain interesting dimensions, all of which it is important to note.

(a) The necessity of the Scientific Method

The dimension with which we can begin is that both Marx and Engels were insistent upon the fact that they advocated and employed *the scientific method* in the study of nature and human society; they declared themselves 'empiricists'; but in no place whatever did they offer a detailed analysis of what they considered 'scientific method' to be. Some things were said: there were continual *assurances* that the methods of science were employed throughout their work and formed the firm basis of all their propositions; that empirical *facts* were the bed-rock of their theories; yet no clear conception or outline of this 'scientific method' was ever presented with satisfactory clarity or detail.

Marx felt it important, for example, '...to assure the reader conversant with political economy' that *his* results had been 'won by means of a wholly *empirical* analysis...' and, furthermore, that he welcomed 'every opinion based on scientific criticism'. He also took pains to make it clear that his accounts of English factory legislation (and of the conditions of work in the factories) in *Das Capital* were based upon a detailed study of 'blue-books' which were themselves the results of the empirical investigations of factory inspectors and commissioners undertaking governmental enquiries. He had, indeed, a great respect for the competence and lack of bias of these inspectors and for the accuracy of British social statistics. In all this he emphasized his empiricism and his concern for the accuracy of his empirical 'sources'.

The claim was made that the new system of analysis formulated by Marx was to be distinguished completely from the 'metaphysical' systems of the past in that it rested clearly and fundamentally on *science,* and found its generalizations in the *facts* which were empirically studied, whereas they did not.

Thus, according to Engels, philosophy 'came to an end' with Hegel, but, because Hegel had developed the old metaphysics to their fullest extent:

'...he showed us the way out of the labyrinth of "systems" to real positive knowledge of the world.

'One leaves alone' "absolute truth", which is unattainable along this path or by any single individual; instead one pursues *attainable, relative truths along the paths of the positive sciences...'*

'It is no longer a question anywhere of inventing interconnections from out of our brains, but of discovering them in the facts.'

With this development, science alone produced testable knowledge about all aspects of nature, man, and history, and philosophy was totally displaced. Philosophy was now stripped of any substantive subject-matter.

'For philosophy,' wrote Engels, 'which has been expelled from nature and history, there remains only the realm of pure thought (so far as it is left): the theory of the laws of the thought-process itself, logic and dialectics.' Dialectical Materialism, as a scientific study and knowledge of nature and history..."no longer needs any philosophy standing above the other sciences".'

Indeed, later, Lenin was to echo this position in his claim that the 'philosophy' of Marx, 'Dialectical Materialism,' was all-sufficient as a '*perfected philosophic materialism.'*

Lenin also emphasized the scientific basis of Marx's system of thought, when he claimed that Marx's application of dialectical materialism to the study of man and history:

'...represented the greatest conquest of *scientific thought.* Chaos and arbitrariness, which reigned until then in the views on history and politics, were replaced by *a strikingly consistent and harmonious scientific theory,* which shows how out of one order of social life another and higher order develops...'

It was 'historical materialism', he maintained, which:

'...first made it possible to study *with scientific accuracy* the social conditions of the life of the masses and changes in these conditions.'

Engels, too, emphasized that Marx's system was an extension of the methods of science into the study of man and society.

'For we live not only in nature but also in human society, and this also no less than nature has its history of development and its science. It was therefore a question of bringing the *science of society* into harmony with the materialist foundation, and of reconstructing it thereupon.'

Marx himself was quite definite about the all-embracing nature of science in securing such knowledge as man could achieve.

'*Sense-perception* must be the basis of all science. Only when it proceeds from sense-perception in the two-fold form both of *sensuous* consciousness and of *sensuous* need–that is, only when science proceeds from nature–is it *true* science.

'All history is the preparation for "*man*" to become the object of *sensuous* consciousness, and for the needs of "man as man" to become (natural sensuous) needs. History itself is *real* part of *natural* history–of nature's coming to be man. Natural science will in time subsume itself the under science of man, just as the science of man will subsume itself under natural science: there will be *one* science.'

There is no doubt whatever, then. about the scientific pretensions and claims of Marx and Marxism. Before leaving this initial and simple noting of their basic emphasis upon science, and before moving on to ask what Marx and his followers considered the nature of this science to be, it is worthwhile simply to point out how ambiguities has raised their head even in these apparently straightforward assertions. Only a few points need to be mentioned at this stage.

Firstly, when Marx spoke of 'science *proceeding from nature*'–what exactly did he mean? And when he claimed that only this science is *true* science: did he think that there were kinds of science which did *not* proceed from nature? And that, therefore, there were criteria in accordance with which one could distinguish *true* science from *false* science? Later, we shall see that the *relativity* of its propositions is one characteristic distinguishing science from 'metaphysics', but, given relativity, the question of distinguishing *true* from *false* science raises large problems.

Secondly, it can be seen in these few quotations that the extension of 'science' in the study of nature, man and society seems to be not so much closely associated, as *indentified* with the acceptance of 'materialism', 'dialectical materialism', 'historical materialism'. To accept something called 'materialism' (as against the 'idealism' of 'metaphysics') and to adopt a 'scientific' approach to the study of any kinds of facts, seem to be considered synonymous. But why? No good reasons are given. In this, 'science' seems to be indentified with the acceptance of one metaphysical assertion (*not* argument, let it be noted!) rather than another. And this seems rather an odd and questionable assumption.

These ambiguities are seen to entail even greater elements of confusion when the testability of 'science' is in some way strongly associated, if not equated, with 'practice' or 'pragmatism', and the 'relativity' of systems of ideas, bodies of knowledge, or 'ideologies' is seen in relation to the 'material' basis of social classes and political movements: so that we are quickly transported from a 'scientific study of nature, man, and society' (i.e. involving, presumably, testable theories about various kinds of facts) to something called 'scientific communism' or 'scientific socialism' which now, somehow, gives scientific guarantees and justifications for the destinies of certain socio-political groups.

'Scientific' communism or socialism, it may be noted, is forthrightly contrasted (by both Marx and Engels) with 'Utopian' socialism–as put forward by many of the earlier French socialists; and the 'search after a new social science' on the part of these scholars was denigrated (though not entirely) because *their* social science was not satisfactorily founded on the developing proletariat and its developing material conditions. There are hints here as to how one distinguishes 'true' science from 'false'–but they are rather disquieting ones.

The extent of this ambiguity must not be underestimated or under-emphasized; it is a very real, important, and unresolved ambiguity, and needs to be seen clearly.

Perhaps the most stark statement is to be found in the systematic exposition of Stalin. Having stated the materialistic and scientific basis of Marxism:

'Marxist philosophical materialism holds that the world and its laws are fully knowable, that our knowledge of the laws of nature, tested by experiment and practice is authentic knowledge having the validity of objective truth, and that there are no things in the world which are unknowable, but only things which are still not known, but which will be disclosed and made known by the efforts of science and practice.'

And having explained the extension of this scientific procedure to the study of society and history, Stalin then pronounced the fact that:

'Hence Socialism is converted from a dream of a better future for humanity into a science.'

It is important to see that Stalin did *not* say: 'With this scientific knowledge of society, Socialism will be better equipped to achieve its ends', (and, of course, *any* political movement should be in such a position armed with accurate knowledge), but that 'Socialism' *itself* was 'converted into a science'.

Similarly, V. Adoratsky, in his preface to the selected works of Marx (and Engels) described these works as being 'permeated by the integral world outlook of scientific communism'.

'The struggle of the proletariat', he wrote, 'cannot be successful without a revolutionary theory which completely reflects and explains the whole complicated process of historical movement and serves as a guide in changing the world. Scientific communism includes practical revolutionary activity as an indispensable constituent part. But this activity must be guided by scientific theory...'

Ambiguity on ambiguity! 'Science', it seems, is by some strange logic transmuted into the ideology if the proletariat, the content of which accords with, or is relative to, its practice within its own material conditions. This may seem a strange position, as indeed it is, but it will be seen to derive quite directly from the actual, and very definite propositions of Marx himself as well as his followers. It is enough here, however, to see that the basis insistence upon a *scientific* approach to the study of man and society was very much more ambiguous matter than it was in the work of the other men we have discussed.

Since *science* was so fundamental to this new approach to the study of society, one would have expected Marx to be meticulously careful in making clear the *nature* of science, and, especially, the *nature* of his *science of society.* In fact, however, he says astonishingly little about this. Much is *said* about the importance of science and empiricism, but hardly anything about its nature. Some of the ambiguities creep in here because, as we shall see, such discussions as take place about the distinctive approach of science tend to take the form of a defence of 'materialism' and its suppositions. Even so, some of the assumptions–whether correct or not–of Marx and Engels about the nature of science, can be drawn from their indirect remarks. And some of these are of considerable importance for a critical assessment of their system.

(b) The nature of the scientific method and basic epistemological assumptions

Practically all the points which I wish to emphasize in this section occurred in the discussion about the nature of 'dialectics' 'materialism', and the like, and were s closely connected with them as to be almost inseparable from them. Even so, I think it better to consider these larger ingredients of Marx's thought later, and I believe each of these points about the nature of science and epistemology to be important in their own right–both for a correct appreciation of Marx, and, more important for our purposes, for seeing the contribution of Marx in clear relation to that of other scholars of the nineteenth century.

(I) SCIENCE PROVIDES KNOWLEDGE OF 'NATURE': EXPERIMENTIAL, TESTABLE, RELATIVE, NEVER FINAL: AKIN TO POSITIVISM

The first thing which is completely clear from the various writings of Marx and Engels is that they rejected earlier 'theological' and 'metaphysical' conceptions of 'truth' as radically as Comte had done. In this, their position was like that of all nineteenth-century thinkers who accepted the new criteria of testable truths adopted in the natural sciences as against any kind of speculative assertion or 'argument' for which there were no kinds of 'experiential' conditions of test. This also entailed for them, as for others, a conscious awareness of the 'delimitation of knowledge' in accordance with the concepts, techniques, and methods of science. In this position it is not too much to say that they simply accepted a Cometean account of the nature and limitations of 'positive science'.

Engels wrote, for example:

'...the demand for *final* solutions and *eternal* truths ceases once for all: one is always conscious of the necessary *limitation* of all acquired knowledge, of the fact that it is *conditioned* by the circumstances in which it was acquired.'

However, both Marx and Engels were more extreme and philosophically less cautious than Comte in the extent to which they conceded, or rather insisted upon, the 'relativity' of knowledge. Comte, it will be remembered, recognized that there were grounds and conditions of 'relativity' in knowledge, but, nonetheless, did not think that the criteria of knowledge which had been, and could be, set up, were 'arbitrary. Engels, however, could write as sweepingly as this:

'...one no longer permits oneself to be imposed upon by the antitheses, insuperable for the still common old metaphysics, between true and false, good and bad, identical and different, necessary and accidental. One knows that these antitheses have only a relative validity...'

–and he never appeared to see what enormous, indeed impossible problems this position opened up before him when he might wish for example, to insist on definitive 'criteria' for the testing of 'truths' within science (let alone metaphysics), or when he might wish to maintain that science is *true* as against metaphysics, or that 'scientific communism' possesses more accurate degrees of 'truth' than does, let us say, 'bourgeois reaction'.

If the antitheses between truth and falsity, identity and difference, necessity and contingency, have disappeared, one wonders what science can possibly be about!

What this amounts to is that Marx and Engels adopted and accepted 'positive science' as a method of achieving knowledge, but paid insufficient attention to clarifying its nature, and were careless to (quite literally) an unspecified degree with regard to its 'relativity'.

(II) SCIENTIFIC KNOWLEDGE IS KNOWLEDGE OF 'REALITY'– WITHOUT PHILOSOPHICAL LIMITATION

There was one important sense, however, in which the claims made by Marx and Engels for the nature and extent of 'scientific knowledge' went for beyond the claims of other nineteenth-century thinkers. Comte, Mill, and Spencer, for example, accepting the 'delimitations' of scientific knowledge and rejecting the claims of 'truth' of metaphysical speculations about the nature of things, nonetheless recognized a necessary limit of 'philosophical agnosticism'. In one way or another, they all accepted the fact that we can ask more questions about the nature of things than we can answer, and that there are, most probably, dimensions of 'reality' that man–with the limitations and confining characteristics of nature and conditions–can never know. He can, at least, never be sure that he has knowledge of all dimensions of the world because he knows that he perceives, observes, connects, generalizes, thinks, through the conditions of his own nature. In one way or another, they all accepted that, though we cannot go beyond 'scientific knowledge', we cannot, either, claim that such 'scientific knowledge' as we have is to be taken without qualification, as knowledge of 'reality'. Indeed, they all chose not to speak of 'reality' in this sense–because it was, in its own way, a metaphysic!

Marx and Engels, however, in strong opposition to the 'reality' of the metaphysician, seemed to want to juxtapose a 'material reality' of their own. Whereas the other scholars we have mentioned took heed to the caution of Hume (in his sceptical empiricism) and Kant (in his limited knowledge of 'phenomena' and his recognition of unknowable 'noumena'–'things-as-they-are-in-themselves'), Marx and Engels outrightly rejected them, but again, it must be said, with a cavalier setting aside of anything approximating to philosophical argument.

Agnosticism, or Neo-Kantian Agnosticism, was no more, Engels wrote, than 'shame-faced' materialism, whatever that was supposed to mean.

There is no doubt whatever that though his 'materialism in his theory of society was a complicated and much qualified matter, Marx quite definitely conceived 'matter' to be the primary 'reality' in 'nature', and the human mind and the knowledge it produced to be a 'secondary reflection' of it. It was this, indeed which formed the basis of this opposition to Hegel. Engels too, was agreed about the primary 'reality' of matter, but the essential point here is that both believed that science could produce direct and exhaustive knowledge of such reality.

Drawing upon Hegel himself, for example, Engels wrote:

'If you know all the qualities of a thing, you know the thing itself; nothing remains but the fact that the said thing exists without us; and when your senses have taught you that fact, you have grasped the last remnant of the "thing-in-itself"...'

But nowhere did he even begin to say by what criteria we can know that 'all' the qualities of a thing have been brought into our knowledge; and nowhere did he begin to apprehend the philosophical problem attendant upon the recognition that the 'qualities' of a thing may be dependent on the 'qualities' peculiar to the perceiver, and that the 'knowledge' pertaining to 'human' perception may be limited on these grounds.

He agreed that the problems raised by Hume and Kant seemed 'undoubtedly hard to beat by mere argumentation' (why *mere,* one wonders?), but he readily brushed this aside with the remark; 'but before there was argumentation, there was action', and then proceeded to show that our sense perceptions could be checked and tested by 'putting them to use'.

'Not in one single instance, so far, have been led to the conclusion that our sense-perceptions, scientifically controlled, induce in our minds ideas respecting the outer world that are, by their very nature, at variance with reality, or that there is an inherent incompatibility between the outer world and our sense perceptions of it.'

But, of course, neither Kant nor Hume wanted to claim that our perception of things or relations of things in the world were at variance with 'reality' or 'incompatible' with it. Hume was only concerned to show that knowledge of the world was knowledge of our experience of this kind, and that it did not possess logical certainty, and Kant was only concerned to claim that such knowledge was not (and had no grounds for claiming that it was) the whole of the story. Engels did not see that his several arguments were simple repetitions of Dr Johnson-like 'kicks against the lamp-post' to prove it was there. But this was no philosophical basis for an unqualified 'realism' of empirical knowledge.

This 'over-stated' claim for the extent of 'scientific' knowledge may not seem a particularly important point to emphasize, but it *is* of the greatest importance when attached to a 'materialistic' dogma, it comes to insist that only 'scientific knowledge at a certain level' (i.e. the basic level of 'material reality') constitutes a 'real' explanation. We are then at the point of a new metaphysical dogma of 'scientific materialism'.

(III) SCIENTIFIC KNOWLEDGE: A SHEER EMPIRICISM

A third characteristic of the nature of scientific knowledge which was closely connected with this 'over-statement' of its claim and the acceptance of the 'objective facts of material reality' was what can be called a 'sheer' empiricism, or what some philosophers of science would call a 'naive inductivism'. It was the view that the generalizations of science, the 'laws' of nature and society, were simply *there* in the facts. No speculation was necessary, the straightforward study of the facts revealed them. As we have seen, Engels argued that, with the abandonment of philosophy, it was no longer a question:

'...of inventing interconnections from out of our brains, but of discovering them in the facts.'

No detailed examination was undertaken as to what methods such a process of 'discovery of interconnections' involved.

(IV) SCIENTIFIC KNOWLEDGE: THE RIGIDITY OF 'LAWS'

A similar, connected conception in the mind of Marx, Engels and all their followers was that of the 'laws' which scientific knowledge discovered. These were not only thought of as 'interconnections' or 'regularities' of relationship' among phenomena, but also as determinate, constraining forces in nature. Marx, for example, when arguing about the usefulness of the knowledge of a developed industrial society for foreseeing the problems of those which were undeveloped, wrote:

'It is a question of these laws themselves, of these tendencies working with iron necessity towards inevitable results. The country that is more developed industrially only shows, to the less developed, the image of its own future.'

Whether this is a true or false conception of scientific 'laws' we need not here try to decide. What is certain is that this language is unmistakable. It is, without doubt, the language of determinism (what Mill called 'necessitarianism'); the language of 'inevitability.

(V) SCIENTIFIC KNOWLEDGE: THE LIMITED CONTROL PROVIDED BY FORESIGHT

This 'deterministic' emphasis was also reflected quite clearly and definitely in the fact that Marx believed that, even with the foresight which a knowledge of scientific 'laws' provided, the extent to which man could control or change the expected events was decidedly limited.

'Once nation can and should learn from others,' he wrote. 'And even when a society has got upon the right track for the discovery of the natural laws of its movement, it can neither clear by bold leaps, nor remove by legal enactments, the obstacles offered by the successive phases of its normal development. But it can shorten and lessen the birth-pangs.'

Like Comte, Marx clearly thought that in the pursuit of science we seek 'to see, in order to foresee,' but, even when we *could* foresee, the extent of our controlling action was very limited.

(VI) SCIENTIFIC KNOWLEDGE: EXPERIMENT AND PRACTICE

The nearest that either Marx or Engels came to a clarification of what they took scientific method to be was the emphasis that they placed upon 'experiment' and 'practice' as modes of testing theories. With regard to both notions, however, what they said was very limited, and, in what they said about 'practice' in particular, the issues became clouded again in ambiguity.

Marx undoubtedly thought 'experiment' to be crucial in the scientific method, and it is interesting to see how he himself thought he was using this in his study of society. Though Marx saw his 'materialist' conception and method as having application to all kinds of societies, his chief focus of concentrated study was the nature of 'industrial capitalism', the laws of which he sought to 'lay bare'. In undertaking this study, however, his focus was even more concentrated than that. In fact, he devoted himself chiefly to the study of industrial Britain.

He outlined, in *Capital* his 'theoretical laws' by a precess of definition and analysis, and then exemplified them in what might be called a specific 'case study' of capitalistic Britain. But he quite consciously regarded this as a specific 'experimental' instance, and, indeed, as an approximation to the experimental method of the natural sciences.

'The physicist' he wrote, 'either observes physical phenomena where they occur in their most *typical form* and most free from disturbing influence, or, wherever possible, he makes experiments under conditions that assure the occurrence of the phenomenon *in its normality*.

'In this work I have to examine the capitalist mode of production, and the conditions of production and exchange corresponding to that mode. Up to the present time, their classic ground is England. That is why England is used as the chief illustration in the development of my theoretical ideas.'*

As we have seen earlier, having clarified the 'laws' of this 'type' of social system, Marx went on the say that they served as guide to those societies which were 'developing' towards it.

What this amounts to is that in his 'science of society', Marx quite distinctly maintained that societies could, like other phenomena, be classified into 'types'— each having its own 'laws' of relationships between its parts–and that these 'typical' characteristics could be clarified by considering in detail the most 'normal' case. Again, we see that the *experimental* and the *comparative* method were conceived as being part of each other in the science of society, and, of course, since the whole force of Marx's 'dialectical materialism' was to the effect that societies, like all other phenomena, were *processes* in relation to their material conditions, the *historical* method was also essentially involved in experiment and comparison. All these considerations of the elements of a science of society, though never clearly stated and elaborated, can be seen to be common to the writers we have already discussed, and to others who were to follow.

Considerable difficulty was introduced, however, by the further element of testability—namely, 'practice'. Marxism is in some essential way 'pragmatic in its emphasis, and the scientific implications of this seem far from clear. Everyone after Marx used the same kind of phraseology. Engels wrote of :

'practice—viz. experiment and industry'. Stalin later wrote of the laws of nature and society—tested by experiment and practice'. And one meaning of this is , of course, quite clear. In so far as men put their knowledge to use in their technology, in their practical methods of industry, they will have continuously to be relying upon, and continuously testing, its truth and adequacy. It was in this same sense, for example that Comte believed that the new industrial proletariat would be more receptive to the knowledge and methods 'positive science'—because they were quite directly involved in *using* them; the effectiveness of their working activity *depended* upon them. This can be both understood and accepted; but it is quite clear that this is no more than saying that those who must continuously *use* and *apply* the knowledge of empirical science will be most sensitive to its adequacy. There is no problem here; practice is simply a kind of extension of 'experiment'.

Marx himself, however, raised conceptual problems here which are much more difficult to understand. He clearly wished to distinguish a conception of science as an intellectual effort to establish knowledge of the world and so *understand* it, from a conception of science as part of a sensuous activity of man, in creatively *changing* the material conditions of nature and society in a process of gradually and progressively creating his own, distinctively human nature. This, I shall try to be as clear as possible about, later; but here we might simply note the great difficulty and ambiguity of this point. The most simple statement of this (though not the best) is to be found in Marx's often-quoted 'Theses on Feuerbach', of which the most relevant are :

(I)

'The chief defect of all hitherto existing materialism—that of Feuerbach included—is that the object, reality, sensuousness, is conceived only in the form of the *object* or *contemplation* but not as *human sensuous activity, practice*, not subjectively. Thus it happened that the *active* side, in opposition to materialism, was developed by idealism—but only abstractly, since, of course, idealism does not know real sensuous activity as such. Feuerbach wants sensuous objects, really differentiated from the thought-objects, but he does not conceive human activity itself as activity *through objects.* Consequently, in the *Essence of Christianity,* he regards the theoretical attitude as the only genuinely human attitude, while practice is conceived and fixed only in its dirty-Jewish form of appearance. Hence he does not grasp the significance of "revolutionary", of practical-critical, activity.'

(II)

'The question whether objective truth can be attributed to human thinking is not a question of theory but is a practical question. In practice man must prove the truth, i.e., the reality and power, the "this-sidedness" of his thinking. The dispute over the reality or non-reality of thinking which is isolated from practice is a purely scholastic question.

(VIII)

'Social life is essentially *practical.* All mysteries which mislead theory to mysticism find their rational solution in human practice and in the comprehension of this practice.'

(XL)

'The philosophers have *interpreted* the world in various ways; the point however is to *change* it.

These, really, are garbled and confused statements. It is quite clear in them that a 'theoretical' attitude to the 'understanding' of 'objective' facts in the world and society is set against 'human sensuous activity' or 'revolutionary, practical-critical activity' which somehow 'proves the truth in practice' not by 'theoretically understanding', but by 'changing' the world. But what on earth does all the mean? What are the *criteria* whereby truth is proved in practical sensuous activity? And in what ways do they differ from the scientific criteria of 'theoretically understanding' the world ? We are never told this, not by Marx himself, or the many from Engels, Lenin, Stalin to hundreds of thousands who quote from these 'theses' as though they contained the light of the ages. But until we *are* told this, these notions can only be regarded as nonsensical.

Their assertiveness, too, however, needs noting. Whoever asks about the 'reality or non-reality of thinking'? Who says that social life is *essentially* practical; or that *all* mysteries find their rational solution in practice ? And there *may* be a point in *changing* the world—but to whom? Some people who *understand* some aspects of the world may see *no* point in changing them. On what criteria are they held to be mistaken ?

Apart from its immediate intellectual ambiguity, this particular emphasis of Marx has increased the ambiguities which have drawn together the 'scientific' pretensions and the 'pragmatic' aims of Communism. By this twist, 'scientific' validity is claimed for the pragmatic programme of a political movement. It is surely very clear too, and patently dangerous, that there is an 'anti-intellectual' element in this position. I think there are elements in Marx's emphasis upon the 'sensuous creative activity of man' which can be understood, and with which one can very deeply sympathize, and this we shall come back to later; but there seems to me no doubt that to introduce *this* dimension of practice as something significantly qualifying the nature of scientific method and knowledge is both obscuring and dangerous in its outcome.

(VII) SCIENTIFIC KNOWLEDGE : CLASSIFICATION

One aspect of the last point is worth selecting for brief special emphasis. We saw that Marx—when thinking of experiment and comparison—insisted upon a central concern in science for the clarification of 'types' or, indeed, 'typical forms' which could exist 'in their normality' or affected by 'disturbing influences'. It is worthwhile simply to stress the fact that—upholding their 'dialectical materialism' (which saw the world as an interdependent multiplicity of forms of process) as against 'metaphysics' (which—as they thought —saw the world as an arrangement of distinct, separate objects)— Marx and Engels emphasized this procedure of *classification* in scientific method. Engels, for example, wrote :

'. . . While natural science up to the end of the last century was predominantly a *collecting* science, a science of finished things, in our century it is essentially a *classifying science*, a science of the processes, of the origin and development of these things and of the inter-connection which binds all these natural processes into one great whole.'

As we shall see, Marx's 'materialism' led to the classification of certain 'types' of social system; but here it is enough to see that with Marx and Engels, as with Comte, Mill, and Spencer, The methods of science included classification as well as observation, description, analysis, comparison, experiment and a historical account of process and development.

(VIII) SCIENTIFIC KNOWLEDGE: PROBES BEYOND SURFACE APPEARANCE TO 'HIDDEN LAWS'

One other point which deserves very brief mention here is especially relevant to the science of society. It is enough, for now, simply to say that both Marx and Engels thought it necessary that realistic science should seek those motives, forces, 'laws' which lay *hidden behind* what *appeared* to be a teeming multiplicity of disconnected faets.

Society *appears* to be complex, accidental, in many ways a prey to chance, but *really* 'it is always governed by inner, hidden laws and it is only a matter of discovering these laws'. (Engels) Also, men *appear* to act in society according to their views, or ends, or principles of moral, religious, political, etc., nature—but *really* there are *class-interests behind* these motives which must be discovered by analysis for any realistic and satisfactory explanation. Again, Engels attacked the 'old materialism' for taking the 'ideal driving forces which operate there (in history) as ultimate causes'. Instead, he argued, one should investigate '. . . What is *behind* them, what are the *driving forces of these driving forces.*'

Now obviously, science delves below appearance, and may well discover deeper connections where, on the surface, there appear to be none. Even so, one does not have to be a genius to smell both a dogmatic metaphysic and an infinite regress here, unless care is exercised.

What this conception could amount to is that one continues to uncover the 'driving forces behind the driving forces' until one arrives at the *kind* or *level* of driving forces which one considers to be 'ultimate'—i.e., which is stipulated by one's metaphysic. It only needs someone with a *different* metaphysic to arrive on the scene, however, for the proposition to be made: 'Ah, no! I beg to differ! We must uncover *the* driving forces behind the driving forces behind the driving forces. . .'

Ultimately, one way get back to the first flip of God's finger—and then one might have an *explanation*.

Certainly the Marxian dogma of 'materialism' lends itself to the danger of this error.

(IX) SCIENTIFIC KNOWLEDGE: THE SIGNIFICANT CHARACTERISTICS OF NINETEENTH-CENTURY DEVELOPMENTS

Finally, it is worthwhile to see clearly that — whether they expressed it clearly or not—the emphasis upon the scientific method and it its nature adopted by Marx and Engels was seen, by them in exactly the same context as that recognized by the other thinkers we have considered. There is one passage in Engel's essay on Ludwig Feuerbach which sets out with complete clarity a perspective of nineteenth century scientific influences and developments which might well have been set out by Herbert Spencer. It is this :

'Above all, there are three great discoveries which have enabled our knowledge of the interconnection of natural processes to advance by leaps and bounds : first, the discovery of the cell as the unit from whose multiplication and differentiation the whole plant and animal body develops —so that not only is the development and growth of all higher organism recognized to proceed according to a single general law, but also, in the capacity of the cell to change, the way is pointed out by which organisms can change their species and thus go through a more than individual development. Second, the transformation of energy, which has demonstrated that all the so-called forces operative in the first instance in inorganic nature—mechanical force and its complement, so-called potential energy, heat, radiation (light or radiant heat), electricity, magnetism and chemical energy — are different forms of manifestation of universal motion, which pass into one another in definite proportions so that in place of a certain quantity of the one which disappears, a certain quantity of another makes its appearance and thus the whole motion of nature is reduced to this incessant process of transformation from one form into another. Finally, the proof which Darwin first developed in connected form that the stock of organic products of nature surrounding us today, including mankind, is the result of a long process of evolution from a few original unicellular germs, and that these again have arisen from protoplasm or albumen which came into existence by chemical means.

'We have now arrived at the point where we can demonstrate as a whole the interconnection between the processes in nature not only in particular spheres but also in the interconnection of these particular spheres themselves, and so can present in an approximately systematic form a comprehensive view for the interconnection in nature by means of the facts provided by empirical natural science itself. . .

'But what is true of nature, is also true of the history of society in all its branches and of the totality of all sciences which occupy themselves with things human.'

This attempt to sift through the many comments made by Marx and Engels on the importance and nature of the scientific method which they sought to apply to the study of society may well have seemed rather painstaking. However, it is undoubtedly necessary if we are properly to assess their theory of society, and, apart from this, I hope it has shown conclusively that the elements involved in their approach to the making of sociology were very much the same in Marx and Engels as in the other thinkers who were seeking the same objective. The 'Marxian' attempt to construct a 'science' of society took place in the same context of nineteenth-century influences, was one attempt among others—and similar to them, and utilized many similar conceptions of theory and method. I hope it has also been made clear, however, how insufficiently Marx's 'scientific assumptions' were worked out, when compared with those of Comte, Mill, and Spencer, and what awkward and potentially dangerous ambiguities were used, though unclarified and unresolved.

We are now in a position to move to the substantive theory of nature and society which Marx, with all the corollaries of Engels, put forward.

Dialectical Materialism

Marx's entire theory of nature and society, his whole 'system' of thought, can best be introduced and presented as a *contradiction* to that of Hegel. Whereas Hegel is the best representative of an 'IDEALIST' philosophy of history, Marx is the best representative of a 'MATERIALIST' philosophy of history. Our first step in understanding Marx must therefore be to become clear about his disagreement with Hegel, and what exactly he meant by 'materialism' and 'dialectical' materialism.

In this, as in every item of Marx's thought, there are ambiguities. Because of this, it is possible to give, on the one hand, a superficial interpretation which is open to caustic criticism and outright rejection, or, on the other, a sympathetic and profound interpretation— which takes care to delve beyond the ambiguities--and which, though extremely difficult to assess, seems to contain elements, insights, reorientations, emphases, of very great importance. There is a sense in which Marx is genuinely like an intellectual iceberg. The one fifth, which stands starkly above the surface is brilliant and striking, but it is also disturbing and disquieting because one is aware of the large and labyrinthine nature of the four fifths which lie, as the supporting reality, below–every single part of which presents considerable difficulties of exploration and navigation in moving towards a full and accurate knowledge of the whole. In this presentation, I shall try to give a clear and fair outline of each necessary component—trying to indicate both its superficial and profound aspects, the ambiguities that attend it, and the different interpretations which arise. But the concentration will be upon *clear exposition*. Our *critical assessment* can follow in a separate section.

What, then, were Marx's disagreements with the dialectical account of nature and history from an 'Idealist' point of view put forward by Hegel?

In a complete and radical manner, Marx first of all rejected the 'idealist' basis of Hegel's system. For him, there was no evidence whatever to suggest the existence of a 'World Spirit' prior to the existence of the material reality of nature; or that the vast, changing panorama of the world and of man's history within it were an 'actualization' of this previously existing 'Idea'. On the contrary, all our evidence was to the effect that the material reality of nature existed prior to the emergence of man, and prior to the subsequent emergence, within nature, of all those qualities of life and mind which, active in all men's activities—in art and music and literature, as well as in the making of societies—we have come to call 'Spiritual'. This meant a complete over-turning of Hegel's system which had many very important dimensions.

First of all, the *material reality of nature was primary* in the nature of the world and history, and '*mind*' or '*qualities of the spirit*' were *secondary*. In *some* way, *matter* had given rise, in its intricate processes, to the emergence of animal organisms, the human species, human society and its historical transformations, and the conscious, creative activities of *mind*. Because of this order of the facts, the order of *explanation* and *understanding* was the same. It was a knowledge of the nature, conditions, and processes of *material reality* which could explain the subsequent qualities of life, mind, and conscious human creativity, *not* vice versa. Hegel had got *both* the order of the facts, *and* the necessary order of the explanation, the wrong way round.

Secondly, however, this error of Hegel's also entailed a false attributing of qualities of '*reality, truth, eternity*' to '*mind* and *spirit*', and a relegating of the actual activities of natural processes, and the actual struggles of men in history to a level of *contingency* only. The *real* qualities had existed from eternity in the 'Idea' of the 'world Spirit', and the vast scene of nature and history, with all its vicissitudes and tribulations, was no more than a fabric of *means,* whereby the 'World Spirit', came to enjoy the full consciousness, in created actualities, of its original potentialities. Nature and men were borne upon a kind of vast tide of divine intentions and divine realities. Once this perspective was overturned, however, many interpretations were fundamentally changed. The 'ideas' of the human mind and spirit, and the concepts (such as 'beauty', 'truth', 'justice') which were implicit in them, no longer possessed 'reality, absoluteness, eternity', but were seen to be relative to man's actual activities in nature and society; they were 'reflections' of the material reality of nature and society and relative to men's historical conditions in that context. Man's actual activities in changing nature and society were seen to be the creative *reality* of human affairs, and 'ideas' and 'knowledge' were a relative part of these. Qualities of mind, though not absolute and eternal, were, nonetheless, in *this* perspective, seen to be *won* from the struggles with material nature. They therefore had a new status and dignity, despite the 'lower' or 'lesser' metaphysical claims that could be made for them.

This might especially be seen if one considers a particular

'idea' and 'actuality' such as 'Freedom'. Both Hegel and Marx 'measure' the dialectical 'advances' of history in terms of ever-increasing degrees of "Freedom. With Hegel, however, 'Freedom' is an initial 'Idea' within the potentiality of the World Spirit, and , after all the swirls of historical conflict, comes to be 'conscious' of its actualization when men, in the morality of the state, experience it. The atoms and organisms of the world have been woven in kind of jazz about the underlying theme, or melody, of 'Freedom', which was stated at the outset by the 'World Spirit'. With Marx, 'Freedom' is an achievement of consciously worked out creative, personal activity in society, which men have *won,* have *struggled for,* have *accomplished,* in suffering, learning about, and then directing the material conditions and vicissitudes of nature and history. This is a very different perspective.

There is another element of this which Marx thought important. The Hegelian 'Idealist' system, of interpreting 'reality' in terms of certain 'categories' or 'ideas' and their (logical) dialectical unfolding in the actualities of nature, led to the imposition of a demand for theoretical understanding in terms of '*abstractions*'. 'Actualities' in nature and history were '*externalizations*' of 'ideas', and therefore to '*understand*' them was to uncover the '*abstract idealities*' which interpenetrated them. Marx radically opposed such 'theoretical understanding' in terms of 'abstraction', too. The *actualities* are the *material struggle,* he argued. The *practicalities* of the nature and society are the basically real facts, and the 'ideas' are an outcome of, and can only be understood in terms of the *practical* activities. Marx, then, advocated a fundamentally opposed method of understanding and explaining nature and history in terms of practical activities within a context of material conditions and processes, including an understanding of men's 'ideas', 'knowledge' and 'theories' as part of this. And it is clear that really was, and is, something vitally important in this 'overturning' of the earlier philosophical approach. This was viewpoint which not only proposed a vast reversal of order in philosophy and science itself, but was also of very basic importance for the making of sociology, and the statement, and criticism, of sociological theories.

Again, the sharp difference between Hegel's and Marx's

position here can be made meticulously clear by briefly considering one matter—the nature of 'alienation'—which both men took to be of central importance for understanding the conflicts and contradictions at the heart of society and its many relationships. For Hegel—'alienation' is a matter of the mind, or spirit (i.e. the World Spirit itself, and its partial actualization in man in any historical epoch) feeling separated from, and distanced from, the 'objectification' of its real 'essence' in the institutions of 'civil society' and the 'state' (and other 'actualizations' of nature). This experience of 'estrangement' is an important factor in the ongoing struggle in nature and history until the full conscious experience of the essence in the actuality is accomplished. For Marx—'alienation' is the distance and estrangement man comes to experience in the limiting, constraining conditions of his practical creative activity in the context of nature and society. In working on nature, he creates necessary material objects and material conditions and relationships (with other men) of labour. These themselves constrain his 'essential' activity—i.e. of creativity—and especially because, in history, they include the necessary emergence of 'property relations' which not only set man at a distance from the objects of his creativity, but also set man against man in relationships of exploitation, conflict, and power. These material, economic, and social aspects of 'alienation' are the mainsprings of historical struggle for Marx. The difference between the 'Idealist' and the 'Materialist' positions therefore seems very fundamental.

One other important dimension of this is difficult to state, but a great deal hangs upon it, and the perspective it provides is, properly understood, of the highest importance for understanding the historical significance of the 'modern revolution' of the past two hundred years or so, and is entirely compatible with the viewpoint of Comte, Spencer, and others who attempted to place the period, and the human dilemma to which it gave rise, in perspective. It is this :

The Hegelian 'Idealist' position rested on the unquestioned assumption that the spiritual 'essence' of man existed prior to his emergence in the world, and that there was therefore a kind of ultimate spiritual bedrock of absolute truth on which the entire fabric of the universe and human society was solidly based. In the smoke and confusion of history, men saw through a glass darkly, but, behind the troubled obscuring details, behind the 'temporal' sufferings, the rock-like eternity was there. The Marxian 'materialist' position–one among several which emerged with the questioning of modern science—maintained not only that there was no such rock, but that the true perspective contained dimensions which it was most important to realize in properly estimating man's contemporary dilemmas of destiny. Marx's position really maintained that the intricate material processes of nature and history were really the ground out of which *man made himself. Man did not have a nature prior to history.* On the contrary, man, as one species amongst others, emerged in a material nature over which he had no control, but in which he had to struggle. *The historical conditions of this struggle, which were the complex developments of societies, were actually the long process of creation of man's own nature.* The material conditions of historical change, too, have hitherto been beyond man's control, but with the emergence of modern science and modern industrial technology, man is increasingly conscious of his historical perspective, increasingly able to direct the future of his own creative efforts, and thus able to *make himself,* consciously and freely. In this way, Marx regarded the entirety of previous history, during which man had been subordinated to his material conditions, as the 'PRE-HISTORY' of man. Only from this point on could man impose his own spiritual values and purposes upon history.

It will readily be seen that this view is strongly in keeping with Comte's picture of the culmination of history in the 'positive' stage, in which man must assume responsibility for the direction of his own affairs, and also with Spencer's idea of the 'Ethical' condition of society now before us—when the more mundane, economic problems of mankind have been resolved. But it will also readily be seen how firmly such a system of ideas provides a programme for *progressive political action,* whereas Hegel's system—with its eternal verities to uphold—leads itself to political conservatism and reaction. It is easy to see how and why Marx became a plank for political revolution; but it is also clear that—whatever one may ultimately accept or reject in his system—Marx was one very important voice among others stating a vast change of perspective—both of thought and action—in the modern world.

I may say that, in my opinion, both Marx and Engels either misunderstood or misrepresented some aspects of Hegel. For example, to argue that, for Hegel, the actualities of nature and history were simply '*externalizations*' (which is not the same as 'objectifications') of the 'World Spirit', and that 'matter' was a kind of secondary vehicle only, which Spirit used to 'externalize' itself, is a misunderstanding. For Hegel, matter itself is a creation of Spirit, always in a creative turmoil in the actualization of its forms; there is no 'externalization' in it; the entirety of existence is creative process in which spirit is *itself-becoming*. Consequently, to think that the understanding of all this is a matter of 'abstractions' at the level of logic and 'rational theory' in the ordinary sense, is, itself, not to do justice to Hegel; not to penetrate his language and conceptions sufficiently. In short, Hegel himself is much more involved in the 'practical, sensuous activity' of nature and history than Marx gives him credit for : he is no cardboard figure of metaphysics. It can also be argued that—no matter how Hegel himself might have been *used* ideologically, consciously or otherwise, by various groups and social classes—there is nothing *necessarily* conservative or reactionary in an 'Idealist' philosophy of history. Neither, by the way, is there *necessarily* anything progressive in a 'materialist' one. At any rate, these issues are still open to debate at the deepest philosophical level and we must touch upon them again at the and of this chapter; but this need not prevent, or hold up, our exposition of Marx's 'materialism' *as if it were* a completely valid *opposite* to the system of Hegel.

It is necessary, now, to look with care at specific aspects of this in order to see all the elements of Marx's position, and, especially, to see where the ambiguities, superficialities, and profundities show their several faces.

(*a*) *The over-turning of Hegel*

It is perfectly clear that Marx himself, Engels, and all who followed, regarded the position of 'Dialectical Materialism' as a complete reversal of Hegel. Marx wrote, in the preface to the second edition of *Capital* :

'My dialectic is not only different from the Hegelian, but is its direct opposite. To Hegel, the life-process of the human brain, i.e., the process of thinking, which, under the name of "the Idea", he even transforms into an independent subject, is the demiurgos of the real world, and the *real* world is only the *external, phenomenal form of* "the Idea". With me, on the contrary, the ideal is nothing else than the material world *reflected* by the human mind, and translated into forms of thought.

The italics in this passage are mine, and seek to emphasize firstly, the superficial conception of Hegel which we have noted earlier, and secondly—an important point to which we shall return—Marx's quite definite conception that the human mind *reflects* the material world, which is itself *real.* This too, of course, is a philosophically superficial and unwarranted position.

At the same time, we must notice that Marx did not *reject* Hegel, as did many critics of the time. On the contrary, he defended him against those who, as he put it, treated Hegel as 'a dead dog'. Though he *reversed* Hegel's 'Idealism', he nonetheless upheld and praised the 'dialectical' conception of nature and history—the conception of all the elements of nature and history as parts of a vast, interdependent, conflictful, developmental *process* of things—which Hegel had put forward and examined so systematically. In opposition to the totally destructive critics, he wrote :

'I therefore openly drowed myself the pupil of that mighty thinker, and even here and there. . coquetted with the modes of expression peculiar to him. The mystification which dialectic suffers in Hegel's hands, by no means prevents him from being the first to present its general form of working in a comprehensive and conscious manner. With him it is standing on its head. It must be turned right side up again, if you would discover the rational kernel within the mystical shell.

There is no lack of clarity here. The 'dialectical' conception was retained, but its 'Idealist' basis was rejected. Reality was *material* reality, and out of *this* had all secondary qualities of life and mind emerged; by *this* were all qualities of life and mind determined. To see the clear, didactic way in which this position came to be held, it is interesting to note the statement of Stalin.

'Contrary to idealism, which regards the world as the

embodiment of an "absolute idea", a "universal spirit", "consciousness" . . . Marx's philosophical materialism holds that the world is by its very nature *material*, that the multifold phenomena of the world constitute different forms of matter in motion, that interconnection and interdependence of phenomena . . . are a law of the development of moving matter, and that the world develops in accordance with the laws of movement of matter and stands in no need of a "universal spirit"... '

It is when one comes to consider in detail the actual nature and processes of '*material reality*' and the ways in which it is thought to be causally '*determining*' of the nature and content of mind that difficulties and ambiguities arise.

(*b*) *Materialism: Matter and Mind*

It seems, to my mind, completely correct and fair, despite qualifications which were made later in their thinking, to say that the position of Marx and Engels was quite emphatically that the material processes of nature constitute the objective reality of the world, and that mind—in all its forms—is, and remains, as 'reflection' of this; and is '*determined*' by it. Indeed, I want to show, at the outcome of our argument, that if this position is qualified to the extent that they later wished to qualify it, it ceases to be distinctive theory of 'materialism' in the radical sense that they claimed.

Matter is the primary reality, and it brings into being, and determines the nature and changing content of mind. For any satisfactory explanation of any events in nature, we must look for the causal factors in material reality. Mind is always secondary and dependent; a reflection of this. This was the definite and undeniable position of Marx and his followers.

We have already seen his own words :

'With me, the ideal is *nothing else* than the material world *reflected* in the human mind, and *translated* into forms of thought.'

Similarly, though I do not want to introduce too much, as yet, the consideration of the *material reality of society*, Marx also wrote :

'The mode of production in *material* life *determines* the social, political and intellectual life processes in general. It is not the consciousness of men that determine their being but, on the contrary, their social being that *determines* their consciousness'.

These are completely definite statements, and they were much reiterated in varying forms and emphases throughout the writing of Marx. Engels, as always, was much more pedantic, and very specific indeed.

The real unity of the world, 'he wrote, consists in its materiality. . .'

'. . . the material, sensuously perceptible world to which we ourselves belong is the only reality; and our consciousness and thinking, however suprasensuous they may seem, are a product of a material, bodily organ, the brain. Matter is not a product of mind, but mind itself is merely the highest product of matter.'

' . . . the dialectic concept of the concept itself becomes merely the *conscious reflex* of the dialectical motion of the *real* world, and the dialectic of Hegel is placed upon its head. . .'

'*It is impossible to separate thought from matter that thinks*. This matter is the substratum of all changes going on in the world. . .

Again, there can be no doubt about this position. In attacking the 'Idealist' emphasis upon the *primacy* of mind, it was thought necessary to demote the role of mind in nature, and to insist upon the primacy, the totally dominant determining powers, the reality, of *matter*. Both Marx and Engels emphasized too, that all the 'theoretical outlooks' of men were 'derived from their material conditions'.

'Does it require deep intuition,' they wrote in the Communist Manifesto, 'to comprehend that man's ideas, views and conceptions, in one word, man's consciousness, changes with every change in the conditions of his material existence. . .?'

No, one might reply, but is requires a good deal more than deep intuition, and something much more susceptible to test, to demonstrate that it is always the latter that *determines* the former; and that only the latter is *real*, whist the former is no more than a '*reflection*' of it. It is apparent at once where ambiguities rush in upon a position of this kind. For though it *may* be plausible to reject an 'Idealist' metaphysic, and though it *may* be plausible to argue that mind has emerged in the world in the context of prior material processes, and remains to some extent constrained by them, it does *not* follow that mind is totally subservient to them, determined by them, or ineffective in 'causing' change. Neither does it follow that mind is, in any sense, less 'real' than matter. It may be that protoplasm emerged in the world *after* atoms and molecules, but no-one would say it was 'less real' than they : it is one quality of the world as we are aware of it, and so are aspects, efforts, purposes, and powers of mind. To replace 'Idealism' by 'Materialism' in the sense stated above, is no more than to *assert* one metaphysic against another.

Again, to see the extent of the solidifying of this metaphysic, we might look briefly at the culminating statements of followers such as Lenin and Stalin. Lenin, for example wrote:

'Materialism in general recognizes objectively real being (matter) as independent of consciousness, sensation, experience. . . Consciousness is only the reflection of being, at best, an approximately true (adequate, ideally exact) reflection of it.*

And :

'Matter is that which, acting upon our sense-organs, produces sensation; matter is the objective reality given to us in sensation. . . Matter, nature, being, the physical—is primary, and spirit, consciousness, sensation, the psychical—is secondary.'

Stalin, with his methodical precision and care, wrote as follows :

'Contrary to idealism, which asserts that only our mind really exists, and that the material world, being, nature, exists only in our mind, in our sensations, ideas and perceptions, the Marxist materialist philosophy holds that matter, nature, being is an objective reality existing outside and independent of our mind; that matter is primary, since it is the source of sensations, ideas, mind, and that mind is secondary, derivative, since it is a reflection of matter, a reflection of being; that thought is a product of matter which in its development has reached a high degree of perfection, namely, of the brain, and the brain is the organ of thought; and that therefore one cannot separate thought from matter without committing a grave error.'

We have noted the ambiguity attending this question of what is, or is not, *real,* and the 'determining' powers of matter, and all that need be said further, here, is that the great importance of realizing these ambiguities will be seen when we come to consider their place in theories about 'Historical Materialism'. They are far from being philosophical, or conceptual issues alone, but lie at the heart of our assessment of Marx's sociology. Before leaving this initial aspect of 'materialism', however, one other point must be emphasized strongly—and this refers to a 'trivial' or 'profound' interpretation of Marx, even though it is, again, but a pointing out of indefiniteness and ambiguity. It is this.

It seems to me true to say that Marx himself always wrote with a broader, richer, vision of things before him than many of the rather narrow, repetitive, parrot-like systematizers who came after him; who rode to prominence and power on his philosophical band-wagon. It is easy to see how 'matter' and 'mind' can be juxtaposed in the most simple-minded of ways, following from the above kinds of statement, and how a naive notion of material 'determinism' can be stated, criticized and totally rejected. And this may be a valid criticism of many Marxists. Marx himself, however, never wrote in quite such naked terms. By and large, Marx did not oppose 'matter' and 'mind' — which, for him would be 'abstractions'; but really thought always of man being involved in practical, sensuous, creative activities *in nature*; and thought of man's 'feeling', 'thinking', 'theorizing' as always being concomitant with these activities—arising in and from them, serving them, and being tested in their application. It was really 'man creatively active in nature; suffering the constraints of material circumstances in nature and society; but coming ultimately to govern them and direct them in the light of knowledge and with the effective power of industrial technology', and this gives very different picture, allowing for a full appreciation of all the qualitative richness of nature; the qualitative richness of 'material reality'. It is also less doctrinaire in its dogmatism. Marx, for example, wrote in this way :

'The worker can create nothing without *nature*, without the *sensuous external world.* It is the material on which his labour is manifested, in which it is active, from which and by means of which it produces. . . '

To say that : '. . . Man *lives* on nature—means that nature is his *body,* with which he must remain in continuous intercourse if he is not to die. That man's physical and spiritual life is linked to nature means simply that nature is linked to itself, for man is a part of nature.'

It is at least obvious, and this is all we need note for now, that an account of man's creative activity in nature, and an account of the historical making of societies and of systems of thought, belief, and artistic imagination which are significantly related to this activity is a much richer and more acceptable programme of description, analysis, and explanation, than a simple 'matter-versus mind' determinism. And this must be borne in mind. Some insights and dimensions of Marx may be more true and important than some criticism of the determinism which can be constructed from his statements would seem to suggest. And yet we must note that this, even so, is really a defence of profundity in terms of ambiguity—which is an odd kind of defence, and really leads to nothing firm. For it means, really, that in so far as Marx can be interpreted as asserting a metaphysic of narrow 'materialistic determinism' he can be shown to be philosophically shallow; but in so far as he can be interpreted as possessing insights of profundity, he can be shown *not* to be putting forward a tight 'materialism' at all. The problems of deciding upon 'superficial' or 'profound' interpretations, and the ambiguities which vex any attempt at fair and correct judgment, begin to swarm about us !

So much, at any rate, for materialism and its emphasis upon the 'determinism' mind by material reality.

(c) Dialectical Materialism : contrary to 'Metaphysics'

One other claim made on behalf of dialectical Materialism by Marx, Engels and their followers which contains ambiguity, and should be seen clearly, was that it is somehow (by insisting upon the basic reality of material processes) contradictory to, and an advance upon, 'metaphysics'.

Thus, when writing of the application of (Hegel's) dialectics to the 'materialist conception of nature', Engels maintained that :

'. . .modern natural science . . .has proved that in the last analysis nature's process is *dialectical* and not *metaphysical.*'

We need not dwell on this point since it is so obvious an error, but, again, to emphasize how far the error has gone in doctrinaire expositions, let us briefly note some of the repeated statements of Stalin :

'Dialectics is the direct opposite of metaphysics.

'Contrary to metaphysics, dialectics does not regard nature as an accidental agglomeration of things... unconnected with, isolated from, and independent of each other, but as a connected and integral whole...

'Contrary to metaphysics, dialectics holds that nature is not a state of rest and immobility, stagnation and immutability, but a state of continuous movement and change...

'Contrary to metaphysics, dialectics does not regard the process of development as a simple process of growth...'

And so—on and on. In this way of arguing (if that is the right word) something called 'metaphysics' is derogated as a kind of musty old lumber-room full of old ideas of 'reality' as being 'static', 'stagnant', 'accidental', isolated collections of objects', and the like, whereas dialectical materialism' shines by its side as all that is scientific, seeing 'reality' as a rich, ceaselessly changing, growing, progressive process of things.

But this, of course, is completely misguided. 'Metaphysical' theories (which are about the nature of 'reality)' as distinct from scientific theories (which are about the testable interconnections among facts of our experience) do *not* necessarily assert 'static' accounts of 'discrete, isolated objects, etc. *Some* metaphysical theories might, but certainly not all; and the term 'metaphysical' is certainly not to be *equated* with the holding of such notions. But also —Dialectical Materialism *is itself* a theory of reality; indeed, a very pugnacious one, attacking the 'Idealist' account of 'reality' and seeking to replace it very definitely with another. There must, then, be no doubt or confusion whatever about this. 'Dialectical Materialism' was a new *Metaphysical theory;* and it will be important to see that its supposed *'scientific theories* of society' are in large part no more than an assertive insistence upon the adoption of *this* metaphysic rather than others.

We are clear, then, about 'Materialism' as a new, ambiguous metaphysic; but we have come to use the adjective 'dialectical'. What, exactly, was meant by this? And why, and in what ways, was it thought to be an 'advance' ?

(*d*) *Materialism : Dialectics*

Dialectical materialism was distinguished from what Marx

and Engels called the 'Old' Materialism by two important characteristics, both of which were held to imply fundamental differences in what constituted scientific 'explanations' of events in nature and history. These two features were therefore new features of *method,* as well as new conceptions of the nature of reality. First—Dialectical Materialism regarded all the 'entities' or 'events' of the world *not* as disparate, concrete 'things', existing in a set of eternal, external, spatial relations to each other, but as mutually interpenetrating and interdependent parts of one vast, continuous process. Objects (and their 'distinctive natures') could only be understood in their close interdependence with surrounding objects, and, essentially, as part of an all-pervading process, in continuous interaction and change. Second—Dialectical Materialism specified the nature, the determinate characteristics, *of this process of change;* it was, in fact, a process in which sequences of *additive, quantitative* change gave rise, at certain specific 'nodal' points to *qualitatively* new forms of reality. These two features taken together, however, led to a third point which I wish especially to emphasize : namely that Dialectical Materialism was, in fact, a materialistically based *theory of evolution* : scarcely distinguishable from that of Spencer. Its claims to be distinctive in this respect were, as we shall see, unfounded. It was, in fact, one expression among others of the nineteenth century evolutionary perspective. It also contained exactly the same ambiguities concerning 'evolution' and 'progress'.

The new insistence which was placed upon *process* has already been noted in the fact that Marx, whilst rejecting Hegel's 'idealistic' basis, nonetheless accepted his 'dialectics' as being a reorientation of the greatest importance. The same emphasis is to be found in all the expositions of Engels.

'What distinguished Hegel's mode of thought,' he wrote, 'from that of all other philosophers was the enormous *historical sense* upon which it was based . . .

'He was the first who attempted to show an *evolution*, an *inner coherence* in history. . .

'This epoch-making conception of history was the direct theoretical prerequisite for the new materialistic contemplation. . .

The fundamental contribution which Marx and he had

made in 'rescuing' Hegel's dialectical conception and applying it to the materialist conception of nature, was, claimed Engels :

'The great basic thought that the world is not to be comprehended as a complex of ready-made *things,* but as a complex of *processes*, in which the things apparently stable no less than the mind-images in our heads, the concepts, go through an uninterrupted change of coming into being and passing away, in which, in spite of all seeming accidents and of all temporary retrogression, a progressive development asserts itself in the end. . .'

And in this dialectical conception of materialism, he maintained :

'. . . nothing is final, absolute, sacred. It reveals the transitory character of everything and in everything; nothing can endure before it except the uninterrupted process of becoming and of passing away, of endless ascendancy from the lower to the higher.'

This, it is very clear, is almost exactly the endless process of 'transformation of forms' put forward by Spencer; and the terms 'progressive development', 'endless ascendancy' from 'lower to higher' make the implicit *evaluative* element in Engels' conception clear beyond all doubt. In order to make this identity (I do not think this is too strong a word) between Engels and Spencer meticulously clear, we might look at the statement which Engels made when trying to emphasize the difference between 'dialectical' and 'old' materialism by insisting that *matter* simply could not be conceived independently of *process, of motion.* In *Anti-Duhring,* he wrote :

'*Motion is the mode of existence of matter.* Never anywhere has there been matter without motion, nor can there be. Motion in cosmic space, mechanical motion of smaller masses on the various celestial bodies, the motion of molecules as heat or as electrical or magnetic currents, chemical combination or disintegration, organic life—at each given moment each individual atom of matter in the world is in one or other of these forms of motion, or in several forms of them at once. All rest, all equilibrium, is only relative, and only has meaning in relation to one or other definite form of motion. A body, for example, may be on the ground in mechanical equilibrium, may be mechanically at rest; but this in no way prevents it from participating in the motion of the earth and in that of the whole solar system, just as little as it prevents its most minute physical parts from carrying out the oscillations determined by its temperature, or its atoms from passing through a chemical process. Matter without motion is just as unthinkable as motion without matter. Motion is therefore as uncreatable and indestructible as matter itself; as the older philosophy expressed it, the quantity of motion existing in the world is always the same. Motion therefore cannot be created; it can only be transferred.'

The first distinctive feature of 'Dialectical Materialism'—the insistence on a perspective of *interdependence* and process—is therefore very clear, and we shall emphasize again, later, that this was, in fact, the nineteenth century theory and perspective of 'evolution'. The second feature, however—the 'quantitative-qualitative' process of change in material reality—is even more important for our critical assessment of Marx's theory of nature and society. And it is important to insist that this central conception of the transformation of 'quantity' into 'qualitative difference' was, in fact, held by Marx himself (not only by Engels) and did, in fact, constitute a basic principle of analysis and explanation in all his work. It is sometimes held that it was the *followers of* Marx, rather than Marx himself, who made much of this conception, and this principle of explanation, and it is true that Engels (and later Lenin and Stalin) articulated it much more pedantically than he did. Still—he stated, accepted, and adopted it fully himself, and his system is based upon it, and open to criticism in terms of it.

In fact, Marx derived the conception from Hegel—that, in nature and history, additive elements of a *quantitative* nature reached certain 'nodal points' at which they became *qualitatively* newly emergent substances, forms, entities. The *essential* nature of change and creation in material reality was this emergence and unfolding of qualitative difference, out of cumulative quantitative change. And in *Capital* Marx wrote of social transformations of this kind, and also referred to the same kinds and sequences of change as uncovered in the molecular theory of chemistry.

It was Engels, however, who—in his *Dialectics of Nature* and his polemics against Herr Dühring—amassed examples to illustrate these 'quantitative-qualitative' dialectical process, and it is most important to see these examples clearly and to see the mode of explanation which they clearly imply, and insist upon.

In the *Dialectics of Nature,* Engels wrote :

'In physics. . . every change is a passing of quantity into quality, as a result of a quantitative change of some form of movement either inherent in a body or imparted to it. For example, the temperature of water has at first no effect on its liquid state : but as the temperature of liquid water rises or falls, a moment arrives when this state of cohesion changes and the water is converted in one case into steam and in the other into ice. . . A definite minimum current is required to make a platinum wire glow; every metal has its melting temperature; every liquid has a definite freezing point and boiling point at a given pressure, as far as we are able with the means at our disposal to attain the required temperatures; finally, every gas has its critical point at which, by proper pressure and cooling, it can be converted into a liquid state. . . What are known as the constants of physics are in most cases nothing but designations for the nodal points at which a quantitative (change) increase or decrease of movement causes a qualitative change in the state of the given body, and at which, consequently, quantity is transformed into quality.

And in *Anti-Dühring :*

'This is precisely the Hegelian nodal line of measure relations, in which, at certain definite nodal points, the purely quantitative increase or decrease gives rise to a *qualitative leap,* for example, in the case of water which is heated or cooled, where boiling-point and freezing-point are the nodes at which—under normal pressure—the leap to a new aggregate state takes place, and where consequently quantity is transformed into quality.'

In *Anti -Dühring,* too, Engels gave examples of a number of acids—formic acid, acetic acid, propionic acid, butyric acid, and valerianic acid—which, he showed, constituted :

'. . . a whole series of *qualitatively* different bodies, formed by the simple *quantitative* addition of elements and in fact always in the same proportion. . . Each new member comes into existence through the addition of one atom of carbon and two atoms of hydrogen, to the molecular formula of the preceding member, this *quantitative* change in molecular compostion produces at each step a *qualitatively* different body.'*

Again, to see how firmly this doctrine of conception and explanation came to be laid down, let us see how Stalin framed it :

'Dialectics,' he wrote, 'does not regard the process of development as a simple process of growth, but as a development which passes from insignificant and imperceptible quantitative changes to open, fundamental changes, to qualitative changes; a development in which the qualitative changes occur not gradually, but rapidly and abruptly, taking the form of a leap from one state to another; they occur not accidentally but as the natural result of an accumulation of imperceptible and gradual quantitative changes.'

This conception, and this principle of explanation in 'Dialectical Materialism' are undeniably clear. Material reality is primary; qualities of life and mind are dependent, and secondary. All particular elements or aspects of material reality can only be understood and explained as interdependent parts of a continuous process of transformation and change. And in this process, change is brought about by a sequence of cumulative, additive, quantitative changes which, at certain points, undergo, or manifest a 'qualitative leap' to a newly emergent entity. The explanations of 'Dialectical Materialism' rest upon the fundamental foundation of this conception.

Here, we will not stop to enter into criticism, but move forward to see some other ways in which this 'Dialectical Materialism' was thought to constitute an advance.

(e) Materialism: Dialectics an advance on 'Old' Materialism

We have already noted, in passing, the ways in which 'dialectics' was thought to have surpassed the 'old' materialism, but, for the sake of precision, let us simply note that there were *three* or these. First, the 'old' materialism was thought to be 'mechanistic', whereas the new conception saw reality as a complex, interwoven process. Second, the 'old' materialism had a 'static', 'eternal', frame of reference (the 'metaphysical' conception) whereas the new perspective was one of dialectical, quantita-tive-qualitative change, essentially historical and develop-mental, and, as Lenin put it later, applied 'the standpoint of evolution consistently and all-sidedly'. Third, the 'old' materia-lism conceived of men still in 'abstract' terms, and focused its efforts upon 'understanding' and '*interpreting*' the world, whereas the new conception saw historical man in his essentially practical activities, and focused its efforts upon '*changing*' the world.

We need not note again the ambiguities attending some of these points. The other claims for the *advancement* over earlier theories of 'dialectics' are more interesting.

(f) Materialism: dialectics an advanced Theory of Evolution

Already, we have seen, and have argued, that the Marx-Engels formulation of 'Dialectical materialism' was, in fact, a Spencerian theory of evolution in (in many respects) scarcely distinguishable terms. But it is worthwhile to note quite specifically that this is how followers of Marx themselves came to regard it. Indeed, this is what they insisted on claiming for it. The best example, after Engels, was Lenin, who wrote as follows :

'In our times, the idea of development, of evolution, has almost fully penetrated social consciousness, but it has done so in other ways, not through Hegel's philosophy. But the same idea, as formulated by Marx and Engels on the basis of Hegel's philosophy, is much more comprehensive, much more abundant in content than the current theory of evolution. A development that repeats, as it were, the stages already passed but repeats them in a different way, on a higher plane; a development, so to speak in spirals, not in a straight line; a spasmodic, catastrophic, revolutionary development; "breaks of gradualness"; transformation of quantity into quality; inner impulses for development, imparted by the contradiction, the conflict of different forces and tendencies reacting on a given body or inside a given phenomenon or within a given society; interdependence, and the closest, indissoluble connection between all sides of every phenomenon (history disclosing ever newer and newer sides); a connection that provides the one world-process of motion proceeding according to law—such are some of the features of dialectics as a doctrine of evolution more full of meaning than the current one.'

This, with absolute clarity, claims not only that. 'Dialectical Materialism' Is a theory of evolution, but that it is a *better*, more thorough, more comprehensive, theory of evolution than others of the time. But, equally clearly, it speaks in almost complete ignorance of the evolutionary theories of men like comte and (especially) Spencer which were, in many ways, very similar. As I have said earlier, I want to emphasize this very strongly because, on the one hand, many recent critics have tended to deplore the insufficiencies of 'evolutionary' theories, and have held up Marxism as a 'revolutionary' theory which has sharper explanatory 'teeth', so to speak. And they do not seem to realise that Marxism was, and is, one 'revolutionary' theory among others. But also, on the other hand, 'Dialectical Materialism' has come to be thought, by many, quite a unique, startlingly new outlook of 'process and change', and quite a distinctive basis for the making of satisfactory sociology—different from all others. And this, of course, is simply untrue, and cannot be upheld for a moment. 'Dialectical Materialism' is not distinctively different from the evolutionary perspective of Spencer *expect* that it asserts, within—indeed, in the heart of—this context, a materialist, quantitative–qualitative metaphysic and dogma. And this turns out to be its most vulnerable, indeed its insupportable, component.

(g) *Materialism : Dialectics an advanced Social (as well as Natural) Science*

Finally, we may simply note that one claim made on behalf of 'Dialectical Materialism' was that it provided a completely new basis and perspective for the creation and development of a 'science of society' which was an improvement on anything achieved before. Lenin has stated this claim very clearly, but all 'Marxists', from Marx and Engels to the present day, have shared it. In his encyclopedia article on 'Karl Marx', Lenin wrote :

'*At best*, pre-Marxist "sociology" and historiography gave an accumulation of raw facts collected at random, and a description of separate sides of the historic process. Examining the *totality* of all the opposing tendencies, reducing them to precisely definable conditions in the mode of life and the method of production of the various *classes* of society, discarding subjectivism and arbitrariness in the choice of various "leading" ideas or in their interpretation, showing how all the ideas and all the various tendencies, without exception, have their roots in the condition of the material forces of production, Marxism pointed the way to a comprehensive, an all-embracing study of the rise, development, and decay of social economic structures.'

Though one would agree that it was an improvement in the scientific approach to the study of society of study 'all sides' of the historic process, the 'totality' of social facts in their interdependence, and the like, it is, of course quite false to think that pre-Marxist 'sociology', and historiography ignored these things. The outlook of 'Dialectical Materialism' was simply *not* new in these respects at all. What it *could* claim was to have laid specific emphasis upon the primacy of *material* conditions in nature and society. Even here, it was not new in being 'materialistic'; it was new and different only in specifying the quantitative-qualitative process of change, and the primacy in this cause and effect determinacy of the *material* facts.

So much, then, for 'Dialectical Materialism' as a conceptual approach to the analysis of, and statement of theories about '*Nature*'. For Marx and his followers, the 'World Spirit' was totally removed from the scheme of things and from the apparatus of explanation. The entirety of 'Nature' was a *material* process which changed in accordance with quantitative additions and accumulations, and qualitative 'leaps', and which was simply '*reflected*' in the emergent processes of life and mind.

The most interesting matter, from our point of view, is the way in which this clear 'analytical apparatus' of Dialectical Materialism then came to be applied to the study of society and history—thereby coming to be called 'Historical Materialism'. This, especially, was the contribution of Marx to the making of sociology, and we are now completely ready both to state this theory and to achieve a critical assessment of it. In this section especially, I want first of all, to confine myself to the fairest *exposition* of Marx's theory, and, only secondly, after this, to come to a scrupulous *criticism* of it. Before launching into this, however, one point must be made. In Marx himself, of course, there was, strictly speaking, no distinction between 'Dialectical Materialism' and 'Historical Materialism'. It was one of Marx's major emphases that man was a part of nature; that human society was developmental outcome of the material activity of man in nature; and that the history of society was a determinate sequence of these material activities and the institutional fabric built about them. So this must be borne in mind. It is really, again, the Marxian *'expositors'* — Engels, Lenin, Stalin, who clarify *firstly* 'Dialectical Materialism' as a system of conceiving and explaining the world ('nature'), and then *secondly* 'Historical Materialism' as a system of conceiving and explaining society and its development. However, in my opinion, this 'pedagogic' dichotomy has, in fact, done a great service, because, in trying to be meticulously clear, it has meticulously clarified the *analogies* which, in Marx, are taken to be real *identities* (e.g., between the material aspects (basis) of natural processes, and the 'material conditions' of society; between the 'quantitative' addition of molecules in the changes of nature, and the 'quantitative' additions of technological inexactitudes (ambiguities) which lead, in my view, to theoretical—and even descriptive and analytical—falsity. All this may well sound unnecessarily complex, but I do not think it is. These ghosts really do need laying, and I want to do my best to lay them.

Let us move then, to Marx's theory of society, his 'Historical Materialism' and let us work through his argument systematically both in order to be exact in our understanding of it, and to make clear all those components of analysis and theory which are common to those other theoretical positions we have considered so far.

Historical Materialism

(a) As matter is the primary objective reality in Nature, so Man's relations to the material world, Man's material con-ditions of life, are the primary objective reality in Society.

This was the first major principle of the application of 'Dia-lectical Materialism' to the scientific study of society, and there were really two aspects of it—not, strictly speaking, identical with each other—which are emphasized by Marx and Engels.

The first of these was a stated priority of need : that man had, of necessity, to sustain himself economically, to win a livelihood from the material resources of nature, and so survive—before he could devote himself to 'secondary' social experiences and activities : religion, art, family organization and the like. In his speech at Marx's graveside, Engels said :

'Marx discovered the law of evolution in human history; he discovered the simple fact, hitherto concealed by an overgrowth of ideology, that mankind must first of all eat and drink, have shelter and clothing, before it can pursue politics, science, religion, art, etc.; and that therefore the production of the immediate material means of subsistence and consequently the degree of the economic development attained by a given people or during a given epoch, form the foundation upon which the state institutions, the legal conceptions, the art and even the religious ideas of the people concerned have been evolved, and in the light of which these things must therefore be explained, instead of *vice versa* as had hitherto been the case.'

Also, the same point was emphasized in Engels' biographical note on Marx :

'History was for the first time placed on its real basis; the obvious but previously totally overlooked fact that men must first of all eat, drink, have clothing and shelter, therefore must *work,* before they can fight for domination, pursue politics, religion, philosophy, etc.'

This, strictly speaking, was simply a statement of historical *order*; of temporal *sequence* : that the wresting of livelihood from the material resources of nature had to come *before* the development of the more complex fabric of social organization.

The second aspect of this point was distinctively different, though it might be said to be inclusive of it. It was that, quite apart from historical sequence alone, it could be shown to be *always* the case in society that man's practical activity in making products from the material resources of nature formed a basic set of social and (especially) property relations which *determined* the nature of all the other institutions of law, government, religion, education, etc.—which came into being to serve its particular pattern of interests and power. In this sense, man's practical relations with the material world were the *primary*, *objective* reality in society, and all other institutions were *secondary reflections* of it; the former constituted the *material basis* of society, the latter—the '*super-structure*' of institutions.

Marx wrote that when criticizing Hegel's philosophy of law, he was driven to the conclusion :

'. . .that legal relations such as forms of the state are to be grasped neither from themselves nor from the so-called general development of the human mind, but rather have their roots *in the material conditions of life*. . . the anatomy of civil society is to be sought in *political economy*.

Also, in he first volume of *Capital*, he insisted :

'*Technology* discloses man's mode of dealing with nature, the process of production by which he sustains his life, and thereby also lays bare the mode of formation of his social relations, and of the mental conceptions that flow from them.

But here it is best to look carefully through Marx's own 'classical' statement of his theory—because it contains, both implicitly and explicitly, practically all the elements which we shall want to draw out, examine, and emphasize as separate points.

'In the social production which men carry on they enter into definite relations that are indispensable and independent of their will; these relations of production correspond to a definite stage of development of their material forces of production. The sum total of these relations of production constitutes the economic structure of society—the real foundation, on which rises a legal and political superstructure and to which correspond definite forms of social consciousness. The mode of production in material life determines the social, political and intellectual life processes in general. It is not the consciousness of men that determines their being, but, on the contrary, their social being that determines their consciousness. At a certain stage of their development, the material forces of production in society come in conflict with the existing relations of production, or—what is but a legal expression for the same thing—with the property relations within which they have been at work before. From forms of development of the forces of production these relations turn into their fetters. Then begins an epoch of social revolution. With the change of the economic foundation the entire immense super-structure is more or less rapidly transformed.

In considering such transformations distinction should always be made between the material transformation of the economic conditions of production which can be determined with the precision of natural science, and the legal, political, religious, aesthetic or philosophic—in short, ideological forms in which men become conscious of this conflict and fight it out. Just as our opinion of an individual is not based on what he thinks of himself, so can we not judge of such a period of transformation by its own consciousness; on the contrary this consciousness must be explained rather from the contradictions of material iife, from the existing conflict between the social forces of production and the relations of production. No social order ever disappears before all the productive forces for which there is room in it have been developed; and new higher relations of production never appear before the material conditions of their existence have matured in the womb of the old society itself. Therefore, mankind always sets itself only such tasks as it can solve; since, looking at the matter more closely, we will always find that the task itself arises only when the material conditions necessary for its solution already exist or are at least in the process of formation.

In broad outlines we can designate the Asiatic, the ancient, the feudal, and the modern bourgeois modes of production as so many epochs in the progress of the economic formation of society. The bourgeois relations of production are the last antagonistic form of the social process of production—antagonistic not in the sense of individual antagonism, but of one arising from the social conditions of life of the individuals; at the same time the productive forces developing in the womb of bourgeoise society create the material conditions for the solution of that antagonism. This social formation constitutes, therefore, the closing chapter of the prehistoric stage of human society.

In this statement it is perfectly clear that the materialist basis of society was held to determine all other 'secondary' qualities of it, and that the dialectical process of change in the history of society, as in nature, was one accumulative quantitative additions in the material basis of society, accompanied, at certain points, by 'qualitative leaps'—revolutionary transformations—to new 'super-structures' of institutions. Each of the components of this theory must now be separately stated.

(b) Man's practical relations with the material world are man's 'economic' relations. The economic structure is the material basis of society

This is a distinctive step of argument which is not always made clear in Marx's theory. To speak of man's sensuous practical activity in nature, or man's relations to the material world, is *one* thing; to equate all this with man's *'economic'* relations; the 'forces of production'; and then to claim that the nature of the *latter* determines all the dimensions of the *former*—is quite definitely another; but in Marx these are not at all distinguished. We shall come back to a criticism of this point later, but here it is enough to note and emphasize that the '*primacy of material reality*' in nature maintained by dialectical materialism, is, in its application in 'Historical Materialism' interpreted as the principle that, *in society, men's relations to the material world are the primary reality which determines all the rest*; and, further, that these relations to the material world are men's *economic* relations.

Marx treated the two terms—'material' and 'economic'—as being synonymous. Thus, in a letter to Annenkov, he wrote, concerning the 'social history of men' :

'Their *material relations* are the basis of all *their relations*.'

And in the first paragraph of the last quotation, he maintained that the sum-total of the 'definite relations' of 'social production' :

'. . .constitutes the *economic structure* of society—the *real foundation,* on which rises a legal and political super-structure... '

Men's material relations with each other and with the material world were clearly identified with the *economic* structure of society—which was the material basis; the real foundation; which determined all the institutions of the super-structure. And this material, 'economic' basis of society consisted, according to Marx, of the *'forces of production'*.

(c) The Economic Structure of Society : The 'Productive Forces' ***By the 'material forces of production', Marx meant a number of specific and closely related things.***

(I) PRODUCTS, AND INSTRUMENTS OF PRODUCTION

In working upon the material resources of nature to satisfy their needs, men created material products (houses, roads, vehicles, 'commodities') which formed a material basis of regulated social life. These products were a material embodiment, a material 'objectification' of the social labour of the population in a community, and , as members of the community, men had to be related in some regulated way to them. Also, in working upon their material environment, men developed certain *'instruments'* or *'means'* of production; a certain technology which was of a definite material nature at any given period in society. The energy and activities of men in working upon nature were always 'patterned' or 'channelled' through this technology. The *products* of a communal labour and the *means* of production therefore constituted a fundamental material basis of society.

(II) THE RELATIONS OF MEN TO THEIR PRODUCTS AND INSTRUMENTS OF PRODUCTION

This definite nature of the products and the instruments of production in society meant, also, equally definite ways in which *men were related to them.* The making and distribution of *products* meant some necessary *'property relations'* among men. The existence of definite *means of productions* meant that men must be related to these means of production in definite ways : again, in certain *'property relations'*, but also in a specified *'division of labour'*. The members of a small community of Bushmen in the material conditions of the Kalahari Desert with limited techniques for seeking water and such sources of food as were available; the Lord of a medieval village and the peasants who worked the land with limited techniques of farming; the Manager, administrative staff and colliers who operated a modern coal-mine, with specific techniques of mining; would obviously all have a different set of relations to their material conditions and means of production. The distinctive division of work; the distinctive regulations of property; would be related to the technical apparatus of the society.

The Definite Relations of men to their products and means of production in any social and historical situation were held to be a corollary of, to be concomitant with, the material products and techniques themselves; and they patterned the material activi-ties and energies of men into certain, determinate forms. The relations of men to their products and means of production were therefore a determinate part of the material 'productive forces'.

(III) THE RELATIONS OF MEN TO EACH OTHER : SOCIAL CLASSES

Since men were related to their products and means of production in determinate ways, it followed, of necessity, that they were related to each other in definite ways. In their division of labour and in their property relations—in short, in their relations to the means of production—men held definite positions: of power or lack of power; of status or lack of status; of property lack of property. Men sharing the same positions in this economic order would also share an identity of interests. The relations of men to the means of production led directly to the formation of *class relations*, and to *class conflict.* The 'social being of men determines their consciousness', Marx claimed, and therefore the different interests which arose from being differently placed in relation to the means of production, gave rise to *'class consciousness'*.

On the basis of their material products and means of production, then, men came to have determinate class relations to these means of production, and thus to have determinate class relations. A system of social classes was established as a necessary concomitant of each system of technology (each 'economic system'); and this system of classes was therefore a part of the 'productive forces' of society; a part of the material, 'economic' foundation of society.

The material basis of society, then, the primary objective reality forming the foundation of the social order, was the 'economic' structure, consisting of the 'productive forces'—and these consisted of (a) the material products and the means of production, (b) the relations of men to them (the property relations and the organized relations of labour), and (c) the system of social classes. This basic reality then came to be 'reflected' in the 'secondary' superstructure of institutions.

(d) *The 'Super-structure of Social Institutions*

Just as the material reality of nature came to be 'reflected' in the qualities of life and mind which were 'secondary', sc—in 'Historical Materialism'—the material basis of society (its productive forces) came to be 'reflected' in the qualities of a super-structure of institutions. Legal institutions were built upon the fundamental property relations and reflected the interests of social classes. Institutions of marriage and family relationships reflected the nature of personal relationships within the system, and indicated the 'level' of sensitivity reached in such relationship. Religious institutions reflected the material structure of society and sanctified property and the hiearchy of authority in economic relationships. The institutionalization of art, philosophy, education provided an 'ideological' reflection of class interests and a systematization of the 'knowledge' underlying the technical skills and practical degrees of control over nature in society.

That the 'super-structure' of other institutions was regarded as the qualitative reflection of the material, economic basis, subordinate to it in terms of causal determination, was made perfectly clear by Marx and all who followed him.

'The mode of production in material life *determines* the social, political and intellectual life processes in general,' he wrote. 'It is not the consciousness of men that determines their being, but, on the contrary, their social being that determines their consciousness.'

Again :

'. . . the economic structure of society is the *real* foundation, on which rises a legal and political superstructure and to which correspond definite forms of social consciousness.

Engels was equally definite—though we shall consider his qualifications to this later. He quite specifically refers to legal, political, and all 'ideological' institutions and conceptions as being only '*reflexes*' of the material basis of society.

'. . .the jurist imagines he is operating with a principle', he wrote, 'whereas they are *really only economic reflexes. . .*'

In the same letter he wrote of the :

'. . .political, legal and moral reflexes' of the economy.

And in his essay on Ludwig Feuerbach, he also wrote of the 'state' as being :

'. . .only a reflex . . . of the economic needs of the class controlling production. . .'

The same emphasis has continued to be a firm plank of the Marxist position. Lenin, for example, in his essay on the 'Sources and component Parts of Marxism', made this standpoint of Historical Materialism very clear :

'Just as the cognition of man reflects nature (i.e. developing matter) which exists independently of him, so also the *social cognition* of man (i.e. the various views and doctrines—philosophic, religious, political, etc.) reflects the *economic order* of society. Political institutions are a super-structure on the economic foundation.'

This is a perfectly clear example of the application of the persuasions of dialectical materialism to historical materialism.

Before leaving this point, it is worthwhile to remind ourselves that the relations of men in the 'material basis' of society, as part of the 'productive forces' of society, were held by Marx to be :

'. . .*indispensable* and *independent of their will*. . .'

If this is so, and if the qualitative elements of the super-structure are so specifically determined by the material base—then all the qualitative characteristics of the life, mind, and institutions of men in society are held to be completely determined by the material means of production. This is a social determinism resting solely on material products and the technological means of producing them. It is an economic and technological determinism.

(e) The 'State' as the central institution in the 'Super-structure'

It needs to be emphasized, as the next component in the argument, simply that among all the institutions of the super-structure, the 'State' is the one most central and of greatest importance. Indeed, it is , in a sense, the collective embodiment of all the others; or, better, all the others are parts, dimensions, of its whole nature. Thus the law, in all its detail, is centrally upheld in the form of the State. The doctrines, values, and practices of Religion centrally serve the form and stability and sanctity of the State; and so with each major element of the super-structure. But since all these are 'reflections' of the economic basis and the established 'class-system', the State is, crucially, the embodiment of the interests, ideology, values, and power of the ruling class. It is the focal point of all these institutions which reflect, justify, protect, serve, and uphold the existing material basis of society.

Thus, in the Manifesto of the Communist Party, Marx and Engels wrote :

'The executive of the modern state is but a committee for managing the common affairs of the whole bourgeoisie.'

And, again :

'Political power, properly so called, is merely the organized power of one class for oppressing another.'

Engels himself, too, in *The Origin of the Family,* wrote that the State is the organ of :

'. . . the most powerful, economically dominating class that, with the help of this state, becomes also the politically dominating class, and thus acquired a new means of subduing and exploiting the oppressed masses. The ancient state was thus the state of the slave-owners for subduing the slaves, just as the feudal state was the organ of the nobility for subduing the serf-peasants, and as the modern representative state is a tool for the exploitation of wage-labour by capital.'

The State, then, becomes the political organ serving class-domination, and is the central element in the entire super-structure which reflects the economic order, the material base.

(f) A Structural-Functional Model of Society

It will be clearly seen that Marx had outlined, in this analysis, a very clear model of the nature of society, of the 'social system' as a whole, and that this was in 'structural–functional' terms. In Comte's terms, Marx provided a very clear analysis of 'Social Statics' : an analysis of the main elements of a social system and the functional interdependency between them. The clarity of this model might be emphasized with the aid.

After our earlier discussion, I do not think this diagram requires any comment. The main components of the social and their close functional interconnections with each other are luminously clear. Only two brief points may be added.

The first is that Marx himself was quite explicitly aware that he was conceiving 'the social system' as a functionally interdependent set of parts in this way, and had quite clear definitions of the nature of a 'society' in his work. A clear definition of this kind is to be found in his letter to P. V. Annenkov on the nature of Historical Materialism.

'What is society', he wrote, 'whatever its form might be? The product of men's reciprocal action. Are men free to choose this or that form of society for themselves?' By no means. Assume a particular state of development in the productive forces of man and you will get a particular form of commerce and consumption. Assume particular stages of development in production, commerce and consumption and you will have a corresponding social order, a corresponding organization of the family and of the ranks and classes, in a word a corresponding civil society. Presuppose a particular civil society and you will get particular political conditions which are only the official expression of civil society. . .

It is superflous to add that men are not free to choose their *productive forces*—which are the basis of *all* their history.

The structural–functional model of society is perfectly clear in this statement, as also is the conception of 'types' of societies resting on differing stages of development of the productive forces—a separate point to be separately emphasized shortly.

The second point worthy of additional emphasis is that this structural-functional model was outlined by Marx in such a way as especially *to explain the nature of social conflict, social transformation, and social change.* And these aspects of conflict and change were not *contingent or additional*—when looking at actual societies; they were seen as *essential characteristics* of social systems. As with Comte, the model of 'Social Statics' which Marx constructed was such as to lay emphasis upon the fact that human society was *essentially* a historical process; *essentially* a *changing* and *cumulatively* developing process; and that this process was *essentially* a process of *conflict.*

The structural-functional model was one of conflict and change. This point cannot be emphasized too strongly.

(g) The Quantitative-Qualitative Process of Historical Change

This model of society resting upon the material basis of the productive forces was then used to provide an explanation (a 'theory') of social change, and again this was a direct application of Dialectical Materialism to the facts of history. Just as gradual, quantitative additions accumulate in nature, and suddenly give rise to determinate 'qualitative leaps' into new substances or forms, so in history, gradual quantitative additions accumulate within society, suddenly compelling 'revolutionary leaps' to qualitatively new total social systems. The argument of Marx was this.

Since the basic reality of society was its material, economic foundation, the factors making for change were to be sought in these productive forces. Gradually, over a long period, changes were brought about in the means of production . Technological changes occurred. These material changes in the means of production were additive and cumulative. In ways unforeseen by the people who brought them about, however, these many cumulative changes came gradually to *transform* the relations of men to the means of production, and thus their class-relations. The material basis of society became transformed within the ever more constraining system of an old super-structure of institutions. At a certain point however, this old set of institutions could no longer adequately contain, or deal with, the new productive forces and the new class interests they entailed. A 'revolutionary' situation suddenly forced radical changes; the old super-structure was burst asunder and overthrown, and a qualitatively *new* super-structure came into being, adequately reflecting the new material basis.

Several extremely important aspects of this quantitative-qualitative explanation of Historical Materialism need to be separately made clear and emphasized.

(I) Society, And Any Adequate Explanation of It, Essentially Historical

It is important to see that Marx was in agreement with all the other theorists we have considered in his persuasion that *society was essentially a historical process, and that the explanation of it essentially required a historical method.*

Furthermore, Marx clearly insisted that social *development* was a reality that had to be noted and explained. Change was *not* only *subsequent difference,* it was also the cumulative emergence of new *levels* of technical achievements and social organization which *grew* on the basis of past of past achievements and *advanced* beyond them. Marx's theory was, therefore, a theory not only of change, but also of *development* and *progress.*

(II) SOCIAL EVOLUTION

A second important aspect of Historical Materialism is that it was essentially a theory of social *evolution. It* explained the emergence of determinate types and levels of society which *gradually* developed and succeeded each other, and only changed finally into new forms of society when the new material conditions had become so far developed, so thoroughly developed, as to make the old super-structure no longer (in *fact,* not in *moral principle*) tolerable. This too, is a point deserving emphasis , because the stress laid, for political progress, upon the 'revolutionary' point of social change (the climax of social transformation), has been such as to lead some theorists to assert that the Marxian theory was something radically different from evolutionary theories. Stalin is a particularly good example of this.

'If the world is in a state of constant movement and development, if the dying away of the old and the upgrowth of the new is a law of development. . . we must not base our orientation on the strata of society which are no longer developing, even though they at present constitute the predominant force, but on those strata which are developing and have a future before them. . .

'In order not to err in policy, one must look forward, not backward.

'If the passing of slow quantitative changes into rapid and abrupt qualitative changes is a law of development, then it is clear that revolutions made by oppressed classes are quite natural and inevitable phenomenon.

'In order not to err in policy, one must be a *revolutionary,* not a *reformist.'*

The clear identity of the theoretical analysis of 'qualitative leaps' and the political directive of 'revolutionary' commitment could not be plainer; nor could the quite unqualified identity of 'progress' with 'technological advance'.

A much more careful and judicious thinker—Werner Sombart—saw things very differently and insisted that Marx's was a wiser perspective than that of some idealistic socialists *exactly because* he saw 'revolutions' as the culminations of long 'evolutionary' sequences.

'Marx,' he wrote, 'applies the evolution idea to the social movement. Other conspicuous men have tried to consider socialism and the social movement as in the flow of historic life. But no-one has so clearly, illuminatively, effectively shown these historical relations. That political revolutions and agitations are fundamentally great displacements of social classes. . .The idea was decisive that revolutions could not be forced, but were the outgrowth of specific economic antecedents. . .thus for the social movement the idea of "revolution" passes into thought of "evolutions" .'

Sombart also quoted some of the writing of Engels (published shortly before his death as the introduction to *The struggle of Classes in France*) who claimed of those who had tried to force a proletarian revolution in Europe round about the mid-nineteenth century :

'History has proved wrong us and all who thought similarly . . . We, "revolutionaries", succeed far better by means legal than illegal and destructive.'

Our point here is not, of course, to recommend Marx's specific mode of explanation in all this, but only to emphasize that his theory is a theory of social *evolution*. Indeed it could be demonstrated that this conception of social evolution had almost all the same characteristics as those laid down by Spencer : from Simplicity to complexity, and the like.

(III) Types of Society : Classification And Comparison

A third important point is to see that , following upon his particular model of society, Marx sought a systematic study of all known societies and their process of historical development by exactly the methods recommended by Comte, Mill, and Spencer—namely the methods of careful description, classification and comparison. Again we see the historical and comparative method proposed and used in necessary relation with each other. The difference in Marx was only that, with a different conception of the significant causal factor in social change (i.e., the central hypothesis for 'social dynamics')—in his case the 'material basis' of society—he classified 'types' of society in terms of this criterion, and , more especially, in terms of the class-system which characterized them. He distinguished 'primitive communal' societies which had a minimal social differentiation, and then societies characterized by slavery, serfdom, and wage-slavery (Capitalism) followed by a 'transition' through 'socialism' to 'communism'. Each of these 'types', however, was only *designated* by the criterion of technology and class; each of them consisted of a determinate 'complex' of interrelated institutions which could be uncovered by historical and comparative study.

(IV) Equilibrium-Disequilibrium Analysis

A fourth important characteristic of the method of analysis and explanation employed by Historical Materialism—and again a proposal shared by Comte and Spencer especially—is that of the 'equilibrium-disequilibrium' analysis of social order and social change. The development of a certain set of productive forces gradually brings into being about it an appropriate superstructure of institutions, and this is an achievement of an 'equilibrium' condition, a condition of integration and stability. Within this framework, however, material changes occur, class relations are gradually transformed, class interests are changed, new struggles are born, and so 'diseqilibrium' conditions are comulatively brought into being. These are 'resolved' by the qualitative leap to a new and appropriate 'equilibrium'. The sequence of social and historical change thus permits of analysis in these 'equilibrium-disequilibrium' terms.

Marxian 'Historical Materialism' is, in fact, an 'equilibrium –disequilibrium' analysis of the historical sequences of social order and social change, and the *explanation* of this process in terms of material change, attendant social conflict, and its resolution.

(V) Social Psychology

A fifth quite fundamental and integral component of 'Historical Materialism' is the particular position adopted concerning the *psychological* aspects of human nature in society; the place of psychology in the scheme of sociological explanation; and, indeed, the very conception with is implied of 'psychology' as a science.

These points were not worked out systematically by Marx, and can be dealt with only briefly, but his position concerning them was both patently clear and important.

First of all, Marx—in a way more complex, and more fully conceived than can possibly be sufficiently conveyed here—believed that though one could postulate clearly the 'essence' of man in the sense of indicating the qualities that characterized the *human* as distinct from other animal species, it was quite impossible to speak of a substantive '*human nature*' independent of the creative, cumulative, cultural activity of *society*. As to the 'essential' nature of man distinguishing him from other species, it was the necessity and ability to 'work up', creatively, the resources of nature in such ways as to satisfy *and* explore needs. But this itself meant that man was a 'maker' : his nature was not something there which filled the moulds of 'society'; his nature was something he progressively made, explored, expanded, enriched in the creative, co-operative work with his fellows which essentially constituted the making of history, the creative adventure of history. In short, man's 'essence' necessitated the making of historical society; but this making of historical society was itself the making of '*human nature*'. Also—the creativity of man was *necessarily* a social process in which countless other men were involved; in which any generation of men rested initially upon the achievements of earlier generation; and in which 'unintended consequences' of action had aggregate social effects going beyond men's individual wills. So that the making of *individual human nature* was essentially a process of *society*.

The implications of this viewpoint, and this conception, are of enormous range and importance, but again it is worthwhile to see the fullest agreement between Marx and Comte on this point. To 'Know Thyself', said Comte, it is necessary to study the history of society. All psychology, other than knowledge of relatively simple concomitants of biology, was, for him, 'Social Psychology'; and it may be remembered that he believed that the fullest study of 'Man the Individual' could only come after our fullest exploration of the science of society. Marx was equally definite about all this, and some special implications deserve the strongest, sharpest emphasis.

It is quite impossible, from Marx's point of view to 'explain' society in terms of something called '*Individual* Psychology'. On the contrary, the explanation of the substantive nature of the individual's experience and behavior can only be achieved in sociological terms. *Society* is the creative process—going far beyond the individual—within which the individual comes to be what he is.

Marx takes this point much further , and much more radically, however. It is not only that, conceptually and methodologically speaking, one cannot explain society in terms of individual psychology, but, radically and fundamentally, *there is no such thing as individual human nature, or indeed simply 'human nature' (whether individual or otherwise) in abstraction from the creative process of society.* Society makes and shapes the most basic attributes of man. It might be argued, for example, as against this, that at least *some*—things such as the simple *sense* (sight, hearing, taste, touch, scent) —are *basic* in human nature. . .But no!—Said Marx—they are *not!* And to get this perspective right is fundamental . He wrote insistently as follows :

'Just as music alone awakens in man the sense of music, and just as the most beautiful music has no sense for the unmusical ear—for this reason the *senses* of the social man are *other* senses than those of the non-social man. Only through the objectively unfolded richness of men's essential being is the richness of subjective *human* sensibility (a musical ear, an eye for beauty of form—in short, *senses* capable of human gratifications, senses confirming themselves as essential powers of *man*) either cultivated or brought into being. For not only the five senses but also the so-called mental senses—the practical senses (will, love, etc.) —in a word, *human* sense—the humanness of the senses—comes to be by virtue of its object, by virtue of *humanized* nature. The *forming* of the five senses in a labour of the entire history of the world down to the present.'

It follows from this that any 'psychology' must be couched within this context of the full and rich appreciation of the creativity of society and history—otherwise it will be 'abstracted' out of all realistic awareness of its subject-matter. A science of psychology abstracted from this detailed awareness of society and history in the making of man *is an academic impossibility*. This again is a point of important, and so deserving of our consideration as to merit the utmost emphasis.

'A *psychology,*' Marx wrote, 'for which this, the part of history most contemporary and accessible to sense, remains a closed book, cannot become a genuine, comprehensive and *real* science. What indeed are we to think of a science which *airily* abstracts from this large part of human labour and which fails to feel its own incompleteness, while such a wealth of human endeavor unfolded before it means nothing more to it than, perhaps, what can be expressed in one word—"*need*" "*vulgar* need"?'

This emphasis of Marx is one which was perhaps never more needed than now. The study of human nature must lie within the study of society and history; otherwise it is a vast mistake.

(VI) THE STUDY OF SOCIAL ACTION

Moreover, Marx argued, the psychological and sociological study of man cannot regard men as 'passive agents' in the determinate flow of events. Though men's activities in society are constrained, limited, determined by aggregate forces and material conditions which lie beyond their individual wills, still—they are *activities*. Men are continuously involved in practical, creative action in society. Men make their own history, though within determinate constraints. They work consciously, actively, in conflict , among the interests, attitudes, values and relationships, of the time within which they live. A full understanding and explanation of 'society' and its 'dialectical' processes cannot be achieved therefore excepting by a full understanding of the *social action* of men. This again is a most important emphasis—both in reiterating a point on which Comte, Mill and Spencer had also insisted, and in showing that the emphasis upon the 'understanding of social action' later stressed by weber was already fully recognized among these nineteenth century thinkers—even though they did not look with sufficient sophistication into the conceptual and methodological problems involved.

Engels, perhaps, put this point most clearly and forcibly. In his essay on 'Ludwig Feuerback', he wrote :

'When it is a question of investigating the driving forces which—consciously or unconsciously, and indeed very often unconsciously—lie behind the motives of men in their historical actions and which constitute the real ultimate driving forces of history, then it is not a question so much of the motives of single individuals, however eminent, as of those motives which set in motion great masses, whole peoples, and again whole classes of the people in each people; and here, too, not the transient flaring up of a straw-fire which quickly dies down, but a lasting action resulting in great historical transformation.

'To ascertain the driving causes which here in the minds of acting masses and their leaders—the so-called great men—are reflected as conscious motives, clearly or unclearly, directly or in ideological, even glorified form—that is the only path which can put us on the track of the laws holding sway both in history as a whole, and at particular periods and in particular lands. Everything which sets men in motion must go through their minds; but what form it will take in the mind will depend very much upon the circumstances.'

The study of the 'psychological aspects of men in society' was not, then, a study only of their 'conditioning' by material and historical circumstances, but also an understanding of their considered actions in the detailed working out of events. In insisting upon this point, Marx was also very concerned to *avoid* the conception of *society* as some abstract '*totality*', or some '*entity*' independent of the manifold activities of actual men in their work and their social relationships.

'What is to be avoided above all,' he wrote 'is the re-establishing of 'Society' as an abstraction *vis-a-vis* the individual. The individual is *the social being*. His life, even if it may not appear in the direct form of a *communal* life carried out together with others—is therefore an expression and confirmation of *social life*. Man's individual and species life are not *different*.

The 'dialectics' of history therefore clearly involved *men* in their *actions*.

(VII) UNINTENDED CONSEQUENCES

An additional point which is of importance, and which should be made clear, is that when both Marx and Engels argued that the material changes in the basic economic structure of society *determined* the relations of men and the institutions of the superstructure, what they had very largely in mind was the vast play of 'unintended consequences' in society. This too seemed to underlie what they meant by claiming that these great social transformations were 'independent of men's wills'. The substance of the point is that when countless men make small alterations and improvements in the particular jobs they are doing; when they gradually change their technical means of production; they have nothing further in mind. They are simply wanting to ease their task, or improve the efficiency of their effort, or improve the quality of their product. They have no social transformation in mind. But—in the entirety of society, and over periods of time—these many specific changes accumulate to such proportions as to have aggregate effects which were unforeseen. The entire fabric of the means of production had been cumulatively transformed , and men find that their relationships have been changed accordingly, and that old institutions no longer fit their needs; no longer serve their interests satisfactorily. This 'lack of fit' of institutions becomes increasingly conflictful until a new super-structure is created.

Again, Engels stated this persuasion very clearly. Arguing (in 'Ludwig Feuerbach') that the 'dialectics of nature' were paralleled in the 'dialectics of history', the nonetheless found it necessary to explain the ways in which the dialectical processes of history contained, so to speak, the 'conscious aims and intentions' of men. He wrote in this way :

'In one point, however, the history of the development of society proves to be essentially different from that of nature. In nature—in so far as we ignore man's reactions upon nature—there are only blind unconscious agencies acting upon one another and out of whose interplay the general law comes into operation. Nothing of all that happens—whether in the innumerable apparent accidents observable upon the surface of things, or in the ultimate results which confirm the regularity underlying these accidents—is attained as a consciously desired aim. In the history of society, on the other hand, the actors are all endowed with consciousness, are men acting with deliberation or passion, working towards definite goals; nothing happens without a conscious purpose, without an intended aim. But this distinction, important as it is for historical investigation, particularly of single epochs and events, cannot after the fact, that the course of history is governed by inner general laws. For here, also, on the whole, in the spite of the consciously desired aims of all individuals, accident apparently reigns on the surface. That which is willed happens but rarely; in the majority of instances the numerous desired ends cross and conflict with one another, or these ends themselves are from the outset incapable of realization or the means of attaining them are insufficient. Thus the conflict of innumerable individual wills and individual actions in the domain of history produces a state of affairs entirely analogous to that in the realm of unconscious nature. The ends of the actions are intended, but the results which actually follow from these actions are not intended; or when they do seem to correspond to the end intended, they ultimately have consequences quite other than those intended. Historical events thus appear on the whole to be likewise governed by chance. But where on the surface accident holds sway, there actually it is always governed by inner, hidden laws and it is only a matter of discovering these laws.

'Men make their own history, whatever its outcome may be, in that each person follows his own consciously desired end, and it is precisely the resultant of these many wills operating in different directions and of their manifold effects upon the outer world that constitutes history.'

Similarly, in a letter to Joseph Bloch, Engels wrote:

'History makes itself in such a way that the final result always arises from conflicts between many individual wills, of which each again has been made what it is by a host of particular conditions of life. Thus there are innumerable intersecting forces an infinite series of parallelograms of forces which give rise to one resultant—the historical event. This again may itself be viewed as the product of a power which, taken as a whole, works *unconsciously* and without volition. For what each individual wills is obstructed by everyone else, and what emerges is something that no one willed. Thus past history proceeds in the manner of natural process and is also essentially subject to the same laws of movement.'

In this conception it is again evident how 'Historical Materialism' must seek the 'hidden' patterns of social and historical interconnection which may not be 'apparent' on the surface of events, or in the consciousness of men who are being borne along by them. Much later, we shall see how this has been incorporated into 'modern' sociological analysis under the term 'latent', as distinct from 'manifest' functions.

(VIII) ALIENATION AND IDEOLOGY

There is this further dimension of Marx's analysis in terms of 'Historical Materialism', and it concerns the question : *how* do the aims, intentions, and powerful motives of men come to be intimately related to the material processes of social change, to class-conflict and political struggle? The answer lies in Marx's 'materialist' (as distinct from Hegel's 'idealist') account of 'alienation' and the ideologies which are rooted in this experience. This is an incredibly difficult matter to be both brief and clear about—but still, let us try. The effort is necessary because some sociologists have gone so far as to ask 'What has all this to do with sociology?' But this reflects a very profound lack of understanding of Marx, because this notion of man's 'alienation' and the resolution and elimination of it was not only the basic strand underlying his sociology; it also provided one of the central 'mechanisms' of human motivation in social action. Briefly, Marx argued as follows—his ideas being rooted in the conceptions of both Hegel and Feuerbach.

Hegel had introduced the idea of 'alienation' in a 'spiritual' sense in order to provide an understanding of the felt incompleteness of human experience and the striving for completeness amid the actualities of creation. For him the continuous process of creation in the world was an unfolding of the actualizing of spirit and mind in the concrete forms of nature and history, and each particular step of this—each 'form' being a particulate, limited actuality; a partial 'objectification' of spirit; a partial 'realization' of the 'idea'—entailed a certain 'distancing' of spirit from its degree of objectification, a certain 'estrangement' in that the spiritual essence was not yet fully, richly, realized in the actuality. And the motives of men in their historical struggles (including philosophy, art, religion as well as the political and legal making of societies) were moved, compelled, by this undertone of divine discontent, seeking the fullness of spiritual realization in their creative life in the world. The 'dialectics' of mind and spirit continuously sprang from this spiritual unrest of 'alienation', and this human 'alienation' was rooted in the larger creative entirety of the 'World Spirit'.

Feuerbach, in his *Essence of Christianity,* rejected this large 'Idealist' perspective, and argued simply that the sublimities of religion in society—the ideologies which portrayed spiritually satisfying aims and ends and conditions of human destiny—were simply rooted in human insufficiencies and dissatisfactions. The Gods were wish-fulfillments. Man, in his actual conditions of life in nature and society, suffered a many-sided tragedy—of transience, of continual limitation and frustration, frequently of injustice, and ultimately of death. The creation of religious ideality—of Gods, doctrines, rituals—was the outcome of man's desire to seek a resolution of his dilemmas, a healing of his wounds, a salvation from his limitations and his evils. A religious ideology was, in short, a reflection of the needs of man in the actuality of his conditions.

Marx and Engels had rejected Hegel's 'Idealist' system, and found Feuerbach's more direct explanation a release from it, indeed a kind of deliverance from it, but they needed to take it further : to show, in detail, how 'ideology' in society could be explained in terms of their own dialectical and historical materialism, and how these ideological experiences and motives of men could be shown to be rooted in an 'alienation' accompanying man's practical activities in nature and society. Their explanation of 'alienation' and 'ideology' thus provided a basic understanding of the motivation which underlay 'class-struggles' and the political activity which arose out of it. It *linked* the material basis of society and changes in it with the clash of ideas, values and beliefs at the level of the 'super-structure'. It was therefore a necessary component of the 'dialectical' explanation of history. Marx's explanation was this.

Man's 'essence'—the characteristic which distinguished him, as a species, from all others in nature—was his *social creativity* the co-operative activity with his fellows in working creatively upon nature. Beginning in the necessitous struggle for survival, this then became the historical creation of culture, within the context of which man made the very stuff of his own individual nature. Man the maker; Man the creator; Man who works the manifold qualities of nature into an increasingly rich fabric of culture, and , in so doing, creates in the world, and out of the stuff of the world, the distinctive qualities of the human spirit : this was Marx's picture. Properly understood, Marx's picture of man in the world was one of Creative Humanism. This, then, was Man's 'essence'—to create richly and freely in nature.

'It is just in the working–up of the objective world, therefore,' he wrote, 'that man first really proves himself to be a *species being*. This production is his active species life. Through and because of this production, nature appears as *his* work and his reality. The object of labour is, therefore, the *objectification of man' species life:* for he duplicates himself not only, as in consciousness, intellectually, but also actively, in reality, and therefore he contemplates himself in a world that he has created.'

'In creating an *objective* world by his practical activity, in *working-up* inorganic nature, man proves himself a conscious species being. Admittedly animals also produce. They build themselves nests dwellings, like the bees, beavers ants, etc. But an animal only produces what it immediately needs for itself or its young. It produces one-sidedly, whilst man produces universally. It produces only under the dominion of immediate physical need, whilst man produces even when he is free from physical need, and only truly produces in freedom therefrom. An animal produces only itself, whilst man reproduces the whole of nature. An animal's product belongs immediately to its physical body, whilst man freely confronts his product. An animal forms things in accordance with the standard and the need of the species, to which it belongs, whilst man knows how to produce in accordance with the standard of every species and knows how to apply everywhere the inherent standard to the object. Man therefore also forms things in accordance with the laws of beauty.'

In this creativity 'essential' to his nature, Man actively *needed* objects in nature, indeed, part of his *own* nature was this need to be objectively related to nature for the possibility and fulfillment of this activity. Marx insisted upon this inextricable and intimate relationship between 'human nature' and 'nature' (as constituting the 'essence' of man's nature) in the following way.

'*Man* is directly a *natural being*. As a natural being and as a living natural being he is on the one hand furnished with *natural powers of life*—he is an *active* natural being. These forces exist in him as tendencies and abilities—as *impulses*. On the other hand, as a natural, corporeal, sensuous, objective being he is a *suffering*, conditioned and limited creature, like animals and plants. That is to say, the *objects* of his impulses exist outside him, as *objects* independent of him; yet these objects are *objects* of his *need*—essential *objects*, indispensable to the manifestation and confirmation of his essential powers. To say that man is a *corporeal*, living, real, sensuous, objective being full of natural vigour is to say that he has *real, sensuous, objects* as the objects of his being or of his life, or that he can only *express* his life in real, sensuous objects. To be objective, natural and sensuous, and at the same time to have object, nature and sense outside oneself, or oneself to be object, nature and sense for a third party, is one and the same thing. *Hunger* is a natural *need*; it therefore needs a *nature* outside itself, an *object* outside itself, in order to satisfy itself, to be stilled. Hunger is an acknowledged need of my body for an *object* existing outside it, indispensable to its integration and to the expression of its essential being. The sun is the *object* of the plant—an indispensable object to it, confirming its life—just as the plant is an object of the sun, being an *expression* of the life-awakening power of the sun, of the sun's *objective* essential power.

The essentially 'naturalistic' or 'materialistic' nature of Marx's conception of man's 'essence', as against Hegel's 'idealist' or 'spiritual' conception, was therefore perfectly clear. And, given this, his conception of 'alienation' was also clear.

Just as, in Hegel, the objectification of the thing created was a certain constraining delimitation upon the larger potentiality of spirit itself, so, in Marx, the sensuous, practical activity of man in 'working-up' the materials of nature took the form of 'material objects'; of 'products'. The labour of men in a community became *embodied in products*. A material order of objects was created. But this, in itself, had a certain delimiting constraint upon their creative energies. They were, to a new degree (and a *growing* degree as the material order and the material instruments of production became more complex) set at a distance from the pristine conditions of their creative activity. A certain 'estrangement' was brought about. But this 'alienation' was especially intensified by the fact that, in the conditions of communal production, the individuals who created 'products' did not themselves 'own' them. A new problem of the relation of men to the means of production and to the products created, and to the exchange of these products, arose. In short—production, exchange, and the division of labour in society entailed *property* relations. The objects which men produced, the means of production which they had to use to produce them, did not belong to *them*; they did not themselves have direct control over them; they were owned, controlled, by *others*. Men were therefore 'alienated' from the *essential* conditions for the fulfillment of their *essential* nature not only by the material process of production, but by the complex *relations of production* which set some men over against others and therefore in conflict with others. *Property relations* were conflictful *class relations, property* was *power*.

With this picture, the entirety of Marx's scheme of explanation becomes at once apparent. Each distinctive 'technological' stage in history, each distinctive 'material, economic, basis' of society constituted a distinctive set of property relations, of class-relations in which a certain class 'owned' and controlled the means of production and the 'commodities' produced, and in which the other, subordinate classes were 'alienated' from the conditions necessary for their 'essential human activity and fulfillment. Class-conflict is therefore endemic to human society. The super-structure of institutions reflects (and effectively serves) the domination of the property-owning class over those classes which are 'alienated'. And 'ideologies' in society are the sets of ideas, values, and aims (including the 'wish-fulfillment dimensions' of Feuerbach) which reflect these different complexes of class conditions. In this entire sense, Marx and Engels believed that : 'The history of all hitherto existing society is the history of class struggles.'

It is very important to insist here that, for Marx, this entire historical process of kinds and degrees of 'alienation', and of man's struggle to overcome all forms of 'alienation', was not a kind of morally blameworthy sequence of man's chosen cruelty to man, but, on the contrary, a necessary historical process of the making of man : the necessary sequence of conditions whereby man came to a full creative achievement of his 'essence' as a distinctive species. Thus, *private* property (and its several forms related to certain modes of production) was necessary in the stages of man's social creativity : just as it was also necessary, following upon the emergence of industrial capitalism, to supersede it.

'Precisely in the fact', wrote Marx, 'That *division of labour* and *exchange* are embodiments of private property lies the twofold proof, on the one hand that *human* life *required* private property for its realization, and on the other hand that it now requires the *supersession* of private property.'

This entire process of property-relations, class-relations, alienations and ideological struggles, Marx regarded as the '*pre-history*' of mankind; the long period of struggle in which man had gradually won the recognition and the conditions of his 'essence'. The *future* of man would be his self-directed history. In this picture, and this emphasis, can be seen (again) both Marx's 'turning upside down' of Hegel—in insisting that man's spiritual essence, his creative individual freedom in nature and history, is something that man has *creatively achieved,* rather than something that was initially *there* in the world spirit; and the agreement of this position with Comte's conclusion that Man now had to confront responsibly a self-directed future, and Spencer's conclusion that Man could now create a new 'ethical' society.

However, there is one further point that must be made about the nature of 'ideology' in all this. On the one hand, we have seen that 'ideology' was thought of as 'reflecting' material conditions and real conditions of alienation. The 'general consciousness' of men was :

'. . . only the *theoretical* shape of that of which the *living* shape is the *real* community, the social fabric. . .'

In this sense, it would appear that the several 'ideologies' in society would be considered *true*—in the sense of corresponding with definite aspects of social reality; but, curiously, Marx and Engels tend definitely to regard 'ideologies' as kinds of '*false* consciousness'; as kinds of pictures of social reality which one has got to question and reject—probing, instead, *behind* them with scientific analysis which gets at the deeply hidden *truth*. Engels wrote in a letter to Franz Mehring:

'Ideology is a process accomplished by the so-called thinker consciously indeed, but with a *false consciousness*. The *real* motives impelling him remain unknown to him, *otherwise it would not be an ideological process at all.*'

This is a very odd, assertive point; but here we will not argue with it, only note it. It is necessary to notice briefly just one further dimension of 'alienation' and the conflicts to which it points.

(IX) VALUE, CAPITAL, AND THE CONFLICT BETWEEN WAGE-LABOUR AND CAPITAL

It has already been evident that, in Marx's conception, 'alienation' and 'class-conflict', though *subjectively experienced* things, were also actual material relations, and it is important simply to make clear the way in which Marx analysed this material basis in his explanations of historical change.

We have already seen that, for Marx, 'material products' were the embodiment of human relations. Products of human labour were not just 'things' as other objects in nature were; it was a kind of 'fetishism' so to regard them; they were objectifications of particular sets of productive relationships among men. 'Alienation' too was a reflection of a division of the value of products between the classes concerned. The *value* of a product was the amount of human labour which went into the making of it. The *owner* of the product, however, made a *profit* when *exchanging* the product on the economic market. This 'margin' of difference (the profit) between the price the owner received for the product on the market, and the price he paid the workers for their labour (wages) was therefore thought to be '*expropriated*'. Competition was such as to lead the owner to pay only the *minimal* level of wages (that sum necessary to provide the worker with his *necessary subsistence*) in seeking to *maximize* his profit. And so the conflict between the owner and the alienated took the form of a conflict between capital (stored and expropriated value) and wage-labour. . .and, in capitalism, between *capitalists* (the owners of the means of production) and the *proletariat* (the propertyless wage-earners).

A final aspect of this is that Marx believed that with the changing 'composition of capital', the development of industrial capitalism would lead to a falling rate of profit, and , therefore, to an increasingly intense conflict between 'capital' and 'labour'. Perhaps, too, it is necessary to note that Marx believed that industrial capitalism—whilst leading to larger-scale production —would also become increasingly restrictive on the expansion of production, and the employment of new inventions and new techniques, since these would tend to despoil the markets for their 'successful products'. Conflict would also, therefore, intensify here between 'capital' and 'labour' since the narrow defence of private property and enterprise served the interests of one class, whereas the movement towards the collectivization of property and larger-scale production seemed to be in the interests of the other.

(X) THE PROLETARIAN REVOLUTION : SOCIALISM, COMMUNISM, AND THE CLASSLESS SOCIETY : THE WITHERING AWAY OF THE STATE

In the entire process of history, hitherto, the 'qualitative leaps' of political revolution whereby new super-structures of society had replaced the old, had been accomplished, according to Marx, by rising social classes which had come to power on the basis of changed conditions of production. Hitherto, also, each new dominant class, on achieving power, had found beneath it a subjected class, lower than itself in the economic structure, and which, in the new pattern of material relationships, it had proceeded to exploit. There was, however, a great difference in the specific case of industrial capitalism and its transformation to a collectivized society. It was this.

In the case of industrial capitalism, the productive forces and the property relations were such as to produce a basic conflict between only *two* social classes, as we have seen : between those who owned the means of production—the capitalists; and those who owned none—the wage-earning proletariat. There were professional 'middle-classes', but Marx thought these were related to the means of production in the same way as the proletariat, and would therefore become a part of the new collectivized order as the conflict intensified and the resolution of it became clear.

Consequently, when the industrial proletariat accomplished the revolution—demolishing private property and collectivizing the means of production—*there would be no subjected class beneath them.* All the members of society would be related to the means of production *in the same way.* There would be no class-exploitation. The enormously increased productivity of collectivized industry, and the unrestrained application of science and technology to industry, would eliminate conditions of 'alienation'. Men could now experience their 'essential' creativity freely. Through the transitional period of Socialism, under the guidance of the 'dictatorship of the proletariat', a Communist society would be achieved in which productivity would make it possible to *distribute* wealth in accordance with *need,* whilst asking of men that contribution to society of which they were *capable.* This, it is important to see, would be the *reversal* of inequalities, and a complete transformation in the tone and human values of society.

This is worth much emphasis. Marx—and some may be surprised at this—was *opposed* to what he called a *crude communism.* Simply to transform 'private property and enterprise' into 'public property and enterprise'—whilst retaining the old emphasis of values upon competitive 'getting' and 'having' was, he thought, a travesty of the aims of socialism. The transformation of the material means of society should be to accomplish those new relations among men which could lead to man's experience of his 'essential nature', his creative activity in nature freely enjoyed with his fellows. It was, Marx insisted, a '*human*' society we should achieve, in which all the alienating conditions of material and social organization which had limited the achievement of this had been overcome. Marx's utopian vision has much in it to warm the heart, whether or not one agrees with his explanatory system on which it rested.

At any rate, in *this* revolution—from industrial capitalism to communism—a *classless* society could be achieved, indeed *would* be achieved, and the further corollary of this was that—since the 'State' was the organ of the ruling class, and, now, no social classes existed—the 'State' was no longer necessary, and would 'wither away'. Both Marx and Engels were very emphatic about the several aspects of this. Marx, for example, in trying to make very clear what his own specific contribution had been; what was *not* new, and what *was* new in his own work; wrote in a latter to Joseph Weydemeyer (March, 1852) :

'. . . And now as to myself, no credit is due to me for discovering the existence of classes in modern society, nor yet the struggle between them. Long before me bourgeois historians had described the historical development of this class struggle and bourgeois economists, the economic anatomy of the classes. What I did that was new was to prove : (1) that the *existence of classes* is only bound up with *particular, historic phases in the development of production;* (2) that the class struggle necessarily leads to the *dictatorship of the proletariat;* (3) that this dictatorship itself only constitutes the transition to the *abolition of all classes* and to a *classless society. . .* '

There are no half-measures about this statement. Similarly, there are no half-measures about what Engels said concerning the fate of the 'State' following the proletarian revolution. In *Anti-Dühring,* he wrote as follows :

'*The proletariat seizes the Sate power, and transforms the means of production in the first instance into State property.* But in doing this, it puts an end to itself as the proletariat, it puts an end to all class differences and class antagonisms, it puts an end also to the state as the state. Former society, moving in class antagonisms, had need of the state, that is, an organization of the exploiting class at each period for the maintenance of its external conditions of production; that is, therefore, for the forcible holding down of the exploited class in the conditions of oppression (slavery, villeinage or serfdom, wage labour) determined by the existing mode of production. The state was the official representative of society as a whole, its embodiment in a visible corporation; but it was this only in so far as it was the State of that class which itself, in its epoch, represented society as a whole; in ancient times, the state of the slave-owning citizens; in the Middle Ages, of the feudal nobility; in our epoch, of the bourgeoisie. When ultimately it becomes really representative of society as a whole, it makes itself superfluous. As soon as there is no longer any class of society to be held in subjection; as soon as, along with class domination and the struggle for individual existence based on the former anarchy of production, the collisions and excesses arising from these have also been abolished, there is nothing more to be repressed which would make a special repressive force, a state, necessary. The first act in which the state really comes forward as the representative of society as a whole—the taking possession of the means of production in the name of society—is at the same time its last independent act as a state. The interference of the state power in social relations becomes superfluous in one sphere after another, and then ceases of itself. The government of persons is replaced by the administration of things and the direction of the process of production. The state is not "abolished", *it withers away.*'

Nothing could be clearer or more emphatic.

In this way, then, a classless, stateless society will be created on the basis of the new material conditions now possible. And in this way, Marx and Engels completed this application of 'dialectical materialism' to the study of society and history : producing a systematic theory of the way in which man, in the making of both his society and himself, has moved creatively out of the early bondage of material necessity, through the many constraining, alienating conditions of the various stages of 'pre-history', to a self-directed society in which individual men can freely enjoy the creative activity in nature and human relationships which is their distinctive essence. Spiritual freedom, out of long suffering and struggle, has been achieved, and can form the basis for man's future consciously directed life.

(XI) SPECIFIC HISTORICAL AND COMPARATIVE STUDIES

It remains only to say that both Marx and Engels undertook specific and searching studies of particular historical situations in various societies in order to demonstrate the utility and validity of their system of analysis. The extent to which Marx studied the many reports on the material conditions and the productive relations existing in Britain may be seen in sections of *Capital,* but also, in very telling fashion, in his address to the Working Men's International Association in September 1864 (at St. Martin's Hall in London). His studies of the 'Eighteenth Brumaire of Louis Bonaparte', of 'The Civil War in France', of the 'Class Struggles in France : 1848-1850,' are very substantial examples of his analysis of the 'social action' of men pursued within the context, within the grip, of changing, aggregate conditions larger than themselves. And, to a more limited extent, both Marx and Engels, had quite substantial comments to make about material conditions, class-relations, and political situations in Ireland, India, and even Russia. So that historical and comparative studies were entered into and achieved to some considerable extent.

So much, then, by way of systematic exposition of Marx's 'Dialectical and Historical Materialism'. We must now turn to the task of critical assessment.

Criticisms

I shall try to be quite exhaustive in enumerating the several criticisms of Marx, though some of them are of relatively minor and others of major importance. We are now in a position to assemble and to judge these criticisms quite fully and clearly, and we must try to make our critique as definitive as possible so that we can properly assess the place of Marx in the making of Sociology.

(a) Dialectical Materialism : Not New

A first criticism levelled at Marx was that the 'Dialectical Materialism' with which he countered 'Idealism', was not *new*. Heraclitus, it has often been said, and other scholars of the past, had already put forward the idea of the world as a continuous material process; an ongoing, ever-changing flux of events. Marx had therefore made no contribution here.

This criticism, of course, is of no consequence whatever. A theory is not to be judged according to its age, or, indeed, according to the number of times it has been stated in history. If Heraclitus was *right;* if his theory was *true;* then it was a contribution of Marx to have re-stated it. But, of course, Marx's 'system' of explanation of the world in materialistic terms was quite different in its detail from the views of thinkers in earlier historical periods. As such, it was undoubtedly a contribution. The question is—is it true or false? And this cannot be decided by noticing that other people have said something similar before.

This criticism is, in short, pointless and trivial, as well as being, in quite basic respects, untrue.

(b) *Dialectical Materialism: too simple a theory of nature*

A second criticism, often associated with the first, is that 'Dialectical Materialism' was not only not new, but that it was so large-scale and simple a theory as not really to explain anything much. On the surface, to speak of 'quantitative changes' leading to 'qualitatively new substances and forms' in nature, seems very factual, measurable, scientific, and especially when the illustrations given—such as an additional molecule of hydrogen leading to a qualitative change from a gas into a liquid—seem so telling. But as soon as this apparently clear statement is *questioned*, and as soon as the processes of nature are examined in more detail, the more questionable becomes this *dictum* that all 'qualitative' change is brought about by a number of gradual, additive, quantitative changes. Consider, for example, the explanation of the emergence of a new biological species offered by the 'theory of evolution'. It seems true that a small accidental change in the genetic constitution of the germ cell of an animal brings into being a qualitatively new offspring, and if this offspring is favoured by the natural environment, it may give rise to a qualitatively new species; but it does *not* seem true that this process is characterized by a long sequence of gradual, cumulative, quantitative additions (a kind of 'incremental' material process) which, at a certain 'nodal' point suddenly gives rise to a qualitatively new phenomenon. Genetic changes, genetic 'mutations', seem rather to be unusual, arbitrary changes which are, immediately, qualitatively new phenomena. And many of them, of course, are *unfitted* for survival, they are, in fact, fatal for the offspring which results from them. Dialectical materialism, as stated by Marx and Engels, with its basic process of 'quantitative-qualitative' change, is therefore far too large-scale and simple, far too all-embracing a theory, to give us a really satisfactory explanation of all the processes of change in nature. Whereas it *seems* to fit with changes such as the quantitative additions of molecules, or with the increase in the temperature of a liquid which will bring it to the condition (i.e., at boiling point) of a vapour, it certainly does not fit all kinds of change in nature. Strictly speaking, Dialectical Materialism is the large-scale assertion of a specific philosophical (a metaphysical) viewpoint; it is *not*, in itself, a scientific theory.

(c) *Dialectical Materialism : the distinction between 'Quantitative' and 'Qualitative' change questionable*

This questioning of the scientific utility and accuracy of 'Dialectical Materialism' also leads to a third criticism which *appears* (and indeed is, though not wholly so) *terminological,* but which is of quite basic importance. It is this. Is there not something fundamentally questionable about the whole distinction between the '*quantitative*' and '*qualitative*' elements of change, and, consequently, upon the whole weight which comes to be placed upon the 'quantitative' (as being '*material*' the '*primary* reality', the fundamentally '*real*') basis in that *order* of causal explanation which, alone, is taken to be satisfactory? Consider this carefully.

In the simplest case—if I add one molecule of a certain chemical element to an acid, and thereby produce another acid, is it strictly correct to say that a quantitative addition has produced a 'qualitative leap' to a new substance ? Or is it more correct to say that the addition of the molecule is, *simultaneously, both a quantitative and a qualitative* kind of change; and that the use of the words 'quantitative' and 'qualitative' refer only to *the ways in which we regard* that change : 'quantity' being used when we are thinking of the measurement of the unity of 'analytical components' and 'quality' when we are referring to 'perceptual differences' or 'properties' (in some perceptual sense). But, strictly speaking, the change is *both* quantitative and qualitative simultaneously.

This is more apparent if we take other examples given by Engels—let us say the boiling or freezing of water (or liquids). If we increase the temperature of water, for a long time nothing happens excepting a quantitative increase (parallel with the units of temperature) in the rapidity of circulation of the molecules. When a certain temperature is reached, however, ('boiling point', and 'nodal' point), any further quantitative change brings about the *qualitative* change from a liquid to a vapour. But let us think about this carefully. Why should the *heating* of the water (because we can *measure* it in *degrees*) be termed a *quantitative* change? Why should the increasingly rapid circulation of the molecules of water be termed only a *quantitative* change ? Are not the *heating* and the more rapid circulation of molecules simultaneous *qualitative* changes too? We certainly think so if we put our fingers in the water; or if, for example, we are heating a baby's feeding bottle or a tin of soup. But also—why should we speak of '*qualitative* change' *only* at the point when the water changes to steam? Surely, all we are doing here is taking the *most evident perceptual difference,* from the point of view of our own sense-experience, as a qualitative 'nodal point' in nature. Perhaps the difference in terms, of 'heat' or 'rapidity' of circulation of molecules' is still only a gradual, incremental change; and it is only that *from the viewpoint of our own (human) perceptual awareness* that a qualitatively striking change has, with relative 'suddenness', occurred.

Certainly to speak of something *quantitatively additive causing* something *subsequently qualitative* is a questionable, indeed highly dubious, way of describing what is happening. Again, it can be seen, really, to be of the nature of a metaphysical *assertion.* The arguer wants to insist that what he takes to be *qualitative attributes* are not objectively or basically real, but are only subjectively experienced phenomena which are *dependent* upon, secondary to, more fundamental *quantitative* facts which are objective and *are* real; and therefore he conceptually separates quantitative and qualitative attributes, and *asserts* that it is the former which always *cause* the latter. It is a metaphysical sleight of hand !

This may seem, when arguing about water and acid, to be only a small, even a petty, linguistic point, but we shall see that when we come to the distinctions drawn between the 'material, quantitative' elements of *society,* and the 'qualitative' elements of the super-structure, it is a point of the most fundamental importance.

(d) The Transition from Dialectical Materialism to Historical materialism : too simple

The fourth criticism is with regard to the supposed *application* of Dialectical Materialism to Historical Materialism, and is—that the transition from the one to the other is conceived and undertaken in far too simple-minded a manner : without a satisfactory appreciation of either the different levels of subject-matter involved or the conceptual and methodological problems of studying them.

It is one thing to speak of molecules of various acids, or the circulation of molecules of water, and quite another to speak of human beings—thinking, feeling, purposefully acting beings—involved in complexities of social relationships. These are two quite different levels of phenomena; *the nature of the subject matter is so qualitatively different* that the *same* concepts and methods *do not* apply; or at least, are not *immediately seen to apply*.

Some detailed consideration of the *appropriateness* for the more complex level, of the concepts and methods which are satisfactory for the more simple level, is clearly necessary. Yet these matters are never worked out satisfactorily by either Marx or Engels. Comte, it may be remembered, had *insisted* upon the importance of recognizing *levels* of facts, and qualitatively different *kinds of consensus,* for the proper formulation of the methods appropriate to the several sciences. Marx and Engels well–nigh ignore all this.

It is true that they recognize, as we have seen, that men are consciously active in changing both nature and society; that material reality is actively reflected in their minds; and that the explanation of social change at least includes the understanding of men's interests and purposes; and yet the basic assertion of *materialism*; of the sequence and weighting of '*quantitative-qualitative*' change remains the same with regard to men in society as with regard to molecules and cells in nature. We shall elaborate the many deficiencies of this position in the separate points which follow, but one crucial point might be noted and emphasized here.

Bearing in mind this difference in level between the compounding of molecules in various substances, and of men grappling with their material environments in various societies, it is quite clear that any discussion of the *material reality* or the *material conditions* of both must be *only an analogy*. If we speak about the quantitative basis of material reality' which underlies the emergence of vapour as a phenomenon qualitatively distinct from a liquid, that is one thing. If we then speak of the *quantitative basis of the material conditions* of the activities of men in seeking to satisfy their needs in nature and society, as (for example) giving rise to capitalist society, as a phenomenon qualitatively distinct from feudal society, that is quite another thing. If we seek to emphasize the role of the *material basis* of one (in bringing about qualitative difference) by illustrative reference to the other, we are *employing an analogy*. No more.

If we regard the two sets of phenomena as examples of *the same materialistic process,* then we are indeed mistaking an *analogous* for a *homologous* relationship, and are in error. And in applying their metaphysical assertion of materialism to explain equally *both* natural *and* social and historical processes, it seems to me beyond doubt that Marx and Engels committed this error—which was even more powerfully and didactically reinforced by later teachers such as Lenin and Stalin.

Spencer, it may be noted, had at least been meticulously clear about the analogies which he used, but Marx and Engels seemed blind to theirs, and so have been most of their followers. The force of this point can be more fully seen as we explore all the more *specific* doctrines of 'Historical Materialism'.

(e) The Material Basis of Society : The Identity between Men's 'Relations with the Material World' and men's 'Economic Relations' unwarranted

The first set of vagueness which terminate in an unjustified dogma are Marx's considerations as to the 'material conditions' of men's 'sensuous, practical activities' which constitute the 'basic reality', the 'objective reality', the 'economic structure' which is the foundation of society. It is best to state this criticism quite baldly, and to say that it is an error to equate men's 'relations to the material world' with men's 'economic relations' and, thereafter, to claim that these 'determine' everything else in society.

It is a truism that men act in relation to '*nature*', or the '*material world*', in seeking to satisfy their needs or in exploring the many dimensions of their experience and their purposes. But let us stop at once and consider all that this involves. Surely, it covers, in fact almost every element in human experience.

When men are bewildered by the magnitude and apparent

infinity of the world; when they are afraid of all its powers that can be so destructive of security and happiness; when they are both amazed at its grandeur but distressed at its lack of meaning for them; and when they enter into both collective and private rituals, practices, beliefs, speculations about the nature of it all—surely all this is one aspect of their relations to the material world? When men lose those they love in death, and are aware of their transience, and are afraid of death for themselves and others, and desire beliefs and rituals to give some meaning to personal life, this is surely part of their relations to nature? When men and women form sexual relationships and know love, affection, loyalty; and when in parenthood, they share concern and responsibility for their children; surely these, too, are aspects of their relations to the material world? When men feel aesthetically excited, moved, calmed, by the various moods of skies, landscapes, seas, and the varieties of living forms in the world, all this artistic experience and activity is surely part of their relation to the material world? But none of these can be said, as such, to be men's '*economic* relations'. To say that men's relations to the material world, or even men's *activities* in relation to the material world, are the same as men's economic relations is an absurd over-simplification and quite an unwarranted identity. And yet it slips into Marx and Engels almost unnoticed.

This is where the looseness of Marx's language leads to real difficulty. For to speak of men's 'sensuous, practical activity' in '*nature*' can easily be held to be *inclusive* of all these qualitative details, and I am sure that Marx *did* wish to include them. But to speak of 'the material world' and men's 'economic relations' as determining all the qualitative aspects of human experience gives a different kind of picture; and it also gives rise to quite a false premise for the analysis and understanding of social institutions and the explanation of social change.

(f) The Material Basis of Society : The 'Primacy of the 'Material' or the 'Economic' relations in society : an error of causal sequence'

The first aspect of error here may be called the error of historical order, or of causal sequence. We have seen that, with this false identity between men's activities in relation to the material world and men's *economic* relations in their minds, both Marx and Engels maintained that men's *primary economic problem* had to be solved *first, before* other aspects of experience and activity could be pursued. *First*, it was argued, men must eat and drink, have shelter and clothing; and *then, thereafter,* they could pursue politics, science, religion, art. The *first* economic achievements formed the foundation for all which followed. The politics, science, religion, art, *reflected* the primary material, economic reality, and were therefore to be explained in terms of it.

Something regarded as a material economic problem was clearly regarded as being *primary* in this sense of historical order. And though this seems, on the face of it, to be plausible, it is, in fact, quite false.

Clearly, human groups must struggle for survival; to win material sustenance from nature is necessary; *but* — it is a marked error to assume that there are certain 'material needs', or 'economic needs' *independent of all other human needs* which are in some sense more basic than they, which constitute an economic problem prior to them, and in terms of which they can be explained in a relationship of *subsequent dependence.* Man's 'economic activity', even in the earliest pre-historical periods would already be patterned in accordance with the many simultaneously feit facets of their experience. For example, men do not have 'raw' (so to speak) individual needs for food, drink, shelter; they exist in *groups* bound together by ties of sexual involvement, parenthood, relations and dependencies of kinship, so that what we might call their *familial* bonds actually pattern their activities in relation to nature. They experience the need for food, drink, shelter *for their families.* Similarly, men are aware of death and the dead; they come to bury the dead in certain ways; they bury food, weapons, implements with the dead in accordance with some conceptions of life beyond the grave; they may colour the corpse with red powder in order to recover the semblance of life; and all these will be activities undertaken in relation to nature; they constitute (among other elements of experience) a certain *patterning* of 'economic' activity. Men allocate certain resources to the dead !

What this amounts to is that man's 'economic problem'

is *always* a problem of utilizing the resources of nature in seeking to meet a *multiplicity* of needs and desires. Familial needs, religious needs, aesthetic needs, needs for material sustenance and shelter. . .*all* are experienced simultaneously; and men's activities in relation to the material world are always *patterned* accordingly. It is not true, therefore, that some *primary* economic problem has to be resolved *before* other, secondary, needs can be entertained. *All* needs are experienced, and the 'economic problem' is itself always shaped by the simultaneity of competing needs; it is itself woven of these manifold needs.

Any question of 'explanation' must therefore be pursued by an analysis of this 'interdependency of factors', *not* by the asserted dominance of one factor over others. But it is also very important to notice here that there are no grounds at all for distinguishing something called '*economic* needs' or '*economic* relations' from all other needs and relations in human society. *All* human needs and desires—sexual, parental, artistic, religious, etc.—are of telling importance in *their own right;* they all involve relations with the material world; they all affect the patterning of economic activity; but they are not *subsidiary* to, or *subordinate* to, or *determined* by, some more basic necessity called '*economic reality*'.

It is interesting to notice that historically—in terms of that is known in archaeology and anthropology—this seems to be borne out without question. The earliest archaeological records, not only of *homo sapiens,* but even of earlier groups such as the Neanderthalers, show that, besides having a simple technology, they wore magical charms of fertility; produced art of a ritual and utilitarian kind; practised burial rites; and appear to have lived in family groups. The 'economic' activities of these communities were permeated by, and patterned in relation to, this entire complex of experience and behaviour. With this continuous, simultaneous, interdependency of social elements in mind, all talk of 'primary' and 'secondary'; of 'substructure and super-structure'; can be seen to be fundamentally questionable, and indeed, to be really the outcome of metaphysical assertion. It declares the presence of an 'a priori' assumption which is not explicit, and not warranted.

There are two other points worth making before leaving this. The one is that 'materialist' theory such as that of Marx and Engels, if it is really consistent, faces a very difficult question. If material conditions *determine* the qualitative super-structures of societies, how is the theory to explain the fact that the same material conditions are often accompanied by *widely differing* super-structures? But this is a *question* which may simply be noted.

The second point is more important, indeed of the greatest importance, and we shall return to it as a matter of crucial concern in sociological analysis : namely , that *the material , institutional life and activity of a people in community is, in fact, interpenetrated by values*; *it is an organized embodiment of values.* In some way, it has come to be thought that to speak of *material* activities, or *organized* activities is somehow concrete, factual, real, measurable, whereas to speak of *values* or *morals* in society is to speak of something relatively vague, evanescent, secondary, of no real efficacy in the pressing tide of historical events. What we are now saying is that this might well prove to be an unwitting supposition stemming from a false dichotomy. It may be that the structural institutions of a society, including its 'economic' relations, *are* the actual embodiment of a simultaneous definiteness of values, springing from multiple sources of group experience. But this we shall come back to later. It is an issue of crucial importance : to assess the place of values in society, and later, we shall see that there are good grounds for assuming the *centrality* of values in society.

For now, we have seen that the *historical, order* of economic and material primacy held by Marx and Engels, and the *causal sequence* which they rest upon it, is without basis. But this point needs to be pressed home in one additional way, so that its full and quite definitive force can be seen.

(g) The Material Basis of Society : The 'Primacy' of the 'Material' or the 'Economic' relations in society : also an error of conception

So far, we have emphasized that the 'economic' basis of society does not possess the 'primacy' attached to it by Marx and Engels in the sense of *historical order,* but it needs to be clearly seen (as has implicitly become clear in what we have said) that, quite apart from any question of temporal sequence, this 'primacy' of the 'economic order' in society is a *fundamental conceptual error.*

There is a sense in which it is true that the religious, educational, political, artistic, legal institutions (the 'superstructure') of a society always *reflect* the 'economic structure' of society. They are all closely involved in the allocation of resources in society, and their manifest nature and development is shaped and constrained within this context. But it is a simple conceptual error to assume, from this, that the 'economic structure' *determines* them. On the contrary, the fact that all institutions are 'reflected' so intimately in the economic life of society—in its division of labour, in its rules of property, in its corporate organization—is due simply to the fact that *every institution has its economic aspects, and must engage in demands for resources among the demands arising from all other institutions.* Religion is not just a matter of mystical hot air : it requires buildings, and symbols, and vestments and books and instruments of music. Art itself is not aesthetic contemplation *in vacuo:* it *makes* statues, pictures, and harmonious sounds on sinews and hair and wood and taut leather. The Law is not only a list of rules : it is a set of courts and court procedures, and a profession which requires long and careful education and training. In short, it *is not* something *basic* called the '*economic structure*' which determines all these other institutions, which can then be said to 'reflect' it. On the csontrary, the 'economic structure' of society is the actual embodiment of the many simultaneous demands upon resources actively made by all these institutions. Of course the 'economic system' reflects the many institutions of society, and *vice versa;* it is called into being and shaped according to their many-sided activity; it *is* one aspect of their many-sided creative activity.

Now this is an extremely important conceptual point, and it makes it clear that to abstract *one part* of the entire, interwoven complexity of a social system and to say that it determines all the rest in an absurd procedure. It is a determinism by assertion which *appears* to be supported because 'reflections' of it in society at large can easily be indicated. But there is a conceptual error at the heart of this. Later, we shall look at the efforts made by Marx and Engels to extricate themselves from this bald error of 'economic determinism', but we shall see, too, that these proposals, if accepted, only mean the entire abandonment of their theory. Meanwhile, however, there are one or two further aspects of this point which require separate and special emphasis.

(h) The 'Quantitative–Qualitative' account of social change is untenable

This, in my opinion, is one of the most fundamental criticisms of Historical Materialism and it follows upon the points made so far and is a very important additional dimension of them. We have seen that the 'quantitative–qualitative' distinction is of very dubious validity and value even as a basis for a 'materialist' account of 'nature'. We have seen too, that to equate the 'material basis' of *natural* phenomena with the 'material conditions' of *social* phenomena is an analogy of dubious validity and value. And we have seen that to equate the 'material activities of men in relation to nature' with men's 'economic' relations, and then to claim that this 'economic structure' determines all other institutions in the 'qualitative' superstructure is both historically and conceptually unjustified. But the insufficiency of Marx's and Engels's system of explanation is revealed with a total and overwhelming clarity when we look with exacting care at what constitutes the supposed '*quantitative change*' which, as the primary change in the material basis of society, is of the utmost importance and determines all else.

What are these basic 'material', 'quantitative' changes? What are these 'material' mainsprings of history? They are, in fact, *inventions*. They are no more and no less than the *application of man's ingenuity and knowledge to his practical activities*. They are changes in the 'productive forces' which men, in their ongoing experience and cumulative knowledge, bring about. Gradually, the theory continues, these primary changes, in a long, cumulative process, and with unintended consequences, come to change men's 'relations' in production, therefore changing their 'class relations' and their class-interests, until ultimately a new, entire super-structure of institutions becomes necessary.

But let us stop and consider the exact nature of this point, and the other clear points which immediately arise.

First: why is this proclaimed a '*material*', '*quantitative*' change, as distinct from any other kind of change in any other kind institution? It is, in fact, a *qualitative* matter, and a *qualitative* change entirely. It is the application of man's cumulative *knowledge* to the *improvement* of his tasks. It is with complete astonishment that one has to conclude that Marx, no less than Comte and Mill, offers an explanation of social change in terms of the *cumulative achievements of human knowledge and the increasing degree of control over the environment which it makes possible.* There is nothing *materialistic,* nothing *quantitative,* about this. But several things immediately follow.

It might be said that Marx in distinctively and justifiably 'materialist' in his emphasis because he insists that it is the application of knowledge to *practical, material, economic* tasks which turns out to be the mainspring of social change. Also, that he is justified in speaking of 'quantitative' change in the sense that these many technical changes *quantitatively accumulate* over periods of time. And he is justified in saying that the *quantitative* precedes and determines the *qualitative* changes in society in the sense that the qualitative effects or consequences of these cumulative changes are *not foreseen.* But then—what a strange tissue of ideas, assumptions, assertions, this has become, and in what tell-tale concepts it has been dressed.

First, knowledge applied in technology is, as we have seen, a *qualitative* matter. Never mind, we are told, it is concerned with the *material* conditions of society, with *economic* reality. But *why* should this be asserted? And on what grounds should we accept it? As we have seen: *every* human, institutionalized activity—religious, artistic, etc.—has its economic aspects. And if men can effectively apply their knowledge and experience to *some* activities, they can apply them to all. They can think and act inventively in their family relationships, in their political constitutions, in their churches, and so on, and these changes may all have economic implications. . . But *why* is the one application of knowledge *material* and *quantitative* and the others not? And why must we suppose that the changes in other institutions are bound to wait upon changes in the material, economic sphere, and never in any other order? There is, of course, no reason whatever. And as to 'unintended consequences'—no one would want to deny that social change is full of these, but (*a*) to say that the application of knowledge has unintended consequences is and (*b*) why should it be only the unintended consequences of '*technological*' knowledge which are emphasized? The changes which men make in other institutions may have their unforeseen repercussions on the rest of social organization too.

Furthermore, though men may never be able to foresee all the consequences of the immediate changes they bring about, and though they *may* not be concerned even to *try* beyond the range of their present interests, *nonetheless* it cannot be assumed that men may not foresee *some* consequences, and that they, or some of them, may not come to wish and seek to see the consequences of change beyond the range of their *own* interests and institute certain social and political provisions accordingly. There is also reason to suppose, according to this conception of the ingenuity and inventiveness of men, that, as knowledge accumulates, such foresight and conscious control might be extended.

Quite plainly, the 'quantitative–qualitative', 'materialist' account of social and historical change dissolves, upon critical reflection, into a mere verbal mist, and, again, we can see clearly that, through all the details, it is the assertion of the strong *materialist metaphysic* which persists. Historical Materialism is not a scientific theory of society; it is a metaphysical dogma dressed up in appropriate concepts and select illustrations. No more.

(i) Institutions of the 'Super-Structure' important in their own right: even as determining influences on 'economic activity'

It follows clearly from all the points we have made that it is quite untenable to claim that some institutions—those in the 'super-structure'—only 'reflect' the material reality of society and are determined by it. There is no reason why we should not suppose that each institution—family, religion, law, education, etc.—is of importance in its own right in society; contributing something distinctive in the entire nature of society; and, indeed, having some determining influence upon the structuring, the patterning of economic activity.

(j) The entire structure of society interpenetrated by interests and values : not only 'Economic'. The understanding of Social Action for purposes of social explanation should take account of ALL these.

It also follows clearly from the points made so far that the Marxian insistence on looking *'behind'* stated values and interests (including 'ideological' ones) to the *'real'* material, economic, or class interests which underlie them requires considerable modification. It may be, of course, and often is, that the ostensible aims and reasons offered by men to explain or justify their pursuit of certain actions are specious (whether consciously so or not) and that we have to consider what lies behind these. However, to claim that the only *'ultimate'* data concerning aims and reasons which we can accept as social scientists are *'economic'* ones, is simply the re-assertion of the metaphysical dogma to which we have pointed before. It is just as possible for an overt 'economic' and to be a 'reflection' of an underlying 'religious' persuasion, as vice versa. It follows from our insistence that all institutions may have their own distinctive *raison d'etre* in society; that all the ends which are important for men in society—their religion, familial, political objectives, beliefs, and motives, etc.—should be fully considered in their own right. It *cannot* be assumed, apart from the materialist dogma, that the *only real* interests are economic, and that , *on intellectual principle,* one must look *behind* all other interests until one can locate (or conjure up !) some economic motives in which they are *really* rooted. If one *does* assume this, then one is embarked on Engels' infinite metaphysical regress of seeking '. . . the driving forces behind the driving forces'.

Lest this should be thought a small point, let us see how strongly Lenin wrote about it. In his essay on the *Sources and Component Parts of Marxism* he stated his position like this :

'People always were and always will be the stupid victims

of deceit and self-deceit in politics, as long as they have not learned to discover the *interests* of one or another of the classes *behind* any moral, religious, political and social phrases, declarations and promises. The supporters of reforms and improvements will always be fooled by the defenders of the old, as long as they will not realize that every old institution, however absurd and rotten it may appear, is kept in being by the forces of one or the other of the ruling classes. And there is *only one* way of breaking the resistance of these classes, and that is to find, in the very society which surrounds us, and to enlighten and organize for the struggle, the forces which can and, by their social position *must* form the power capable of sweeping away the old and of establishing the new.'

It is quite starkly clear in this passage that *any* moral, religious, political ideas of an old order, defended by *anybody, must* be regarded as only the specious defences of class and economic interests. And it is held always to be *stupid* to be misled by them. The ideas have no worth or validity in themselves. One has to get to the *reality behind* them. It is also starkly clear in this passage that what is a *new* economic and class interest must be regarded, without question, as being *better* than any institutional or ideological aspects of the *old.* The political naivety of such a point of view, and the political dangers of it, are, of course, colossal.

(k) A basic error of sociological analysis and 'explanation'

It is time, I think, to draw some of these criticisms together to show how Marxism commits a basic error in sociological analysis and explanation, and is an excellent and informative illustration of it : from which, if we are perfectly clear about it, much can be learned.

We have seen that, for purposes of conceptual clarity, analysis, and description, a certain 'model' of society was adopted by Marx and Engels. The 'social system' as a whole was sub-divided into the 'economic basis', the system of class-relations, and then all the institutional elements of the 'super-structure'—the family, religion, law, government, and the like. A 'structural-functional' analysis was adopted, and specific institutions were analytically defined. Then, however, a *causal explanation* came to be conceived, as a specific '*weighting*' of *one* of these institutional components. It was the '*economic basis*' (the 'productive forces') of society which changed, and , in its changing, determined changes in all the rest.

Now Marx himself especially argued that one should not make the mistake of attributing a misplaced concreteness to 'societies' or 'social institutions' and went so far as to emphasize *individuals* as *social beings* always involved in their many-sided practical activities. And yet, this error of stressing one institutional sector of society as the determining cause of other institutional sectors is one into which the Marxian system fell. Marxism is a *mono-causal* theory of institutional change if we treat its arguments and assertions seriously and consistently. As such, it is an error. I would like to be very clear about certain specific aspects of this.

Firstly—having postulated this institutional definiteness: that the material conditions of productive and class relations are indispensable and independent of men's will, and that they determine other social relationships, Marx then clearly regards the quantitative changes in this material basis as being the application of men's ingenuity and knowledge to their practical tasks. In short, the institutional definiteness becomes a many-faceted application of knowledge and skill by many individuals to their many tasks. The fundamental explanation resides therefore in man's *knowledge* and *creative inventiveness*.

Secondly—there is therefore no reason to suppose that the same knowledge and creative inventiveness should not be applied in *other* institutional areas—in religion, government, law, etc.—so , as we have seen ,we are therefore in a position of regarding all institutions as being of importance in their own right.

Thirdly, therefore, sociological analysis cannot be a vast 'a priori' statement about one specific, 'necessary', cause and effect relation between these institutional elements in all societies and at all times. The relations between all these institutions of society may vary. It is feasible to suppose that in *some* periods, the technological changes in society may have dominant importance; in *some* periods military conquest may have a dominant importance; in *some* periods the detailed establishment and development of law; in *some* periods great changes in religious ideas and groupings; in some periods the development of education; and so on. In short, the specific relations to be found among the several institutions of society may well differ among types of society, and from one historical period to another. The exploration of them waits upon detailed empirical study. The *weighting* of one institution to explain sequences of change amongst all others may be entertained as a *hypothesis* to be *tested*—but not as an overriding metaphysical dogma to be defended by selective illustration.

But fourthly—it is highly dubious, and here we come to the crux, of this problem, whether, *for purposes of social explanation* the *weighting* of one institutional component of society as being a dominating determining *cause* of others, *can* be entertained. There are two points. On the one hand, the 'institutional definiteness' can be seen always to consist of men acting within the framework of organization, so that change is always 'mediated' by them, and the explanation of change must therefore always take them into account.

This is a recognition of John Stuart Mill's emphasis—and an acceptance of his rejection of the idea that 'institutions' can have 'causal relations' between each other independently of individuals; But, and this must be noted, it is NOT a *reduction* of the explanation of social change to '*individual*' psychology. But also, though 'institutional sectors', 'elements of social structure', may be conceptually distinguished for purposes of social analysis and description, *men in their social activities participate in them all.* The actuality of human action is always a many-faceted pattern of behaviour in which all these institutional aspects are involved. A man, for example, works for his family, in which he is a father, who brings upon his children in certain ways because he is a Methodist, and encourages them to take political thought seriously, and to pursue their education devotedly, and so on. In his nature and conduct he is *continuously* drawing upon values, aims, attitudes, constraints, etc., from all these institutions simultaneously. He is never *separately* familial, religious, political, educational, etc.; he is *always* acting as a kind of summation of all these in his own individual experience. And when men collectively support (say) one political party, this is, at once, in relation to concerns for family, education, welfare services, religious belief, etc. The *social action* of individuals and groups derives from *all* institutional influences and is something more than the institutional entities themselves.

The upshot of all this is that : *the concepts necessary for the careful ANALYSIS and DESCRIPTION of the institutional organization of society may not be sufficient for CAUSAL EXPLANATION. For EXPLANATION, other concepts such as the understanding of sequences of social action may be necessary, and this may always have to include a consideration of individuals and the ends for which they strive.*

This is a most important point to which we must ultimately return at the end of our study, but I hope it is sufficiently clear that, though certain concepts may be necessary for *descriptive* and *analytical* purposes, it is an error to think that *causal* explanation can be satisfactorily achieved by a process of *weighting* any one of them. Thus, it is not only the *mono*-causal emphasis of Marx which is an error, but even the *nature* of his explanation : i.e., the attributing of causal determinacy to an institutional component of society as such.

Marx has often been praised for achieving an 'autonomous' sociology; for having lifted sociological explanation to an institutional level in its own right, and to have avoided any 'reductionism' in terms of individuals of 'psychology'. Karl Popper, for example, so praises him. But Marx is at fault here. In so far as he insists upon an 'institutional' causal explanation, he is in error. In so far as, in fact, his explanation turns out to be one in terms of the application of knowledge by individuals, his error, true, evaporates—but so does his distinctive theory.

Much later, when we have critically assessed the ideas of Durkeim in particular, we will consider this entire question of 'institutional' versus 'individual', 'sociological' versus 'psychological', explanation down to the roots. It is a difficult issue, into which ambiguities easily creep. For now, however, our concern is specifically with Marx and his theory.

(l) The negative, conflictful aspects of Social Class too much emphasized

To return to Marx's specific doctrines concerning social change : once the deterministic tie between 'economic basis' and 'super-structure' is radically questioned and rejected, then the further corollary must also be seen : that the Marxian metaphysic places its emphasis almost entirely on the *negative, conflictful,* economically *repressive* aspects of any hierachy of class and status in society. Any positive functions which class and status distinctions may serve in the social order : of achieving a certain distribution (allocation) of authority and responsibility, of establishing a beneficial organization of the division of labour in society, of sustaining an appropriately differential system of education, training and recruitment in society, come to be regarded as inhumane and repressive. They *must* be so regarded, because the foundation of each ruling class is secured by *exploiting* the classes beneath it; by *expropriating* the products of their labour.

Now in this, one does not want to seem to be upholding all the evils that have been attendant upon class divisions in society; but it is the case—as soon as one recognizes that the establishing of political order, legal provisions, religious, institutions, education and training, and the like, are activities having ends, motives, functions which are *not* to be identified with *economic* interests, and which are something *more* than a *reflection* of them—that distinctions of status and class in society can be said to make positive and worthwhile contributions. They may, indeed, be such as to *qualify* and *govern* the raw economic and class interests which might otherwise ride roughshod over all considerations of justice and morality. This is not a popular view—but it is true.

That : 'The history of all hitherto existing society is the history of class struggles' is an absurdly over-simplified statement, and one that emphasizes 'the oppressor' and 'the oppressed'. It could equally well be written that all societies, past and present, have had their appropriate orders of status; that these divisions of social class have often entailed inhumanity; but, also, that frequently those of higher status in society have contributed as much to the benefit of those of lower status, as those lower in the hierarchy have contributed to those more highly placed. Members of *all* clásses may be their own ways and in relation to different functions, and those of a higher class may create conditions of security, and wealth which positively benefit those lower in the society. In this sense, Spencer's analysis of ranks, classes, and the insigma of status in society may be said to be better balanced than that of Marx—which, again, really derives from his all–pervading metaphysical dogma.

(m) Alienation: too much emphasized

In exactly the same way, Marx can be said to erect 'alienation' into a metaphysical overstatement of a useful idea, and, by so doing, to give it an unwarranted and peculiarly one-sided emphasis. It is obviously the case that the productive activity of men can come, and does come, to create a material order of property, with established rules of property, which place some men in the power of others. In this, property-owners can ill-treat the property-less whom they employ; the property-less can feel that they are being denied their essential human dignity and are being used as units of labour to create profits for their employers. Problems of power, virulent feeling of grievance, and of hatred at the humiliations and the sheer sufferings and hardships involved, are certainly there in plenty. In this context, the sense of 'alienation' from the essential conditions of human dignity has a real meaning for men so placed. And yet—fully and readily agreeing with this—it must be said that Marx's conception of 'alienation' goes *beyond* this, and , in so far as it does, seems unwarranted, and such as to give a one-sided slant to the analysis of the relations of men in production (and in classes and in society).

As we have seen earlier, Marx definitely opposed Hegel's 'Idealist' notion of 'alienation of spirit' in the process of creation with his own 'materialist' notion of man's alienation from his essential ('species-distinctive') condition of needing creative activity in and upon the natural world to accomplish the fulfilment of his own nature. In this sense, every new technological stage in the development of the productive forces of society, every new set of property and class relations, was (despite increased productive) a new repressive expropriation, until, in industrial capitalism, the worker was propertyless—stripped of all the conditions necessary for his essential fulfilment; a de-humanized unit of mechanical manufacture; geared up to the maximization of profit and therefore suffering the minimal return for his work.

Now apart from the fact that there seems *never* to have

been a condition of society in which man enjoyed a life *free* from alienation (for Marx claimed that in the very production of *objects,* man created a material order which 'alienated' him, and so began the long trek to history—or 'pre-history') it is surely possible that the enterprise of some men (set us say the 'Merchant Adventurers' towards the end of the Middle Ages, or present-day oil companies exploring the resources of Alaska) may create totally new conditions and relations of production which may be positively beneficial in every way to wage and salary earners. To put this even more baldly : may it not be that enterprise based upon a joint aggregation of capital can be such *not* as to benefit the entrepreneurs *at the expense of,* and *to the humiliation of,* wage-earning employees, but, quite literally, to the improved benefit of all concerned? Once the *dogma* of Marx is discarded, there seems no reason whatever why this should not be so. But the *negative* dogma only sees the *end* (i.e. the termination) to such 'alienation' in the collectivization of property. But here one enters Marx's 'Utopia' which is as perplexing as any other.

(n) Marx's 'Theory of Values' : false

A final point to be touched in on this entire matter of 'class-conflict', 'alienation', 'expropriation', etc., as a set of concepts for the materialist explanation of social change, is with regard to the 'underpinning' basis of economic theory which Marx thought firm and conclusive : namely his 'Labour Theory of Value'. We have seen that, following upon a critique of the work of Adam Smith, Jean Baptiste Say, Roicardo, and others, Marx adopted a 'Cost of Production' theory of the value of commodities—maintaining that the value of a commodity was the amount of labour which went into the making of it. 'Profit' was the amount expropriated by the entrepreneur after he had paid 'wages' to the labourer, which had, at least, to be equal to his cost of subsistence. 'Capital' was 'stored labour' put to use by entrepreneurs. The entire system of production, distribution and exchange was therefore a war for the products of labour (accumulated or otherwise); a war between 'profit' and 'wages', between the 'owners' of the means of production and the 'property-less' proletariat.

The fact is that this theory of value put forward by Marx

was false. And on this, there is little to be said. The 'value' of commodities is as much a function of the effective demand for them, as of the cost of the factors which have gone into their production, so that, to be brief, the 'profit' derived from the production and sale of a commodity is *not* a margin subtracted from the labour embodied in it. This can become a complex matter of economic analysis, but it seems perfectly clear, without going further, that this theory of value does not provide the explanatory plank for a fundamental conflict of interest between capitalist and proletariat that Marx thought it did. A basic factor underlying 'alienation' and 'class-conflict' therefore disappears; and it becomes possible, at least, that a certain *identity,* as well as *difference,* of interest can exist between owner and non-owner of the means of production.

This part of Marx's system was criticized and rejected quite definitively by Professor Bohm-Bawerk in his essay : *Karl Marx and the Close of his System.* In this essay, Bohm-Bawerk showed himself quite sympathetic to Sombart's careful and constructive appraisal of Marx, but even so, was quite definite in his detailed rejection of the 'Labour Theory of Value' and all its entailments in Marx's system.

With this critical rejection of Marx's one-sided emphasis upon class-conflict, his overstated claims concerning the nature of 'alienation' and, finally, his labour theory of value, it can be seen that Marx's entire conceptual apparatus for explaining the sources of essential conflict and change in the economic order proved inadequate, and falls to the ground.

(o) The relations between mind and matter, between ideology and material reality, dubiously conceived

We have seen in their entire system that Marx and Engels relegated 'mind' to a 'secondary' role in nature and society. In nature, the experiences and concepts of life and mind only 'reflect' material reality. In society and history, 'ideas, beliefs', all that constitute the 'ideological' element in the social order, 'reflect' the basic material conditions, the productive forces. They are not of importance in their own right, but derive their nature and virility from 'the driving forces behind' them; and, furthermore, they are 'false' ideologies, because they stem from hidden relations, conditions, and historical accumulations of which even those who are driven by them may not be aware. Always, mind and its ideas are subjected to the more powerful determining influence of 'material reality'.

This conception can be criticized on many levels. The first thing is that neither Marx nor Engels ever considered seriously the critical philosophy of Kant which presents very telling grounds for the view that—Idealism aside—the human mind does not by any means simply 'reflect' something 'external to it' called 'objective reality', but, on the contrary, that it brings with it *to* experience certain categories—such as time, space, etc.—which do not appear to be *provided* by experience but without which perceptual and conceptual experience would be impossible. Without in any sense leaving the rigorous and sober level of critical philosophy and empirical science (i.e. without taking flight into questionable Idealist metaphysics the Marxian conception of mind as being 'reflective' *only* seems very ill-considered and superficial).

The second point is that , although it may readily be agreed that forms of life and mind have emerged in nature *after* the existence of material processes, and that the explanation of this emergence must be, in some sense, in terms of these material processes; and though, indeed, it may be readily agreed that mind, as far as we know it, only operates upon a basis of materially existing organic life; nonetheless *it does not follow that mind, given its accumulation of knowledge, remains subservient to material reality and 'determined' by it.* Once mind has emerged; once it has become conscious *of* its context in nature and society; once it has accumulated knowledge and attendant degrees of control; then it may *govern* nature and society increasingly in accordance with its own needs and purposes. It can become *directive,* and *self-directive,* at least to some degree.

Thirdly, all we have said about the importance in their own right of all the specific areas of institutionalized life in society—religion, art, law, government, education, family, and the like—makes it clear that the development of knowledge, ideas, plans, and purposive social action can all result in growing degrees of control of mind *over* material reality; even to the point of consciously changing the structure of property relations, class relations, and forms of economic organization (e.g. company organization) in important respects.

The determining influence of matter over mind, of economic relations over ideology, is therefore much over-emphasized by Marx and Engels. And again, it is odd to recall that their 'material' changes in the 'economic structure' of society turn out to be nothing less than the ingenuity of mind in achieving technical improvements. There are quite radical inconsistencies here.

(p) The social relations of men are NOT independent of their will

It follows from all we have said that the social and economic relations of men are *not* independent of their will as Marx and Engels claimed. It is true enough that when children are born into a society and grow to adulthood in it, they find the productive forces of society *there already,* with a definite nature and set of constraints; and it is true that by a simple effort of will they cannot change them. But this is not to say that the consciousness of men is *determined* by these material conditions, and that they are independent of their will in any final, or crucial sense. Men can and do learn about their conditions; they strive to change them, and they *do* change them. Gradually, no doubt; with much resistance, no doubt; with much frustration and disillusionment certainly, but, nonetheless, men are not only and always determinate pawns on a kind of chess-board of history, placed here or there willy-nilly by irresistible economic forces.

In this respect, of course, Marxism itself has encountered its own inconsistencies—for if men are *determined*, how can it be worthwhile to exhort them to support the proletariat and the Communist Party?—especially if they are products of the professional middle classes—like Marx and Engels and Lenin ! It is an impossible inconsistency.

(q) The State cannot wither away: it creates the conditions of man's freedom

The strange naivety consequent upon their economic and class determinism is further shown in the conclusions of Marx and Engels as to the future of 'The State' (the organ of government) in society. For them, since 'the State' was that element in the super-structure which functioned as the organ, or 'committee', of the ruling class, once a classless society was achieved the State would no longer be necessary and would 'wither away'. But to contemplate a society (Whether with or without social classes) in which men did not make claims and counter-claims on each other, did not enter into disputes, did not have to create and preserve generally acceptable procedures for ensuring order over factions, is to be Utopian indeed. For my part, I find even Hegel himself, certainly Kant, much more convincing when they speak of the freedom of the individual as being something only possible within the objective conditions of morality achieved in the State. The achievement of individual freedom (*including economic* justice) *requires* the achievement of a just form of the state; the State is creative of the conditions (*including* the qualification of economic power) which alone make individual freedom possible; nothing of freedom can be accomplished by waiting for the State to wither away.

It also follows from all we have said about the importance and forcefulness of all the institutions of society *other* than economic institutions alone, that the creation of the State is, at all times, a constructive activity involving all these dimensions, and , at all times, going far beyond a simple 'reflection' of economic or class interests alone. The state is a necessary component of society. It has always existed (even, in rudimentary form, in the most simple societies), and it must always exist.

This naivety of Marx and Engels concerning the nature and necessity of the 'State', indicated their lack of attention to, or sympathy with, political theory and philosophy going beyond the bounds of their own doctrine. Although it is true that the organ of government in any society will be much influenced by the power and interests of the privileged class in that society, it is too simple to say that it is nothing more than the 'instrument' of the ruling class in carrying out its exploitation. In modern 'bourgeois' societies of Western Europe, the principle of political citizenship and the extension of representative government is linked to the idea that the organ of government must undertake the task of balancing the claims and counter-claims which are made by, or on behalf of, all groups and classes in the community, and , indeed, that it must establish and secure the apparatus whereby all such claims can be freely and frankly made known. Even in a classless society, these claims and counter-claims would still have to be made and dealt with; so that some organ of central government will always be necessary to discuss them and to legislate as equitably as possible in accordance with them; and the central power of the state will always be necessary to deal with the struggles for power and privilege of contending groups and factions within the community.

We might note here, as a very important point, that it is a mistake to identify a *privileged* class in a society with a *ruling* class in any simple sense. It may well be that privileged class exists in the society and that it has a great influence in affairs, but there may also be a system of representative government and a constitutional set of checks and balances against the abuse of power, which constrains and minimizes the political power of this class and ensures that the claims of all other sections of the community are justly treated. Privilege is not necessarily *arbitrary* privilege. Inequality is not necessarily *arbitrary* inequality. Supreme power is not necessarily vested in privileged groups.

(r) The classless society: the naive expectations of proletarian rule

In exactly the same way, the Marxian analysis of the 'post-proletarian-revolution' society shows the naivety of the simple conception of class as being a kind of division in society resting solely on men's relations to the means of production, or their place within the productive forces. According to Marx once the private ownership of the means of production is abolished, and the collectivisation of the means of production is instituted, then men will be related to the means of production, and therefore to each other, In the same way; and therefore no further basis for class divisions and class expropriation will exist. The productivity of the newly organized productive forces will be greatly increased so that, increasingly, men can be provided for in accordance with their needs, *not* their unequal place in society.

On the one hand, as we have seen, the distinctions of status in society have functional elements other than those stressed by Marx—so that the disappearance of class is not by any means a thing to be readily expected. Even in society in which there is a common ownership of the means of production, there will have to be some necessary distribution of authority (in the sense of differing degrees of responsibility in decision taking), and this itself will give rise to a hierarchy of statuses and the danger of the concentration of power in the hands of particular groups. It is a commonplace nowadays that power in society resides, not only with those who *own* property, but perhaps to a greater degree with those whe exercise *control* over it. The training for the differential exercise of responsibility will also involve differential educational requirements—and this too will be a source of status distinctions. Educational *opportunity* may be equal, by the many provisions of education cannot be equal. There are, then, important determinants of social status and social class other than economic factors, and it follows that the emergence of a society in which all men are similarly related to the means of production does not make inevitable the elimination of social class. The problems of power are likely to remain in other forms.

Perhaps even more important, however, is the strange naivety of the faith placed by both Marx and Engels in the 'dictatorship of the proletariat', and this, together with the rejection of 'bourgeois democracy', has hardened into a dangerous creed which has brought all the worst elements of uncontrolled totalitarian power in its train; a totalitarian ruthlessness which seems, if anything (consider, for example, the recent subjugation of Czechoslovakia) to be gaining strength in the world.

What form the dictatorship of the proletariat was to take, Marx and Engels never made clear, but, in effect, it has become the 'dictatorship of the Communist Party'—the 'advanced' party of the working classes. This party, of course, is not deluded, as many members of the working classes are, into accepting 'reformist' or 'moderate' policies which are foisted on them by capitalist propaganda. This party, based upon the science of Historical Materialism, can see 'behind' these ideological facades to the 'driving forces behind the driving forces', to the '*real interests*' of the working class—not those they *think* are their interests at any given moment. This, of course, especially if one smashes 'bourgeois democracy', is *sheer* dictatorship; it is no less than the abandonment of democracy; and I, for one, find myself at a loss to distinguish between the 'World Historical Individual' of Hegel who knows the 'real will' of the 'World Spirit', and the leader of a Communist Party who knows the 'real interests' of the proletariat. The machinegun bullet which each of them puts into lower mortals for the sake of the historic destiny of man does not, one suspects, feel much different to those who are destroyed by it.

If, in the pursuit of the 'classless' society, men destroy 'bourgeois democracy', the 'representative' form of the State, but then find that the classless society is not forthcoming, and that divisions of power remain, they may find that they have destroyed the only political means of safeguarding society from the exercise of such arbitrary power. They may still have a class society, but without, any longer, the political means of dealing with its conflicts. These errors, then, are not by any means of a *conceptual* nature only; they are errors of the greatest potential danger.

(s) Material and economic determinism : The Qualifications of Marx and Engels

All these criticisms have been made of the doctrine of Dialectical and Historical Materialism as we have seen it outlined by Marx and Engels. It must be said, however, that both men tried to deny the kind and degree of 'determinism' which our interpretation of their writings has assumed. Attacking this notion of 'economic determinism', Engels insisted of himself and Marx: 'our conception of history is above all a *guide to study,*' not a lever for construction after the manner of the Hegelians,' and he vituperated against :

'. . . the fatuous notion of the ideologists that because we deny an independent historical development to the various ideological spheres which play a part in history, we also deny them *any* effect upon history.'

In a letter to Joseph Bloch, he stated his position in this way:

'According to the materialist conception of history the determining element in history is *ultimately* the production and reproduction in real life. More than this neither Marx nor I have ever asserted. If therefore somebody twists this into the statement that the economic element is the *only* determining one, he transforms it into a meaningless, abstract and absurd phrase. The economic situation is the basis, but the various elements of the super-structure—political forms of the class struggle and its consequences, constitutions established by the victorious class after a successful battle, etc.—forms of law—and then even the reflexes of all these actual struggles in the brains of the combatants : political, legal, philosophical theories, religious ideas and their further development into systems of dogma—also exercise their influence upon the course of the historical struggles and in many cases preponderate in determining their *form.* There is an interaction of all these elements in which, amid all the endless *host* of accidents the economic movement *finally* asserts itself as necessary.'

This appears to be a qualification of some substance, and yet, when one examines it carefully, it is simply a way of asserting the dogma more moderately. It still insists upon the distinction between the *economic basis* and the *super-structure,* and it still insists that the economic basis of production is *ultimately* the *determining* element in history; the element which *finally* asserts itself. In many other places Engels makes much of allowing a full consideration of other institutions such as the law, political institutions, and even morals, but still he speaks of them all as *'reflexes'* of the economic order and claims that it is the economic conditions of society which are *'finally decisive'*.

There are really two critical responses to be made to this kind of 'apologia'. The first is simply that if nothing has been modified, excepting to insert the words 'ultimate' or 'final' here and there, then the theory remains open to all the criticisms we have stated—and it remains true that the 'material reality' on which all else rests is simply the application of human knowledge to practical tasks : a peculiarly thin basis for a fundamental distinction between the 'material' basis of society and the rest.

The second response is: that if the economic determinism is abandoned—then *there is no distinctive theory of Historical Materialism at all.* There is simply a theory of social change in terms of cumulative knowledge; its application in all institutional spheres; and the tracing of its many unforeseen consequences; with special emphasis upon property relations and class relations as important sources of social conflict and important factors in social change. But in such a theory, all institutions would have to be given full consideration in any analysis of society so that no distinctive 'materialist' hypothesis arises.

These attempts to qualify the claims of 'Historical Materialism' are therefore of very little consequence however they are taken.

Such, then, are the criticisms of the substantive doctrines of 'Dialectical and Historical Materialism'. The verdict arrived at by Professor Action—that Marxism is a 'philosophical farrago'—is correct. Any searching criticism shows that the hotch-potch of concepts drawn together in an apparent 'system' simply do not hang together. And there are, of course, other kinds of criticism which we have scarcely mentioned. Marx and Engels did not avoid the entanglement of 'fact and value', for example, any more than did Comte and Spencer. Their theory encounters, but does not satisfactorily consider, or resolve, the same problems of ethics. Most of us may well agree very strongly with Marx's humane sympathies and his desire to see the arbitrary subjection of man by man ended and removed from society, but still, it is necessary to see that his moral ends and moral principles are in, no way derived from his 'scientific system', and some curious problems and dangers of Marxist ethics result.

For example, Marx speaks of the many changes in economic and class relations throughout history as constituting an 'advance'. They are 'progressive' changes which are part of the 'pre-historic' making of man; they are a necessary process of winning ultimate freedom from 'alienation'. Marx was in a position of having morally to approve of the 'advances' which had brought about slavery, serfdom, wage labour, each·in its turn. But also, Marx claims that these movements in history are inevitable and that the consciousness of men within them is *determined* by their class interests. If this is so—no one in history is either praiseworthy or blameworthy. Men cannot be said to be moral agents. They are not responsible for their moral judgments and social actions. A capitalist cannot help having the views and values he has. In any case, he will inevitably be overthrown by the tide of social change. Why then bother to blame him with most vituperative language that one can command as an evil exploiter and why, on the other hand, extol the values of the worker? He cannot help being a proletarian, any more than the capitalist can help being a capitalist. Why exhort the members of the bourgeoisie to see the errors of their ways? Why exhort the workers to exert themselves in bringing the revolution to a successful outcome? Why, indeed, exhort anybody to do anything? Their consciousness is determined by their social situation. It is all inevitable; and morality is only relative to material and class conditions.

Marx himself is quite definite about this. In the first preface to *Capital*, he wrote :

'I paint the capitalist and the landlord in no sense *couleur de rose*. But here individuals are dealt with only in so far as they are the personifications of economic categories, embodiments of particular class-relations and class-interest. My stand-point, from which the evolution of the economic formation of society is viewed as a process of natural history, *can less than any other make the individual responsible for relations whose creature he socially remains,* however much he may subjectively raise himself above them.

These are very curious inconsistencies. If one maintains that historical processes are inevitable, and that the attitudes of men are determined by their social circumstances, then one removes all grounds for moral praise or blame and all point from moral effort. All that can be said is that the values of one class are on the ascendancy over others in a particular historical situation, but there are no grounds for calling them better or worse and saying that they constitute a moral 'progress'. Furthermore, there are no ethical grounds for fighting on the side of what is *new*. What is *new* is not necessarily what is *better* in terms of ethical standards.

Marxism and Communism also raises difficulties over the distinction between a long term and an interim ethic. In the 'long term' achievement of a communist society, certain ends are held to be not only morally justifiable, but positively sacred. Meanwhile, however, in the struggle which has to be carried on against capitalism, many things are held to be justified as being necessary means to achieve these desired ends. This distinction can, it is clear, justify any kind of immoral behaviour; any kind of deceit, any kind of expediency, any kind of manipulation of others. But, apart from the fact that, if this is so, capitalists are just as much justified in smashing communists as are communists in smashing capitalists, the distinction between means and ends in morality and in political action is never so clear-cut as this. The continuous practice of dubious means may make the character of a political movement, let alone one's personal character, into something far different from the noble conception which the ideal upholds. The 'end' may never be reached. Its character may have been despoiled and destroyed unwittingly in the exercise and the condoning of certain means.

The doctrines of Marx and Engels and the theoretical system which was built upon them contain, therefore, many difficulties. Indeed, far from being 'theoretical' issues alone, they pose, if they have not in part created, some of the gravest political dilemmas and problems of our age; problems which are yet very far from being solved. Again we are brought up against this ever-pressing and ever-important fact: that the making of sociology has not been an 'intellectual' pursuit alone, but has been one activity among others at the heart of the making of modern society; it has been the making of a science which must serve as a necessary basis for dealing with the many-dimensional problems of industrial society. In comte and in Spencer, and in Mill in more moderate fashion, we saw how their sociological systems were used as a basis for positive political proposals. In the case of Marx and Engels, the practical political involvement of their theory was, and remains, even more marked. It is written deeply into the very fabric of peace and war in the twentieth century, and for this reason any 'intellectual' refutation of it will not easily lead to its rejection. The assessment of Bohm-Bawerk was very sound.

'What will be the final judgment of the world? he wrote. 'Of that I have no manner of doubt. *The Marxian system has a past and a present, but no abiding future.* Of all sorts of scientific systems those which, like the Marxian system, are based on a hollow dialectic, are most surely doomed.

A clever dialectic may make a temporary impression on the human mind, but cannot make a lasting one. In the long run facts and the secure linking of causes and effects win the day. In the domain of natural science such a work as Marx's would even now be impossible. *In the very young social sciences it was able to attain influence, great influence, and it will probably only lose it very slowly, and that because it has its most powerful support not in the convinced intellect of its disciples, but in their hearts, their wishes, and their desires.* It can also subsist for a long time on the large capital of authority which it has gained over many people. In the prefatory remarks to this article I said that Marx had been very fortunate as an author, and it repears to me that a *circumstance which has contributed not a little to this good fortune is the fact that the conclusion of his system has appeared ten years after his death, and almost thirty years after the appearance of his first volume.* If the teaching and the definitions of the third volume had been presented to the world simultaneously with the first volume, there would have been few unbiased readers, I think, who would not have felt the logic of the first volume to be somewhat doubtful. Now a belief in an authority which has been rooted for thirty years forms a bulwark against the incursions of critical knowledge—a bulwark that will surely but slowly be broken down.'

However, the 'final judgment of the world' will be some time yet in coming. The ideological hold of this theory in vast areas of the modern world is rooted not most conspicuously in 'oppressed classes', though this certainly is one contributing factor, but in the massive propagandist education which has been institutionalized in nations of enormous population, and now indoctrinates hundreds of millions of previously uneducated people. The battle in the modern world is still, in one large and crucial dimension, a battle of ideas, and will need, for a long time yet, to be fought vigorously and with vigilance. The making of sociology is still at the heart of the making of society.

A Final comment on Marx

I cannot leave this critical study of Marx without making a final comment arising from a point introduced at the outset. The exposition and criticism of Marx's ideas given here seems to me wholly fair. Even so, I am deeply conscious that much of the writing of Marx contains a qualitative richness, and, especially, a deeply moving humanity, which one cannot properly catch in the snare of critical analysis. In a curious way, some of Marx's ambiguities, though not altogether eluding logic, are qualitatively worthwhile. Thus—to take the most obvious example—though one can logically dismantle, and disprove the validity of, the detailed conceptual apparatus, and the metaphysical assertions which it hides, with which Marx insists upon the basic determining importance in society of 'material conditions' and 'class-relations', even so, when one has done this, one finds that Marx's *emphasis* upon these factors has been such as to make one consider them more fully, more seriously, more richly, in sociological analysis than one would otherwise have done. Even when the metaphysical underpinning is discarded, and one resumes sociological analysis in its full sense, giving all elements of society their full place, one finds oneself taking more seriously, regarding as a more telling component, the sum-total of men's practical, technological activities; the property relations they involve; and their close tie with law, politics, religion, and the like, in society. In short, Marx enriches and deepens sociological analysis, even when one has thrown all his dogmas to the winds. And this is a matter worth noting. It is almost as though, with men of peculiarly profound genius, the question of the truth or falsity of their notions is not what supremely matters. It is as though the quality of their outlook, their dimensions of thought, vision, feeling, is something much more than the logical and conceptual apparatus in which they try to snare it. So that, when you have worked with honest judgment through the complex of their work, and in such a way, perhaps, as to have rejected much of its logical shell, you find, nonetheless, that they have *affected* you. Their quality has deepened you. So that you now look with an enriched awareness, a deeper and more many-dimensioned perception, at the same subject-matter you had contemplated before. I cannot put this better. I only know that it is so, and that this deepening of certain dimensions of human nature and human society comes from a study of Marx, even when one has come to discard much of his system.

The humanity of Marx must be apparent to all who trouble to read him, but there are some aspects even of this on which I feel inclined to place much emphasis. His detailed concern for the personal degradation of men in harsh and disgusting situations of economic and social subjection need no further comment; but they were deeply felt beyond a doubt. But it is also worth stressing that the vision Marx had of the kinds and qualities of human relationship and human experience which would come to be possible once a communist society had become 'humanized' was not absurdly 'Utopian' and was as high in its moral standards as those of any other moralist, or even 'idealist'. Though riddled with philosophical dilemmas of 'ethics', the substantive quality of Marx's 'morality' was high. I will give only one example here : the example of Marx's conception of the personalized, 'humanized', relationship of *marriage.*

It is commonly thought (following 'Communist' teaching) that Marx thought 'marriage' a bourgeois institution, and wished to abandon it with the abolition of other forms of 'private property'. In fact, however, Marx only thought in these terms in the sense of desiring the moral *improvement* of the relationship between the sexes. Indeed, he felt that it was in this most intimate of relationships between persons that the entire quality attained by society was reflected. The following passage speaks for itself.

'In the approach to *woman* as the spoil and handmaid of communal lust is expressed the infinite degradation in which man exists for himself, for the secret of this approach has its *unambiguous,* decisive, *plain* and undisguised expression in the relation of *man* to *woman* and in the manner in which the *direct* and *natural* procreative relationship is conceived. The direct, natural, and necessary relation of person to person is the *relation of man to woman.* In this *natural* relationship of the sexes man's relation to nature is immediately his relation to man, just as his relation to man is immediately his relation to nature—his own *natural* function. In this relationship, therefore, is *sensuously manifested*, reduced to an observable *fact,* the extent to which the human essence has become nature to man, or to which nature has to him become the human essence of man. *From this relationship one can therefore judge man's whole level of development.* It follows from the character of this relationship how much *man* as a *species being, as man,* has come to be himself and to comprehend himself; the relation of man to woman is the *most natural* relation of human being to human being. It therefore reveals the extent to which man's *natural* behaviour has become *human*, or the extent to which the *human* essence in him has become a *natural* essence—the extent to which his *human nature* has come to be *nature to him*. In this relationship is revealed, too, the extent to which man's *need* has become a *human* need, the extent to which, therefore, the *other* person as a person has become for him a need—the extent to which he in his individual existence is at the same time a social being. The first positive annulment of private property—*crude* communism—is thus merely one *form* in which the vileness of private property, which wants to set itself up as the *positive community, comes to the surface.*'

A final point I feel it worthwhile to make is that Marx is often thought to have been purely a 'social scientist' and 'political agitator'; a 'materialist' who moved between his study and the British Museum or the working men's political platform. It is not commonly considered that he had a great love of literature, that he saturated himself in Shakespeare and Goethe in particular, and that his 'humanism' had deeper cultural dimensions than was apparent. In this, I myself believe that there lies a very important, indeed a basic, element in Marx's feeling and thinking which has tended always to go unnoticed. And it lies crucially in Marx's love of Goethe. In my opinion, though I do not possess the detailed knowledge to substantiate this, Goethe had an influence of the most telling importance upon Marx.

It must be remembered that the period with which we are concerned—from about the French Revolution to the present day—has not only been significant with regard to the making of sociology; it has also been of crucial significance for the making of modern literature; indeed the two developments have been, and are (properly understood) part of one entire development. They are both a part of man's attempts to come to grips with a new and rapidly changing society, and they constitute a grappling reinterpretation of human nature, experience, relationships, and destiny within this radically changed context. Much could be said about this, but here we may simply note that the beginning of this revolutionary period witnessed the emergence of the 'Romantic' movement in literature; and the great significance of Goethe, as a European figure, was that, in his own mind and work, he himself accomplished a well-considered, well-rounded, well-digested perspective in all this. In all the details of his work, he ranged from classical to modern times; he assessed the strictly modern romanticism within this entire context, and he balanced wonderfully within his thought the several approaches of science, art, and philosophy in man's exploration of the nature of things. But the central thing I have in mind is this.

In 'Faust', the great, long-term, culminating work of his life, it seems to me that Goethe stated his final judgment, following upon his wide–ranging exploration of all intellectual positions which man might adopt. By using the device of the compact with the Devil, Goethe—in Faust—was able to range through all the many dimensions, all the the nuances, all the heights and depths of human experience; through all possibilities which man might dare beyond his ordinary boundaries; and through all the many mythologies and *kinds* of mythologies—including *sheer intellectualism*—which man had tried. From the ruin of his first considered insufficiency of human love, Faust moves majestically through all the many kingdoms of man's mental and historical experience. And, as his quest ranges on for something in experience which he values so much that he would love to see it continuing, all these many avenues of the searching mind in abstraction from humanity become hollow and wearying to him. Ultimately, the judgment of Faust, and Goethe, is that the fullness, the richness, of man's life is to be found not in abstract theorizing or mythologizing at all; not in going *beyond* humanity at all; but in *realization of all the actual dimensions of our humanity in the ordinary, ongoing, shared creative activity of our distinctively human society within the actual richness of nature.* In the acceptance of a distinctively human life of shared, social, creativity in nature; in the acceptance of our human boundaries; in the exploration of our ordinary tasks of working together in society upon a nature of which, properly seen, our own nature is a part; in this lies the true fullness, greatness, beauty of human destiny.

Towards the end of the drama, Faust is still dogged by the images of Want, Guilt, Need, and Care which have driven men into the false direction of turning away, in despair, from the human condition, and seeking their salvation in colourful, mythical, ideological systems which, in fact, are false, misleading, and prevent men from seeing the true basis for their fulfilment—namely the creative improvement of their human lot.

> 'Could I but break the spell,' Faust cries, 'all magic spurning,
> And clear my path, all sorceries unlearning
> Free then, in Nature's sight, from evil ban,
> I'd know at last the worth of being man.
> Such was I once, before dark ways I sought
> And with fell words a curse on living wrought.
> Now teems the air with many a spectral shape,
> So thick that none can shun them or escape.'

Harried still by 'Care' who seeks to divert him, Faust persists in his new vision of humanity; in his effort to break through the created clouds of false ideologies, to pierce the veil which keeps man from a clear sight of his true nature.

> 'My way has been to scour the whole world through.
> Where was delight, I seized it by the hair;
> If it fell short, I simply left it there,
> If it escaped me, I just let it go.
> I stormed through life, through joys in endless train,
> Desire, fulfilment, then desire again;
> Lordly at first I fared in power and speed,
> But now I walk with wisdom's deeper heed.
> Full well I know the earthly round of men,
> And what's beyond is barred from human ken;
> Fool, fool is he who blinks at clouds on high,
> Inventing his own image in the sky.
> Let him look round, feet planted firm on earth :
> This world will not be mute to him of worth.
> Why haunt eternity with dim surmise?
> Things he perceives are his to realize.'
> 'Clear light within my mind shines still;
> And what I framed in thought I will fulfil.
> Ho, you my people, quickly come from rest :
> Let the world see the fruit of bold behest.
> Man all the tools, spade, shovel, as is due,
> The work marked out must straight be carried through.
> Quick diligence, firm discipline,
> With these the noblest heights we win.'

And then, with the 'clash of spades' in his ears Faust seeks to win, by labour, a fertile land (by draining a marshland on a mountain-side) on which men will be able to live the continuous, creative life of a human community.

'I work,' he declares, 'that millions may possess this space,
If not secure, a free and active race.
Here man and beast, in green and fertile fields,
Will know the joys that new-won region yields,
Will settle on the firm slopes of a hill
Raised by a bold and zealous people's skill.
A paradise our closed-in land provides,
Though to its margin rage the blustering tides;
When they eat through, in fierce devouring flood,
All swiftly join to make the damage good.
Ay, in this thought I pledge my faith unswerving,
Here wisdom speaks its final word and true
None is of freedom or of life deserving
Unless he daily conquers it anew.
With dangers thus begirt, defying fears,
Childhood, youth, age shall strive through strenuous years.
Such busy, teeming throngs I long to see,
Standing on freedom's soil, a people free.'

And then, with this final judgment, he commits himself to death by declaring, as had been agreed in his pact with the Devil, that here was something he wished to see continuing because of its worth and beauty.

'Then to the moment could I say :
Linger you now, you are so fair !
Now records of my earthly day
No flight of aeons can impair—
Foreknowledge comes, and fills me with such bliss,
I take my joy, my highest moment this.'

This, of course, is not by any means a total interpretation of 'Faust', but, even going beyond it, is significant that Faust finds his ultimate spiritual sublimity in and through this acceptance of the *essentially human,* and *not* through some intellectualized grandeur which has denied it and sought a realm of ideality unconnected with it. Whatever is possible of sublime experience and attainment for man is rooted in, and created of, the *essentially human;* it is created out of nature by the shared activities of man.

Goethe's ultimate, then, is a 'creative humanism', and my point is that this is essentially the vision and perspective and basis of all value in Marx. I believe that one enormously important strand, perhaps the central strand, in Marx's system of thought is this 'creative humanism'. It contains the same cultural and spiritual qualities as the vision of Goethe. It contains the same considered rejection of all the theoretical mythologies, all the abstract intellectualisms, which have stemmed from man's need, but only serve to hide from him the true basis for his possible fulfilment. It contains the same emphasis upon the ordinary creative activities of man within and upon nature, and the social and historical creation of his own distinctive nature. It sees the sublime in the essentially human; rooted in ordinariness, but stripped of all social falsities which despoil its nature. Whether it was derived from Goethe's influence, or an independent vision shared with it, there is a oneness in the judgments and perspectives of the two men which reveals a quality at the heart of Marx's thinking which is different from that normally attributed to him in terms of his heavy coating of 'materialist', economic, and social scientific concepts.

It is this, I think, which accounts for the ambiguity of feeling which men have in relation to Marx. Sometimes, men see Marx's scientific concepts and theories and are intrigued but yet perplexed by them. Sometimes, however, they catch the flavour of this strong, idealistic, conviction as to the powerful truth of 'creative humanism'—and they are won by it. So that followers of Marx are always well–nigh bound to manifest a passion for all that is humane, couched within a tangle of ideas out of which they try, but fail, to make systematic sense.

For my part, it seems to me that one can do no other than reject the apparatus of Marx's 'system', but that, even so, one can appraise the deepening of one's analysis and understanding of human nature and society that his emphases bring, and—especially—that one can approve entirely of his core emphasis upon 'creative humanism'. But again, it seems to me that this can most valuably be seen within the perspective we are emphasizing in this essay—not as one system of thought satisfactory in itself, but as one very important contribution among others in the making of sociology, the making of modern literature, the making of a new kind of society in this modern era of science and industrialization.

Summary

It will have become increasingly apparent, as our analysis of Marx has proceeded, that his conception of the nature and elements of a science of society, and certain aspects of his approach to the making of it, were similar in all basic ways, to those of comte, Mill and Spencer. We can now make a brief summary statement to make these similarities clear. We have seen that Marx's 'system' was clouded with ambiguities, and riddled with extreme assertions resting on unclarified and unresolved metaphysical assumptions, but here—for the purposes of summary—these can largely be ignored, though they may be noted, in passing, as seems necessary. Our grounds for rejecting them have already been made sufficiently clear.

Scientific Knowledge: a clear delimitation

(a) The necessity and nature of science

Like Comte, Miss and Spencer, Marx insisted that it was the methods of science alone, as distinct from speculative opinion and dogma which were productive of *knowledge.* Science was to be adopted, and metaphysical philosophy rejected. Marx was also agreed that a scientific knowledge of society was necessary as a basis for effective political action and the remaking of modern industrial society. Science was necessary for knowledge and action.

The methods of science were essentially *empirical.* They rested upon the observation and close study of the *facts*, and resulted in the clear, tested statement of *laws* : invariable regularities of interconnection among the facts. Such scientific knowledge was not final or absolute, but relative to men's practical activities, level of advancement, and their material, cultural and historical situation.

(I) AKIN TO 'POSITIVISM'

As a general conception of the nature of science, this was obviously closely akin to the 'positive science' of Comte and others. It lacked, however, any detailed analysis of concepts and methodology of the kind that Comte and Mill had provided.

(II) KNOWLEDGE OF 'REALITY'

Its claims also went far beyond theirs. It claimed, indeed, that science provided knowledge of *'reality'*—without philosophical qualification.

(III) SHEER EMPIRICISM : THE 'LAWS' TO BE FOUND THE FACTS

It was also a sheer empiricism in that it regarded the 'laws' of science as being 'there in the facts'. The mind (which did no more than 'reflect' them) simply uncovered them.

Marx put forward therefore a far more radical and unsophisticated conception of 'empirical science' than that offered by others.

(b) Prediction : but limited control

Marx also agreed that science made possible prediction, and that, on the basis of foreknowledge, effective action should be undertaken to achieve human advantage. However, he viewed 'laws' and 'historical tendencies' as possessing such a degree of rigidity, of inevitability, that the degree of control which men could exercise, even *with* foreknowledge, was distinctly limited. Men could not eliminate, for example, the conflictful; changes from one society to another, they could, at best, only 'lessen the birth–pangs.'

(c) Experiment and practice : the objective being not to understand but to change

Marx agreed, too, that scientific knowledge rested crucially upon factual *testing,* and that this could be accomplished in experiment, and in the trial and error of practice. Here again, he offered no detailed analysis, but his emphasis was upon the testing of theories in *practice* because of his conviction that the primary objective of men was not to *understand,* but to *change* the world. Knowledge was achieved *in* and *for* action. Marx's conception of science was therefore one of 'pragmatism'.

(d) The clarification of hidden laws

One important characteristic and function of science was that it probed beneath the apparent complexities and disparities of the surface of things (of surface phenomena) and produced knowledge of those unsuspected, hidden interdependencies, the 'laws' of a deeper level, by which the interrelatedness of all things could be clearly seen and explained. Science, therefore, gave new, additional, and deeper insights into the nature of things than other kinds of speculation could provide.

Dialectical Materialism and Evolution: guiding conceptions

(a) Basic and unifying conceptions

Exactly as was the case with Spencer, Marx's conception of the actual fundamental nature of things provided a basis for understanding the necessary components of science, and a basic schema for unifying all the science. All phenomena in nature—inanimate processes, organic processes, animal and human species, human societies—were interrelated parts of an ongoing process of material change which manifested a certain developmental and evolutionary pattern. Any specific phenomenon must be seen, and studied, within its actual context of other phenomena; and all were *processes* of material transformation. From relatively simple material processes, more complex forms emerged and developed. Qualitatively new forms rested upon quantitatively changing material processes. Science necessarily operated, therefore, within this over-all perspective of Dialectical Materialism and Evolution.

(b) The classification of the sciences

Within this over-all perspective, all the sciences had a distinct nature and place in that each dealt with a specific field of phenomena—physics, chemistry, astronomy dealing with inanimate phenomena, biology with organic processes and forms, and the science of society with developing systems of social institutions. All science was unified by these guiding conceptions, and all the sciences could be classified in relation to each other within the context of them. An 'arrangement' of the sciences—like the classifications (the 'hierarchy' of the sciences) of Comte and Spencer was clearly implicit in Marx: though more specifically articulated by Engels.

(c) Grounds of 'explanation'

The over-all perspective of Dialectical Materialism and Evolution also gave certain basic principles of 'explanation' in science. In particular : *(a)* because 'mind' emerged from more basic material processes and was a 'reflection' of them ('secondary' to their 'primary' reality) the *explanation* of mental phenomena, ideas, ideologies, must be in terms of the material reality which underlay and determined them. And (*b*) this process of explanation should always take the form of cumulative quantitative changes giving rise, at certain points, to qualitatively new forms. In this sense it was a 'materialist' explanation of 'material' change.

(d) Dialectical Materialism and Evolution equally applicable to the study of society and history : an 'advanced' theory of evolution.

Men and societies part of nature, and the over-all perspective of Dialectical Materialism and Evolution applied to them too, and provided a firm basis to the scientific study of them. In the study of man and society, as well as in the study of all other aspects of nature, Dialectical Materialism was thought to provide a more *advanced* analysis of the processes of evolution.

The scientific study of society

(a) Society : The social system

Exactly as Comte, Mill and Spencer, Marx conceived of a society as an entire 'system' of interconnected institutions; of elements of social structure or 'organization'; distinct from 'systems' of phenomena at other levels—such as the levels of inanimate or organic processes. The scientific study of societies was science of 'social systems', not *just* a study of amalgamations of *individuals*.

(b) A Structural–Functional model of society : Marx's 'Social Statics' and portrayal of the 'consensus' of institutions

In his study of societies, Marx employed a clear structural-functional model of the essential nature of a society, or a 'social system'. This gave a clear picture of the structural components of a society—the material, technological basis; the division of labour and property relations; the system of social classes with the attendant pattern of alienation and ideologies; and the elements of the super-structure : the family, the law, military institutions, religion and the State—and an equally clear picture of the nature of their functions and their functional interdependence. This was Marx's equivalent of a 'social statics'—as the other thinkers had conceived of it; and it gave clear analysis and description of the nature of the 'consensus' which, in Marx's view, obtained among the institutional elements of society.

(c) *Structural–Functional Analysis : a significant grouping of institutions*

Just as Spencer, within his own structural-functional model of society, proposed a significant grouping of institutions—into Regulatory, Sustaining and Distributive—for the purpose of analysing particular patterns of social change, so Marx also proposed such a significant grouping. In his case, it was the significant distinction between those institutions which comprised the *material basis* of society , and those which comprised its *super-structure*. A point which we might simply note, here, is that each theorist emphasized those components in his 'social statics' (in his model of society) which he felt to be most important for the hypothesis of explanation which he wished to employ in his empirical ('Dynamic') studies. If explicitly done, this is a perfectly proper procedure in the construction of theories, and it is a point to which we shall return later. Here it is important only to note that Marx like Spencer and others, did this.

(d) *The Structural–Functional model for the analysis and explanation of social change*

With this model, and with this significant emphasis within the model, Marx then studied specific societies and their sequences and patterns of change. Concentrating chiefly on the study of societies and undergoing 'modern industrial capitalism', he nonetheless, by historical and comparative reference, indicated the application of his model to other kinds of societies. The point which it is important to emphasize here is that Marx's structural–functional model was explicitly constructed on the conviction that society was *changing process,* and that the *order* it assumed was the outcome of *conflicts.* It was constructed especially to accomplish a satisfactory analysis and explanation of conflict and change, as well as of *order,* in societies. These empirical studies of change were what others would have termed the 'Social Dynamics' of Marx, and his treatment of them emphasized several specific points.

(e) Society essentially historical

Clearly, Marx believed that society was essentially of historical nature, and that a satisfactory science of society necessarily contained historical dimensions of analysis. Sociology should include the 'historical method'; it should incorporate detailed historical studies.

(f) Society also an evolutionary, developmental and progressive process of change

Marx held, too, not only that society was a process of *change*—in that the emerging forms of society were *different* from what had existed before; but also that this process of change assumed a *definite pattern in history.* Social *evolution*—the gradual unfolding of new and more complex societies out of earlier and more limited forms—was a *fact* of history. At the heart of this was the reality of *development :* new knowledge, new skills, new techniques, new class systems, and new 'super-structures' of institutions, grew *cumulatively* on the basis of *earlier achievements.* And thirdly—these evolutionary and developmental changes were *progressive,* and in two important ways. They were *technically* and *practically* progressive in that they provided and ever-increasing degree of accuracy of knowledge and range of control over the resources of the environment. And they were *morally* progressive in that they were part of the historical *making of what was distinctively human,* and moved towards the ultimate elimination of human alienation and the achievement of a 'humane' civilization. Marx was therefore committed to all these conceptions.

(g) Types of society : classification and the Comparative Method

Marx's insistence on historical studies was not, however, a request for the study of the chronological events of specific societies; it was a request for *analytical* and *comparative* studies which took the essential historical nature of societies into account. It was in fact, the application of his analytical model to the explanation of societies of particular types (and changes in them). And this clearly entailed the *classification* of *types* of society for the purposes of *comparative study.* In keeping with his analytical model and his hypothesis, Marx classified societies according to the basic criterion of the *material basis,* or the nature of the *productive forces,* which they possessed.

(h) Equilibrium-Disequilibrium Analysis

The study of the sequences and patterns of order, conflict, and change which attended societies, took the form, in Marx, of an *equilibrium-disequilibrium* analysis. This is so clear as to require no further comment—except to add that it also took the form of the *quantitative-qualitative* sequence of dialectical change mentioned earlier.

(i) social Psychology

We may note too, as a special point, that Marx very (indeed decisively) sceptical about a science of psychology. His own persuasion was that distinctively *human* attributes of mind were the outcome of long historical and social processes, and that sociological perspectives were therefore required for their understanding and explanation. Very much like Comte, Marx was convinced that 'all (human) psychology is social psychology.'

(J) The study of social essential within the context of the Structural-Functional model and historical studies

It was also a fundamental insistence of Marx that 'societies' and 'social institutions' should not be regarded as 'entities' in their own right. They were forms of regulation attendant upon the practical activities of men in pursuit of their interests. In the *explanation* of changing societies, then, it was necessary to study the *social actions* of men—to analyse the ends they sought, the means they employed, the interests which motivated them, the tangle of relationships in which they worked out their affairs in any historical period. Again, it is chiefly important to note that *the study of social action* was insisted upon by Marx *within the necessary context of a structural-functional model.* There was no conflict between the two; but, on the contrary, an indispensable and contributive place for each of them within sociological analysis as a whole.

(k) The study of unintended consequences

A final point of importance emphasized in Marx's analysis of society was the necessity of tracing the unintended consequences of particular inventions or particular changes in any aspect of the 'productive forces'. The social actions of men terminated, for them, in the furtherance or satisfaction of their own interests. But these actions, and their achievements, had cumulative repercussions throughout the entire fabric of society which were unforeseen, and probably quite different from what anyone in society had consciously intended. This, as we know, was tangled up with the 'quantitative–qualitative' sequence of 'materialist' change in Marx's and Engels' thinking,; but it stands as an important point apart from this.

By way of summary, this is enough at this stage. It is clear that the 'conceptual apparatus' which Marx had in mind in his attempt to make and to apply a science of society was in all essentials the same as that put forward by the other men we have considered. There was a great similarity among all of them in their notions concerning the 'nature and elements' of a satisfactory sociology.

As we have seen, many criticisms can be made of Marx's emphasis upon the 'materialist' basis of his system, but again, as a final point of summary, we might note that, despite all these well-founded and well-justified criticisms, it was probably true that Marx's emphasis was such as to enrich sociological analysis in this one dimension. The part played in the changing nature of societies by men's practical, technical activities; by their property relations and class relations; and the extent to which the many interests of men which went into the shaping of 'political' society generally were rooted in, or were the unintended consequences of, their 'material' interests; certainly became focuses for sharper, deeper study as a result of Marx's work. The whole extent to which property relations in particular became a firm crystallization of power in society; a constraining force of power which became vested with respectability and authority, and which had to be broken before new progressive forces (which could liberate larger sections of men and women in society) could find their effective expression and development, received a more powerful statement in Marx's sociology than anywhere else. It was not a *new* element in the making of a science of society, but it was a powerfully new *over*-emphasis upon this one dimension. As such, it was of considerable importance and worth.

Bibliography

Ackerman, Nathan W., and Maria Jahoda. *Anti-Semitism and Emotional Disorder*. New York: Harper & Bros., 1950.

Adamic, Louis. *A Nation of Nations*. New York: Harper & Bros., 1945.

Adamic, Louis. "Sitdown," *Nation* (1936), 143:652–654, 702, 704.

Adorno, T. W., and others. *The Authoritarian Personality*. New York Harper & Bros., 1950.

Albig, William. *Modern Public Opinion*. New York: McGraw-Hill Book Co., 1956.

Alexander, Franz. *Fundamentals of Psychoanalysis*. New York: W.W. Norton Co., 1948.

Alexander, Franz. *Our Age of Unreason*. Philadelphia: J. B. Lippincott Co., 1942, Part 3.

Alihan, Milla A. *Social Ecology*. New York: Columbia Univ. Press, 1938.

Allport, Gordon W. *ABC's of Scapegoating*. Rev. ed. New York: Freedom Pamphlet, Anti-Defamation League of B'nai B'rith, 1948.

Allport, G.W. *The Nature of Prejudice*. Cambridge, Mass: Addison Wesley Publ. Co., 1954.

Allport, Gordon W. *Personality : A Psychological Interpretation*. New York: Henry Holt & Co., 1937. Chaps. 4–5, 7.

Allport, Gordon W. "The Psychology of Participation," *Psychological Review* (1945), 53:117–132.

Allport, G.W. *The Nature of Personality: Selected Papers.* Cambridge, Mass: Addison-Weslev Press, 1950. Esp. pp. 1-47.

Allport, G.W. and L. Postman. *The Psychology of Rumor.* New York: Henry Holt Co., 1947.

Altmeyer, A. J. "Outlook for Social Security," *National Conference for Social Work* (1937), 634–644.

Ams Brooks. *The Theory of Social Revolutions.* New York: Macmillan Co., 1913.

Ams C.D. *The Principles of Revolution.* London: Allen & Unwin, 1920.

Anastasi A., and J. P. Foley, *Differential Psychology.* New York: Macmillan Co., 1949.

Anderson, Camilla M. *Emotional Hygiene: The Art of Understanding.* 4th ed., rev. Philadelphia: J. B. Lippincott Co. 1948.

Anderson, Nels, *Men on the Move.* Chicago: Univ. of Chicago Press, 1940.

Anderson, John F. *The Psychology of Development and Personal Adjustment.* New York: Henry Holt & co., 1949.

Anshen, Ruth N., ed. *The Family: Its Function and Destiny.* New York: Harper & Bros., 1949.

Arnold, Thurman W. *The Bottlenecks of Business.* New York: Reynal & Hitchcock, 1940.

Arnold, Thurman W., and others. *The Future of Democratic Capitalism.* Philadelphia: Univ. of Pennsylvania Press, 1950.

Aurousseau, M. "The Distribution of Population," *Geographical Review* (1921), 11:579-585.

Baber, Ray E. *Marriage and the Family.* New York: McGraw-Hill Book Co., 1939. Chaps 6–9, 14, 15.

Barelson, Bernard, and M. Janowitz, eds. *Reader in Public Opinion and Communication.* Glencoe, Ill.: Free Press, 1950.

Barnes, H. E., and N. K. Teeters. *New Horizons in Criminology.* Rev. ed. New York: Prentice-Hall, 1947.

Barnes, Harry E., and O. M. Ruedi. *The American Way of Life.* 2nd ed. New York: Prentice-Hall, 1950.

Barnes, H. E. *Society in Transition*. New York: Prentice-Hall, 1952.

Barnes, Harry E. *Intellectual and Cultural History of the Western World*. New York: Reynal & Hitchcock, 1941.

Barnett, H. G. "Culture Process," *American Anthropologist* (1940), 42:21–48.

Bauer, Wilhelm. "Public Opinion," *Encoyclopaedia of the Social Sciences* (1934), 12:699-674.

Beard, Mary. *Woman: Co-Maker of History*. New York: Longmans, Green & Co., 1940.

Beers, Clifford W. *A Mind that Found Itself*. New York: Doubleday & Co., 1935.

Begardus, Emory S. *Fundamentals of Social Psychology*. 4th. ed. New York: Appleton-Century-Crofts, 1950.

Bendix, Reinhard. "Bureaucracy: The Problem and Its Setting," *American Sociological Review* (1947), 12:493–507.

Benedict, Ruth. *Patterns of Culture*. Boston : Houghton Mifflin Co., 1934.

Benedict, Ruth, and Gene Welthush. *The Races of Mankind*. New York Public Affairs Pamphlet No. 85, 1943.

Benedict, Ruth F. *Race: Science and Politics*. Rev. ed. New York: Viking Press, 1943.

Bernard, L. L. *War and Its Causes*. New York: Henry Holt & Co., 1944.

Bernard, L. L. "A Classification of Environments," *American Journal of Sociology* (1925–1926), 31:318–322.

Bernard, Jessie, *American Family Behavior*. New York: Harper & Bros., 1942.

Bernard, Jessie, *American Community Behavior*. New York: Dryden Press. 1949.

Bernard, William S., and others. *American Immigration Policy: A Reappraisal*. New York: Harper & Bros., 1950.

Bernays, Edward L. *Propaganda*. New York: Liveright Publ. Corp., 1938.

Best, Ethel, and Rebecca Smaltz. *Women Workers in Their Family Environment*. Washington: U. S. Dept. of Labor, Women's Bureau, 1941.

Bettelheim, Bruno. *Love Is Not Enough: The Treatment of Emotionally Disturbed Children.* Glencoe, Ill.: Free Press, 1950.

Bews. I. W. *Human Ecology.* London: Oxford Univ. Press, 1935.

Blaisdell, Donald C., and Jane Greverus. *Economic Power and Political Pressures.* Temporary National Economic Committee Monograph No. 26. Washington: Government Printing Office, 1941.

Blatz, W. E., *Hostages to Peace: Parents and Children of Democracy.* New York: William Morrow & Co., 1940.

Bloch, Herbert A. *Disorganisation, Personal and Social.* New York: A. A. Knopf, 1952.

Blumer, Herbert, and P. M. Hauser. *Motion Pictures, Delinquency, and Crime.* Chicago: Univ. of Chicago Press, 1933.

Boas, Franz, "Race," *Encyclopaedia of the Social Sciences* (1934), 13:25-36.

Boas, Franz. *Race, Language and Culture.* New York: Macmillan Co.,., 1940.

Bogardus, Emory S. *Leaders and Leadership.* New York: D. Appleton Century Co., 1934.

Bossard, James H.S., and Eleanor S. Boll. *Ritual in Family Living.* Philadelphia: Univ. of Pennsylvania Press, 1950.

Bossard, James. H. S. *The Sociology of Child Development.* New York: Harper & Bros., 1948.

Bowman, Henry A. *Marriage for Moderns.* New York: McGraw-Hill Book Co., 1942.

Bowman, H. A. *Marriage for Moderns.* New York: McGraw-Hill Book Co., 1954.

Brady, Robert A. *Business as a System of Power.* New York: Columbia Univ. Press, 1943.

Brameld, Theodore, *Ends and Means in Education; a Midcentury Appraisal.* New York: Harper & Bros., 1950.

Breese, Gerald W. *The Daytime Population of the Central Business Distrid.* Chicago: Univ. of Chicago Press, 1949.

Britt, Steward H. *Social Psychology of Modern Life.* Rev. ed. New York: Rinehart & Co., 1949.

Britt, S. H., ed. *Selected Readings in Social Psychology*. New York: Rinehart & Co., 1950.

Britt, S. H. *Social Psychology of Modern Life*. Rev. ed. New York : Rinehart & Co., 1949.

Bro, M. H. *When Children Ask*. Chicago; Willett, Clark, 1940.

Bromley, Dorothy D., and Florence H. Britten. *Youth and Sex*. New York: Harper & Bros., 1938.

Brown, F. J. "Organizing for Total War," *Annals of the American Academy of Political and Social Science* (March 1942), 220.

Brown, F. J. *Educational Sociology*. New York: Prentice-Hall, 1947.

Brown, Lawrence G. *Social Pathology*. New York: F. S. Crofts & Co., 1942. Chap. 1.

Brown, Lawrence G. *Social Pathology*. New York: F. S. Crofts & Co., 1942. Chaps. 29, 30.

Brown, F. J., J. S. Roucek, and others. *One America. Our Racial and National Minorities*. New York: Prentice-Hall, 1945.

Brown, L.G. *Immigration*. New York: Longmans, Green and Co., 1933.

Bucher, Karl. *Industrial Evolution*. (Trans. from 3rd German ed.) New York: Henry Holt & Co., 1901.

Burgess, E.W. "Accommodation," *Encyclopedia of the Social Science* (1930), 1: 403–404.

Burgess, J. S. "Study of Modern Social Movements as a Means for Clarifying the Process of Social Action," *Social Forces* (1944), 22: 269–275.

Burgess. E. W., and Leonard S. Cottrell, Jr. *Predicting Success or Failure in Marriage*. New York: Prentice-Hall, 1939.

Burgess, E. W., and H. J. Locke. *The Family*. New York: American Book Co., 1955.

Burgess, E. W., and L. S. Cottrell, Jr. *Predicting Success or Failure in Marriage*. New York: Prentice-Hall, 1939.

Burgess, E. W., and Herbert Blumer, eds. *Human Side of Social Planning*. Chicago: American Sociological Society, 1935.

Burgess, J. S. "Study of Modern Social Movements as a Means for Clarifying the Process of Social Action," *Social Forces* (1944), 22:269–275.

Burgess, E. W. "The Growth of the City," in R. E. Park and others. *City*. Chicago: Univ. of Chicago Press, 1949. Pp 47-62.

Burgess, E.W. "The Natural Area as the Unit for Social Work in the Large City," *Proceedings of the National Conference of Social Work* (1926), 53:504-510.

Burgess, E.W., ed. *Personality and the Social Group*. Chicago: Univ. of Chicago Press, 1929.

Burnham, James. *The Machiavellians: Defenders of Freedom*. New York: John Day Co., 1943.

Burnham, James. *Managerial Revolution*. New York: John Day, 1941.

Burrow, Trigant. *The Neurosis of Man*. New York: Harcourt, Brace & Co., 1949.

Bury, J. B. *The Idea of Progress: An Inquiry into Its Origin and Growth*. London: Macmillan & Co., 1920.

Butler, G. D. *Introduction to Community Recreation*. 2nd ed. New York: McGraw-Hill Book Co., 1949.

Calhoun, A.W. *A Social History of the American Family*. New York: Barnes & Noble, 1945. Re-issue of 3 vols., 1917–1919, in 1 vol. Vol. 2, chaps. 6 8, 9: vol. 3, chaps. 4–6, 8.

Cantril, Hadley. *The Psychology of Social Movements*. New York: John Wiley & Sons, 1941.

Cantor, N. F. *Crime and Society*. New York: Henry Holt & Co., 1939.

Cantor, Nathaniel F. *Crime and Society*. New York: Henry Holt & Co., 1939.

Carpenter, Niles. *Hospital Service for Patients of Moderate Means*. Chicago: Univ. of Chicago Press, 1932.

Carpenter, J.R. *An Ecological Glossary*. Norman: Univ. of Oklahoma Press, 1938.

Carr, L. J. *Delinquency Control*. Rev. ed. New York: Harper & Bros., 1950.

Carr-Saunders, A. M. *World Population: Past Growth and Present Trends*. Oxford: Charendon Press, 1936.

Cartwright, D., and A. Zander. *Group Dynamics*. Evanston, Ill.: Row. Peterson and Co., 1953.

Case, Clarence M. "Conscientious Objectors," *Encyclopaedia of the Social Sciences* (1931), 4: 210–212.

Case, Clarence M. *Non-Violent Coercion: A Study in Methods of Social Pressure.* New York: Century Co., 1923.

Cavan, Ruth Shoule. *Criminology.* New York: Thomas Y. Crowell Co., 1948.

Cavan, Ruth S. *The Family.* New Work: T. Y. Crowell Co., 1942.

Centers, Richard. *The Psychology of Social Classes.* Princeton: Princeton Univ. Press. 1949.

Chafee, Zechariah, Jr. *Free Speech in the United States.* Cambridge: Harvart Univ. Press, 1941.

Chase, Stuart. *Democracy under Pressure.* New York: Twentieth Century Fund. 1945.

Chandrasekhar, Sripati. *Hungry People and Empty Lands.* London: George Allen & Unwin, 1954.

Chapin, F.S. *Cultural Change.* New York : D Appleton-Century Co., 1928.

Chapin, F. S. *Experimental Designs in Sociological Research.* New York: Harper & Bros. 1947.

Chase, Stuart, *Idle Money, Idle Men.* New York: Harcourt, Brace & Co., 1940.

Chevigny Hector, and Sydell Braverman. *The adjustment of the Blind.* New Haven : Yale Univ. Press, 1950.

Child, C. M. *Physiological Foundations of Behavior.* New York: Henry Holt & Co., 1924.

Clarke, Helen I. *Social Legislation.* New York: D. Appleton-Century Co. 1940.

Clarkson, J. D., and T. C. Cochran. *War as a Social Institution.* New York: Columbia Univ. Press, 1941.

Cleveland, C.C. *The Great Revival in the West, 1797-1805.* Chicago: Univ. of Chicago Press, 1916.

Coke, F. W. *Democracy, Liberty, and Property.* New York: Macmillan Co., 1942.

Colcord, Joanna C. *Your Community.* Rev. ed. New York: Russell Sage Foundation, 1947.

Cole, Louella. *Psychology of Adolescence.* 3rd ed. New York: Rinehart & Co., 1948.

Cook, Lloyd Allen, ed. *College Study in Intergroup Relations.* Washington, D. C. : American Council on Education, 1950.

Cook, Lloyd Allen. *Community Backgrounds of Education.* New York: McGraw-Hill Book Co., 1938.

Cooley, Charles H. *Social Process.* New York: Chas. Scribner's Sons, 1918.

Cooley, Charles H. "Genius, Fame, and the Comparison of Races," *Annals of the American Academy of Political and Social Science* (May 1897), 9: 317–359.

Cooley, Charles H. *Human Nature and the Social Order.* Rev. ed. New York: Chas. Scribner's Sons 1922.

Coons, Arthur G. "The Nature of Economic Planning in Democracy," *Plan Age* (1939), 5:2.

Corrigan, J. M., and G. Barry O'Toole, eds, *Race: Nation: Person: Social Aspects of the Race Problem.* New York: Barnes & Noble 1944.

Count, Earl W., ed. *This Is Race: An Anthology.* New York: Henry Schuman, 1950.

Coutu, Walter. *Emergent Human Nature : A Symbolic Field Interpretation.* New York: A.A. Knopf, 1949.

Cox, Catharine M., and others. *The Early Mental Traits of Three Hundred Geniuses* (L. M. Terman and others, *Genetic Studies of Genius,* vol. 2). Stanford Univ. Press, 1926.

Coyle, Grace Longwell. *Group Work with American Youth.* New York: Harper & Bros., 1948.

Crowther, J. G. *The Social Relations of Science.* New York: Macmillan Co., 1941.

Cruening, Ernest. "Publicity", *Encyclopaedia of the Social Science* (1934), 12:698-701.

Crystal, David. *The Displaced Person and the Social Agency.* New York: United HIAS Service, 1958.

Cuber, J. F., and R. A. Harper. *Problems of American Society.* New York: Henry Holt & Co., 1948. Chap 1.

Cuber, J. F., and R. A. Harper. *Problems of American Society.* New York: Henry Holt & Co., 1948.

Dahlberg Gunnar. *Race Reason and Rubbish.* New York: Columbia Univ. Press, 1942.

Daugherty, C. R. *Labor Problems in American Industry*. 3rd ed. Boston: Houghton Mifflin Co., 1948.

Davenport, F.M. *Primitive Traits in Religious Revivals.* New York: Truth Seeker Co., 1905.

Davie, Maurice R. *Negroes in American Society.* New York: McGraw-Hill Book Co., 1949.

Davie, Maurice R. *Evolution of War.* New Haven: Yale Univ. Press, 1925.

Davie, Maurice R. *World Immigration.* New York: Macmillan Co., 1936.

Davie, Maurice R. "The Pattern of Urban Growth," in G.P. Murdock, ed. *Studies in the Science of Society.* New Haven: Yale Univ. Press, 1937. Pp. 133-161.

Davis, Kingsley. "A Case of Extreme Social Isolation of a Child," *American Journal of Sociology* (1940), 45: 554–565.

Davis, Allison, and John Dollard. *Children of Bondage.* Washington: American Council on Education, 1940. Part 2.

Davis, Jerome. *Capitalism and Its Culture.* New York: Farrar & Rinehart, 1935.

Davis, Kingsley. "The Sociology of Parent-Youth Conflict," *American Sociological Review* (1940), 5:523–535.

Davies, Stanley P. *Social Control of the Mentally Deficient.* New York: T. Y. Crowell Co., 1930.

de Rougemont, Denis. *Love in the Western World.* New York: Harcourt, Brace & Co., 1940.

Dennis, Lawrence. *The Dynamics of War and Revolution.* New York: Weekly foreign Letter, 1940.

Dennis, Wayne, ed. *Current Trends in Social Psychology.* Pittsburgh: Univ. of Pittsburgh Press, 1948.

Deutsch, Helene. *The Psychology of Women.* New York: Grune & Stratton. Vol. 1, "Girlhood," 1944.

Deutsch, Helene, *Psychology of Women.* New York: Grune & Stratton. Vol. 2, "Motherhood," 1945.

Dewey. John. *Human Nature and Conduct.* New York: Henry Holt & Co., 1922.

Dewey. John. *The Public and Its Problems.* New York: Henry Holt & Co., 1927.

Dickinson, R. E. "Social Basis of Physical Planning," *Sociological Research.* (1942), 34: 51–67, 165–182.

Dodson, Dan W. "Social Action and Education," *Journal of Educational Sociology* (1949-50), 23: 345–351.

Dodson, Leonidas, ed. "The Shadow of War," *Annals of the American Academy of Political and Social Science* (September 1934), 175.

Doliard, John. *Caste and Class in a Southern Town.* New Haven: Yale Univ. Press, 1937.

Dollard, John. *Criteria for the life History.* New Haven: Yale Univ. Press, 1935.

Dollard, John. *Caste and class in a Southern Town.* Garden City, N. Y. : Doubleday Anchor Books, 1957.

Dollard, John. *Fear in Battle.* Washington: Infantry Journal, 1944.

Dollard, John. *Personality and Psychotherapy.* New York: McGraw-Hill Book Co., 1950.

Dollard, John and Neal E. Miller. *Personality and Psychotherapy.* New York: McGraw-Hill Book Co., 1950.

Dollard, John. *Caste and Class in a Southern Town.* Garden City, N.Y.: Doubleday Anchor Books, 1957.

Dollard, John, and Neal E. Miller. *Personality and Psychotherapy.* New York, McGraw-Hill Book Co., 1950. Chaps. 21–23.

Donahue, Wilma T., and Clark Tibbitts, eds. "The Disabled Veteran," *Annals of the American Academy of Political and Social Science* (May 1945), 239.

Doob, Leonard W. *Plans of Men.* New Haven: Yale Univ. Press, 1940.

Doob, Leonard W. *Public Opinion and Propaganda.* New York: Henry Holt & Co., 1948.

Douglas Paul H., and Aaron Director. *The Problem of Unemployment.* New York: Macmillan Co., 1931.

Douglas, W. O. *Democracy and Finance.* New Haven: Yale Univ. Press, 1941.

Doyle, Bertram W. *The Etiquette of Race Relations in the South : A Study in Social Control.* Chicago : Univ. of Chicago Press, 1937.

Drake St. Clair, and H.R. Cayton. *Black Metropolis.* New York: Harcourt, Brace & Co., 1945.

DuBois, Cora. *The People of Alor.* Minneapolis, Minn.: Univ. of Minnesota Press, 1944.

Drake, St. Clair, and H.R. Cayton. *Black Metropolis.* New York: Harcourt, Brace & Co., 1945. Chaps. 19, 20.

Dubois, W. E. B. *Color and Democracy.* New York: Harcourt. Brace & Co., 1945.

Dunlap, Knight. *Habits: Their Making and Unmaking.* New York: Liveright, 1932. Chaps. 1–2, 5, 9.

Durkheim, Emile. *The Division of Labor in Society.* Trans. by George Simpson. Glencoe, Iii.: Free Press, 1949.

Durkheim, Emile. *The Elementary Forms of Religious Life.* Trans. by J.W. Swain. New York: Macmillan Co., 1915.

Eagleton, Clyde. *Analysis of the Problem of War.* New York: Ronald Press. 1937.

Eaton, Joseph W., and Robert J. Weil. *Culture and Mental Disorders* Glencoe, Ill. : Free Press, 1955.

Edwards, L. P. *The Natural History of Revolution.* Univ. of Chicago Press, 1927.

Einzig, Paul. *Economic Warfare.* New York: Macmillan Co., 1941.

Eliot, Thomas D. "Family Crises and Ways of Meeting Them," chap. 22 in R. Hill and H. Becker, eds. *Family, Marriage, and Parenthood.* Boston: D.C. Heath & Co., 1955.

Eliot, Thomas D. *American Standards and Planes of Living.* Boston: Ginn & Co., 1931.

Elliott, Mabel A., and Francis E. Merrill. *Social Disorganization.* 3rd ed. New York: Harper & Bros., 1950.

Elliott, Mabel A., and Francis E. Merrill. *Social Disorganization.* 3rd ed. New York: Harper & Bros., 1950. Chaps. 1, 2, 15, 22.

Elliott, Mabel A., and F. E. Merrill. *Social Disorganization.* 3rd ed. New York: Harper & Bros., 1950. Chap. 22.

Ellis, Robert S. *The Psychology of Individual Differences.* New York: D. Appleton-Century Co., 1928.

Elmer, Manuel C. *Sociology of the Family.* Boston: Ginn & co.,

1945. "The Family," *American Sociological Review* (1937), 2:591–778.

Elmer, M. C. *The Sociology of the Family*. Boston: Ginn & co., 1945.

Eonberg, Morris. "Association," *Encyclopaedia of the Social Science* (1930), 2:284-286.

Epstein, Abraham. *Insecurity: A Challenge to America*. New York: Random House, 1938.

Erikson, Erik H. *Childhood and Society*. New York: W.W. Norton & Co., 1950.

Fairchild, H.P. *People: The Quantity and Quality of Population*. New York Henry Holt & Co., 1939.

Faris, Ellsworth. *The Nature of Human Nature*. New York: McGraw-Hill Book Co., 1937.

Faris, Robert E. L. *Social Disorganization*. New York: Ronald Press, 1955.

Faris, Robert E. L., and H. Warren Dunham. *Mental Disorders in Urban Areas*. Chicago: Univ. of Chicago Press, 1939, Esp. chaps. 2, 10, 11.

Feldman, Herman. *Racial Factors in American Industry*. New York: Harper & Bros., 1931.

Feldman, Herman. *The Regularization of Employment*. New York: Macmillan Co., 1931.

Ferenczi, Imre. "Modern Migrations," *Encyclopaedia of the Social Science* (1933), 10:429-440.

Ferenczi, Imre. "Proletarian Mass Migration, 19th and 20th Centuries," *in International Migrations*. New York: National Bureau of Economic Research, 1929. 1:81-88.

Field, Marshall. *Freedom Is More than a Word*. Chicago: Univ. of Chicago Press. 1945.

Fineberg, S. A. *Overcoming Anti-Semitism*. New York: Harper & Bros., 1943.

Firey, Walter. *Land Use in Central Boston*. Combridge, Mass.: Harvard Univ. Press, 1947.

Fizzier, E. Franklin. *The Negro in the United States. New York:* Macmillan Co, 1956.

Fodor, M. W. *The Revolution Is On*. Boston: Houghton Mifflin Co., 1940.